Managing a Nonprofit Organization

Thomas Wolf

Illustrated by Barbara Carter

A FIRESIDE BOOK
Published by Simon & Schuster
New York London Toronto Sydney Tokyo Singapore

P9-BJH-497

For my parents,
Irene and Walter Wolf,
who have contributed time, money, and
children to nonprofit organizations

FIRESIDE

Rockefeller Center
1230 Avenue of the Americas
New York, New York 10020

FIRESIDE and colophon are registered trademarks of
Simon & Schuster Inc.

Designed by Judith Neuman-Cantor

Manufactured in the United States of America

12   13   14   15   16   17   18   19   20

Library of Congress Cataloging-in-Publication Data

Wolf, Thomas, 1945–
Managing a nonprofit organization/Thomas Wolf;
illustrated by Barbara Carter—1st ed.
p. cm.
1. Corporations, Nonprofit—Management.   1. Title.
HD62.6.W649 1990
658′.048—dc20   89-22807
                                                            CIP

ISBN: 0-671-76415-2

Contents

Preface

This book is based on an earlier volume, *The Nonprofit Organization,* which first appeared in 1983. Of the many people who spoke or wrote to me after reading that book, a large number said that it had helped them to carry out their professional or volunteer responsibilities. I found these comments very encouraging. But there were several people who expressed some disappointment that the book did not cover topics that were crucial in nonprofit administration and they made suggestions on what might be added. The suggestions came from a wide variety of people—staff members of nonprofit organizations, trustees, volunteers, and university professors who used the book in their courses. I listened carefully to what they had to say because they knew better than I how the book could be helpful to the field. As the list of their ideas grew, it became clear that a new, expanded version of *The Nonprofit Organization* was needed, one that not only incorporated suggestions for new topics but that updated the material already in the book.

In this new expanded volume, I have added three new chapters, which include material on marketing, organizational evaluation, and putting together the work force in a nonprofit organization. I have also significantly rewritten all of the other chapters. It was inevitable that after almost a decade, the chapter on computers was completely out of date and had to be entirely rewritten. In addition, since the original publication of *The Nonprofit Organization,* there have been significant changes in the tax code that require changed emphases in the fund-raising chapter. Trustee liability has become an increasingly important topic so there is a new section on that subject as well as an extended section on volunteers. The emphasis in the original book on the nuts and bolts of bookkeeping seemed less crucial, according to many readers, than a fuller treatment of financial planning and the analysis of complex financial statements, so more material on both subjects is included. These and many other changes were discussed with Paul Aron, a senior editor at Prentice Hall Press, who encouraged me to go ahead with this new edition.

Somewhat late in the preparation of this volume, there was one other suggestion that seemed particularly appropriate and has added greatly to the usefulness of this book. The end of each chapter contains a series of questions in the form of a checklist. This is intended partly as a convenience to experienced trustees and administrators who may not want to read the entire chapter. But it is also intended for those who may wish to make sure that their organizations are operating in accordance with the practices I have described, because the checklists provide a convenient summary of the concepts and ideas contained in each chapter.

Why did I write the original book? Quite frankly, I knew there was a great need for a basic manual on the subject of managing nonprofit organizations. As a consultant to nonprofit organizations—and prior to that as the head of a grant-giving foundation—I observed that most staff and volunteers in nonprofit organizations come to this world with very little preparation for their responsibilities. I also knew this to be true from my own earliest experience as a nonprofit administrator. At the age of fifteen, I had my first opportunity to run a nonprofit organization. The organization was a summer music festival with an annual budget of just over $4,000. Like many nonprofit administrators, I had no experience or training in management. My training had been in music. Although this equipped me with the skills to play concerts, it did not prepare me for managing a budget, developing a fund-raising plan, dealing patiently with a board of directors, undertaking a marketing campaign, or any of the other responsibilities that are part and parcel of nonprofit administration.

Twenty-five years later, I am more than ever convinced that my own experience was not unusual. Nonprofit organizations are often run by people who are almost completely unfamiliar with administration. They seem to know a lot about the kinds of activities or services that their organizations offer, but it is probably fair to say that many of them come to their first jobs without any significant management background or training. The good ones use the job as an opportunity to learn, take courses, read books, and play a game of catch-up in learning how to manage. The others become frustrated, burn themselves out, and eventually leave their organizations. As a consequence, the turnover rate among administrators in nonprofit organizations is very high.

It is not only administrators of nonprofit organizations who are largely unschooled. Consider the committed individuals who, after years of service to a hospital (or a museum or a community center), are asked to join the board. Like many who accept positions on boards, these people do so without any concept of the responsibilities of trusteeship. They do not understand their legal and fiduciary responsibilities, they are not willing to give and get money, or, worse yet, they confuse their roles with that of the staff and attempt to involve themselves in the day-to-day operation of the organization. All of these things can cause serious organizational problems. When the governing group does not know how to govern and when roles and responsibilities are not clear, the organization's ability to carry out its mission is compromised.

Finally, there are millions of volunteers who serve nonprofit organizations and this book was also written for them. In 1985, the Gallup organization conducted a survey on volunteerism in America. The results were extraordinary. Forty-eight percent of persons over the age of fourteen had done some volunteer work in the past year. Eighty percent of the volunteer hours had gone to nonprofit organizations. The total number of hours volunteered was the equivalent of 6.7 million full-time jobs and the value of this volunteered time was estimated at around $80 billion, about three-quarters as much as the value of actual paid work in these organizations. For all of these people who give so much of themselves to the nonprofit sector, a basic book about the organizations they serve is a must.

Thus this volume is a primer for staff members, trustees, and volunteers who wish to increase their understanding of nonprofit organizations and hone various management skills. It is also for students who wish to learn about administrative issues in the nonprofit world. It is based on material I originally developed for a seminar that was open to graduate students and working professionals. As a result, the book contains both theory and practical advice. I continue to believe that both are essential if readers are to gain an understanding of the context in which decisions are made and learn the reasons why certain kinds of techniques seem to work.

I am grateful to several people who collaborated with me on this book. Barbara Carter offered her wonderful illustrations, which bring the book's concepts to life with refreshing and humorous visual imagery. Jane Culbert assisted on the financial chapters; Jeanne Brodeur, on the marketing chapter; and Marc Goldring, on the chapter about computers. Doris Frankel, Kaki Gladstone, and Lea Wolf shared their experiences with volunteers and this helped to shape one of the most important sections of the book. Finally, Paul Aron was a patient and encouraging editor who saw the value of approaching an old topic with fresh vigor. To all of these individuals, I owe a great debt of thanks.

1
Understanding Nonprofit Organizations[1]

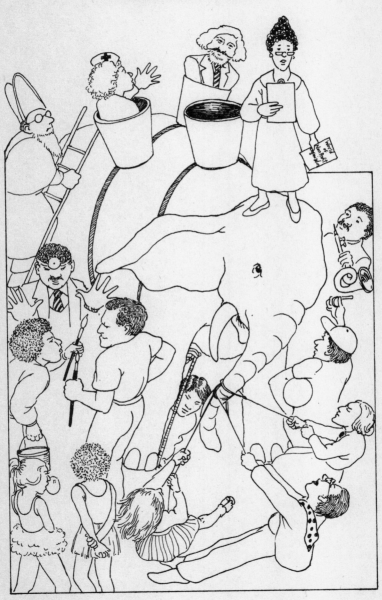

The Spencer family lives in a small city in the western United States. Sam Spencer runs a plumbing supply business; Jane, his wife, teaches at a school for the learning disabled. On a typical day, their lives—like the lives of most Americans—are touched repeatedly by the world of nonprofit organizations.

☐ At 7:30 A.M., Jane takes Sammy, Jr., aged three, to a daycare center housed at the Baptist Church to which the family belongs. She then goes directly to her school, which serves learning-disabled high-school students. The daycare center, the church, and the school are all nonprofit organizations.

☐ At about the same time that Jane leaves, Sam is loading his truck with plumbing supplies for the regional hospital, which is located in their city. The hospital, which employs more than a thousand people, is also a nonprofit organization, one that makes a significant contribution to the local economy.

☐ Before leaving home, Sam reminds son John, aged nine, that he should pack his bathing suit and towel because there is swim practice after school at the local YMCA. The YMCA is the city's principal recreational organization and is organized as a nonprofit.

☐ On this particular day, Jane is on release time from the classroom taking an in-service workshop on language arts instruction at the local college. The college is the largest nonprofit organization in the city.

☐ While Jane is on release time, half of her students from school are on a field trip to the science museum and the other half are attending an open rehearsal at the local symphony. Both of these organizations are nonprofit organizations.

☐ Meanwhile, Sam has completed his delivery of plumbing supplies and drives over to the job-training center where he teaches the essentials of plumbing two mornings a week. Although supported almost exclusively with government funding, the center is a nongovernment, private nonprofit organization.

☐ When school is over, Jane meets with a group of teachers who are working on a special grant proposal that they will submit to a local

3

foundation. They are seeking funds to support a computer-based language arts program in their classrooms. The foundation, whose income is derived mainly from a large endowment and is exempt from taxation, is a nonprofit organization.

☐ After leaving school, Jane drives over to a local nursing home to visit her father. The nursing home is a nonprofit organization.

☐ Sam leaves work early to go to a public hearing. A local builder, one of Sam's customers, has proposed a new development in what was formerly marshland. An environmental group, organized as a nonprofit organization, is opposing the development and is presenting its testimony at the public hearing.

☐ When Jane arrives home, there is a letter from daughter Amy, who is spending the fall of her junior year in South America as part of an exchange program. The exchange was organized by a national nonprofit organization with a local chapter in the city where the Spencers live.

☐ Finally, after dinner, the Spencers receive a call from the public radio station. It is pledge week and the caller asks whether the Spencers will renew their membership in this nonprofit organization. Jane leaves soon after for a planning meeting for the local Girl Scouts' cookie drive. The Girl Scouts is a prominent national nonprofit organization.

According to the Internal Revenue Service (IRS), which keeps the most reliable estimates, there are approximately a million nonprofit organizations in the United States.[2] They range from large universities with assets in the billions of dollars to small all-volunteer, community-based, grassroots organizations that seem to operate on a shoestring. The contribution of nonprofit organizations to the quality of life in this country is immense. But these organizations also contribute substantially to the economy (one estimate puts total nonprofit revenues well over $300 billion annually, which may be conservative). Nonprofit organizations own approximately 2 percent of all the nation's assets, and while this may not seem like a large amount, it represents more than half of what the federal government owns. In terms of the labor force, nonprofit organizations provide employment to between 8 and 10 million individuals; indeed, almost 25 percent of all professional and technical workers in the United States may work for nonprofit organizations.

Despite the tremendous size and impact of the nonprofit sector, it is not well understood by most people. The purpose of this chapter is to describe what nonprofit organizations are, what distinctive features they possess, and what special challenges they pose for the people who manage and govern them.

WHAT IS A NONPROFIT ORGANIZATION?

Suppose you asked someone, "What is an elephant?" and the person answered, "An elephant is a nonhorse." You would probably find the answer unsatisfactory. Yet, the term *non*profit organization describes something that is not something else—it suggests a business enterprise not organized to make a profit. But it tells us very little about the essential characteristics of this type of entity.

It is not easy to describe nonprofit organizations and this is partly what makes managing them such a difficult task fraught with challenges and problems. Unlike management issues in the profit sector, which tend to be clear and related to specific economic measures, issues in the nonprofit environment are more nebulous because they relate to the somewhat abstract concept of *public service*. In a profit-making company, a manager generally knows whether he or she is doing a good job, but it is often less clear in a nonprofit organization in which the primary purpose is not to make money but to serve the public.

Some say that the essential defining characteristic of nonprofit organizations is the fact that they are established to provide a service to the public, and to some extent this is true. But this idea of a public service mission can be misleading. For one thing, there are a number of nonprofit organizations that are not organized to serve the public (for example, country clubs and labor unions). For another, the idea that nonprofit organizations are simply organized to solve some societal problem or deliver some much-needed public service flies in the face of the exclusivity often associated with their respective constituencies. This is perhaps most clear when nonprofit organizations are compared to public (or government) organizations and agencies working in the same field. Although the nonprofit organizations often have a stated public service mission, they do not necessarily have a requirement of equity (that is, a mandate to serve everyone) the way public agencies usually do. As a result, the nonprofit organization's actual constituency may be far more limited than that of a public agency working in the same field.

Others claim that the essential defining characteristic of nonprofit organizations is that their mission is not to make money. Again, this is partly true. But many nonprofit organizations are quite entrepreneurial (again, this distinguishes them from public or governmental agencies working in the same field). Many engage in all sorts of money-making ventures that bear a close resemblance to profit-making entities and this has been cause for some concern among those working in commercial endeavors whose businesses must compete with nonprofits for customers.

In fact, a nonprofit organization is neither in the profit sector nor in the public sector but sits somewhere between the two. This position allows the nonprofit great flexibility in its operation but also requires great skill in its management. On the one hand, managers must learn the same management techniques and analytical strategies that apply in profit-making companies. However, while these techniques are relevant in the nonprofit world, their application is dissimilar. Although both profit-making and nonprofit organizations engage in planning, budgeting, accounting, and marketing; although both have to contend with issues of governance, personnel, and information management; and although both have to raise money from time to time, these activities are carried out in markedly different ways. Similarly, while it may be useful to know about the workings of a public agency and the development of public policy, it is not sufficient preparation for the nonprofit manager or trustee. Governance, organizational accountability, financial reporting, and long-range planning are very different in nonprofit organizations whose special defining characteristics are laid down in state and federal law.

Toward a Definition

In this book, the term *nonprofit organization* refers to those legally constituted, nongovernmental entities, incorporated under state law as charitable or not-for-profit corporations that have been set up to serve some public purpose and are tax-exempt according to the IRS. All must have the following five characteristics:

- They must have a public service mission
- They must be organized as a not-for-profit or charitable corporation
- Their governance structures must preclude self-interest and private financial gain
- They must be exempt from paying federal tax
- They must possess the special legal status that stipulates gifts made to them are tax deductible

Consequently, nonprofit organizations *as described in this book* do *not* include three other categories of organizations:

- Entities that have been set up to make a profit but are failing to do so
- Organizations that are governed informally by a collection of people who, although they have banded together to serve some public good, have been granted no special corporate status by federal and state authorities
- Organizations that are recognized as nonprofit by the IRS but do not have a public purpose (for example, trade associations, labor unions, country clubs, and fraternal organizations)

Because these various classes of organizations do not have *all* the characteristics previously listed, their missions, governance structures, or method of management may be significantly different from what is described in this book.

This chapter considers four major challenges that face nonprofit organizations as a consequence of these special characteristics. The challenges are:

- Articulating a clear public service mission
- Engaging in risk/survival analysis
- Identifying and involving the constituency
- Testing for "Organized Abandonment"

By looking closely at each of these, we will continue to refine our understanding of the special nature of nonprofit organizations.

CONSEQUENCES OF A PUBLIC SERVICE MISSION

An essential difference between profit and nonprofit organizations centers around the concept of mission. The ultimate mission of the profit-making entity is to earn money for its owners. Ownership can come in many forms, of course, from outright ownership of the organization by a single individual to shared ownership (by partners or shareholders or some other group). The concept of *ownership* is completely absent from nonprofit organizations and consequently the nonprofit's mission has a totally different thrust. There can be no owners in a nonprofit organization because such an entity is intended to serve a broad public purpose and the law is clear in specifying that ownership (with concomitant private gain) is incompatible with public purpose. This is not to say that nonprofit organizations cannot make money. Nonprofit organizations can and do make money—in the same way profit-making entities do—but the money that is taken in must be directed toward the public purpose for which the organization was set up, held in reserve, or turned over to another organization with a public purpose.

It is much more difficult to identify and articulate the mission of a nonprofit organization and consequently to develop criteria by which success can be measured. In a profit-making organization, because the mission is clear, success criteria are also clear. The mission centers around profitability; thus the criteria for success (and for decision making) include the bottom line, return on investment, sales, profit margins, market share, and other easily calculated measures. In a nonprofit organization, where the mission centers around public service, it is not only more difficult to define purposes but it can be a bewildering task to try to find the proper yardstick by which to measure success. If the purpose of a school is to produce well-educated citizens, if a peace group is established to oppose the use of military force in Latin America, if a recreation center is to offer constructive activities to urban teenagers, what criteria should each use to measure success? There will always be quantitative measures at hand—college board scores for the school, statistics on attendance at political rallies for the peace group, and numbers of participating teenagers in the case of the recreation center—but these measures are only indirect indexes of success.

Because the missions of nonprofit organizations center on the concept of public service, one might look to the public sector for models that demonstrate how mission statements are articulated and tested. Unfortunately, there is a problem with this approach. In the public sector, as we have already seen, there is an implied or stated mandate of equity in every mission statement. That is, public agencies are obligated to serve anyone who is eligible for assistance. For that reason, quantitative measures of success are often possible on the basis of the numbers of people served, their geographic distribution, their racial and socioeconomic diversity, and the cost-effectiveness of service delivery. For nonprofit organizations, these criteria may be relevant, but more often than not they are only indirect measures of success. Consider a nonprofit university-affiliated teaching hospital. Unlike the public hospital down the street, it cannot directly measure its success by counting the numbers of patients served and the cost-effectiveness of medical treatment. The nonprofit hospital's mission of promoting excellence in medical practice through exemplary training is less concrete, and success criteria are more difficult to establish.

Thus we come to the first major challenge for a nonprofit organization—the challenge of articulating a clear public service mission. The challenge is not only to come up with a statement that defines what the organization is and what it has been set up to do but to state these things in such a way that the organization can evaluate its success in carrying out this mission over time.

Developing a Mission Statement
The challenge of developing a good mission statement is to create a text that is sufficiently broad to encompass the many possible activities that the organization may wish to engage in. This is crucial inasmuch as the law obligates the trustees of the organization to limit their activities to those covered by the mission statement as contained in the organizing charter. However, in addition to a broad statement of purpose, a mission statement is only valuable if it gives some specific guidance on the direction the organization should take in regard to programs, services, and activities.

In designing a mission statement, it is important to remember that whatever is decided on is not cast in stone. Although the filing of the statement of purpose with the organization's incorporation papers is an important step, this document can be updated and changed through a clearly articulated legal procedure. Mission statements should be reviewed and revised periodically. A regular review and revision process is itself valuable in helping to clarify the assumptions and desires of those most involved in the organization. How is a mission statement created? Let's look at a case history.

THE UTOPIAVILLE ARTS CENTER

In the late 1980s, the city of Utopiaville wanted to create a local arts council that would oversee the cultural activities in the community. City officials appointed a committee to look into the question of how best to proceed and the group held public meetings to determine what kinds of activities would be most appropriate for the organization. Initially the group developed a simple mission statement as follows:

The purpose of the Utopiaville Arts Council is to develop, foster, and promote the arts as experiences central to the lives of the citizens of the city of Utopiaville.

While this statement certainly met the standard of being broad, the city council members were not satisfied. They felt the statement was too broad and did not provide enough of a sense of direction and intent. The planning group went back to their notes from the public meetings and the lists of responsibilities and activities that people said should be part of the local arts council's mandate. They rewrote and expanded the mission statement as follows:

The purpose of the Utopiaville Arts Council is to develop, foster, and promote the arts as experiences central to the lives of the citizens of the city of Utopiaville. Toward this end, it will undertake the following activities:

- Initiate programs in art, music, dance, and theater to benefit the citizens of Utopiaville
- Advise the city council on all matters concerning the arts, including pending legislation
- Work closely with the Utopiaville School District, with colleges and universities, and with any other educational institutions in the city on the development of appropriate arts education programs

- Allocate public and/or private funds as appropriate to organizations, agencies, or individuals who can provide arts programs or products of high quality that are deemed beneficial to the community
- Seek and apply for state, federal, and private funds available in support of the arts
- Review and make recommendations on all works of art to be acquired by the city, either by purchase or gift, and make recommendations concerning their proposed locations
- Develop directories of local arts groups, artists, performing and visual arts spaces; assemble calendars and schedules of arts events; and compile other material as appropriate to promote the arts in Utopiaville
- Conduct ongoing planning, researching the arts needs of the city, including new arts facilities, and developing, updating, and evaluating progress against periodic written plans for the growth of the arts in Utopiaville
- Develop an awareness in the business community, in local government, and in the general public of the value of the arts in Utopiaville
- Promote and encourage the cultural diversity of the city and assist in preserving the cultural heritage of the area
- Engage in any other activities that will enhance the arts and cultural life of Utopiaville

This new mission statement was far stronger than the first. Not only did it include a broad opening statement of purpose but it also included a more detailed framework from which the organization could develop a coherent program. And, of equal importance, it provided a structure against which some meaningful evaluation of the organization's effectiveness could be carried out in the years to come.

PUBLIC SERVICE AND RISK VERSUS SURVIVAL

James Sully is the president of the board of a summer camp in northern California. The camp was founded in 1949 primarily to serve the needs of disadvantaged youth and it runs a special program for inner-city teenagers on its pristine acreage in the mountains. The camp's program has been based around a curriculum of outdoor survival skills and teenagers of all ethnic and racial backgrounds have been encouraged to work in groups to foster increased understanding and affection for one another.

Despite the popularity of the camp, costs have been rising and funding has been diminishing for its core inner-city youth program. At a meeting of the board, Sully put the problem plainly: "For several years we've had a serious cash problem and until that's solved we won't be continuing the program for the disadvantaged. We will be taking only full-tuition–paying campers. Balancing the books has become our top priority."

James Sully's survival-and-safety-first attitude suggests that he may have forgotten the camp's original mission or has relegated it to a second-level priority. He seems to be telling us that running a nonprofit organization is just like running a business, that financial problems have to be tended to first. In some ways he may be right. After all, no organization, profit or nonprofit, can lose money forever and survive. But perhaps it is not quite that simple. There may be many ways to meet a financial crisis, some more consistent with the organization's mission than others. As one board member said in response to Sully's statements, "Given the present crisis, it is clear that changes will have to be made; it's the nature of the changes that has people concerned."

Here is a classic manifestation of one of the great dilemmas for nonprofit organizations. Which is more important: To ensure the continuity and the survival of the organization or to stay true to the organization's mission even if this involves certain financial and institutional risks? Consider the following cases:

☐ A legal aid group must decide whether it will begin to charge clients a modest fee in order to generate much-needed earned income (the mission statement talks about providing free legal aid).

☐ A church must decide whether to take a stand on abortion. Regardless of the position it takes, it risks alienating a large number of church members. Yet the minister believes that the mission of the church is to provide guidance on moral issues.

☐ An all-male school, responding to decreasing enrollments, has been advised by a marketing consultant to go coed. Yet the faculty and many alumni feel that the original mission to offer a quality education to young men, is still valid.

☐ A symphony orchestra, organized to improve the quality of the musical life of its city, must decide whether to increase the number of pop concerts and decrease its regular subscription concerts of classical music. The programming change would assist the organization in meeting its payroll but, some say, would compromise the mission of the organization.

☐ A women's health organization, founded as a collective, must decide whether it will reorganize around more conventional management lines in order to increase efficiency and professionalism. Several of the organization's founders believe that collective management is central to the organization's mission.

Each of these examples suggests a choice between risks and compromises. The original missions of the various organizations suggest one direction, prudence and good management sense suggest another. Staying true to the original missions may be risky and expensive, yet focusing only on the relative security of organizational survival may lead to a compromise in principles. The tug between these two competing tendencies is constant in the nonprofit environment, and it becomes extreme when organizations are under pressure, when funds are scarce, and when there is lack of agreement about basic purposes.

purpose v. survival

Once again, the contrast with the public and profit sectors is striking. In the public sector, risk is measured in political terms and agencies generally have a clear idea of how far they can and should go. The authorization to operate comes from elected officials who set limits on what is permissible. To extend those limits requires political persuasion, advocacy, and, in extreme cases, a change brought about by voters who put new people in office. In the profit sector, businesses are constantly faced with choices involving varying degrees of risk. But the risks are almost always measured in terms of the ultimate return or payoff. If the effect of a risky decision today is greater profitability tomorrow, then the decision may have merit.

The situation for the nonprofit organization is different because the standards of value are not stated primarily in political or financial terms. Who can decide how much it is worth to take a moral stand, perform more classical music, preserve a collective decision-making structure, or continue to provide free legal aid? Risk in each case will not lead to greater profitability. In fact, in most cases, risk will place greater financial burdens on the organization. Thus there is no single simple criterion on which to base a decision. It is a judgment call. On one side are the people who say the organization cannot afford to put itself in jeopardy; on the other side are the people who claim that a nonprofit organization that does not stay true to its ideals should not continue to operate. Indeed, as we shall see in chapter 2, it is possible for trustees who do not uphold the mission of an organization to be held legally accountable for their actions.

For all practical purposes, there is rarely a correct place to draw the line between organizational security and a public service mission. A nonprofit organization that is responsibly governed and managed finds itself debating the question continually, issue by issue, decision by decision. This is the second major challenge for a nonprofit organization—risk/survival analysis, or the search for the proper balance between organizational extension and risk taking and organizational security. Meeting the challenge involves the willingness of the governing group:

- To engage in an ongoing planning process
- To analyze future options from both a practical and an idealistic point of view
- To debate the pros and cons of each proposed action in terms of the organization's stated mission and its long-term security

Consider the following example of an organization that successfully met this challenge.

LEGAL EDUCATION SOCIETY

The Legal Education Society has been in existence for several decades. Its mission is to provide legal assistance in a variety of ways—legal aid to individuals who cannot afford it, legal assistance to nonprofit organizations, and scholarly contributions to advance the public's understanding of the law. The multiracial board of directors of the Legal Education Society is composed of lawyers, judges, and private citizens representing different socioeconomic groups. At present, the organization is adequately funded, has a modest endowment, and has a permanent staff of twelve people.

In 1983, the Legal Education Society hired a woman who was widely recognized as one of the brightest young lawyers in the country to be the society's executive director. She had been on the Law Review at a prestigious law school, had contributed significantly to the law literature, and had spent two years clerking for a Supreme Court justice. Her appointment was hailed as a turning point in the history of the Legal Education Society. However, it was a turning point in a way that no one expected.

During the first four years of her tenure as executive director, the young woman pleased everyone. She added programs, secured increased funding, wrote important articles, attracted new staff (including minorities and women), and appeared to be the dynamo that everyone thought she would be when they hired her. After four years, her interest began to shift. With her growing prominence in the field, organizations throughout the country wanted to hire her as a consultant to advise them on setting up legal education programs. At first, she accepted these assignments only on weekends and vacations, having received permission to do so from the board of directors. But as the demand for her consulting services grew, as her own interest in these projects increased, and as the scope of the projects demanded greater time commitments, she asked the board whether she might set up a small consulting program through the Legal Education Society, bringing the consulting contracts through the organization. The advantage, she explained, would be that the Legal Education Society could earn income and expand its influence nationally in the field of legal education.

At first, the arrangement worked well. Two large contracts during the first year netted the organization $42,000 in additional income. The Legal Education Society was cited as a leader in its field. The executive director, with the assistance of several key staff people, continued to be happy with the challenge and growth of the consulting work, but the Legal Education Society's primary constituency back home was becoming restless. The focus of the organization was changing. Individual staff members appeared to be less interested in their constituents' problems as they became more focused on the problems facing people halfway across the country. The board of directors was receiving conflicting signals. The national press and funding agencies throughout the country were praising the work of the Legal Education Society; the local constituency (individuals and organizations seeking legal assistance) were complaining about inadequate service.

On the fifth anniversary of the executive director's tenure, she proposed a major restructuring of the Legal Education Society in which the consulting business would become—within five years—the major activity of the organization. Her plan, brilliant in its conception, saw the organization doubling in budget and staff during that period and becoming far less reliant on grants. Legal assistance would still be provided, but it would be offered through a number of subcontracts and the Legal Education Society would simply act as broker. One of her justifications for the plan was especially compelling. At the time, federal and state governments seemed to be placing less priority on the funding of legal aid programs and the private sector did not indicate enthusiasm about making up the difference. Realistically, there was less money available and greater competition for that money. By way of contrast, the consulting business offered a very promising financial future.

There was no doubt in the minds of those serving on the board of directors that the executive director could pull off the plan. Her ability had been proven time and time again. There was also no debate on the question of the short-term funding outlook. Simply stated, the funding picture for basic legal services looked bleak. However, the board of directors was concerned about what impact the change would have on the organization's central and original mission. Although a consulting business would ensure organizational survival and continued growth, it would also mean a major shift away from basic legal services for the poor and for nonprofit organizations. That need existed, now more than ever, and several community members of the board of directors argued passionately that the organization must return to its original purpose.

The question was debated for two months. Surveys were conducted both among constituents and national authorities. At first, the majority of trustees seemed to favor the executive director's plan. But another group stated unequivocally that it was the legal obligation of the board of directors to safeguard the organization's mission and they threatened to seek the support of the state attorney general to compel the board to reject the plan. In the end, the board of directors, in a close vote, turned down the executive director's request and called for a new plan that would return the organization to its original mission. A year later, the Legal Education Society had a new executive director, a smaller (and mostly new) staff, a smaller budget, many new board members, and a clear sense of its place in the community. The old executive director had started her own consulting firm, which was staffed with many of her former employees. One of her first clients turned out to be the Legal Education Society, which even now continues to draw on her experience and expertise.

Did the board of directors make the right decision? Some people would say yes, some would say no. It is unlikely that the state attorney general would have intervened in the case—although in theory he would have had legal standing to do so had some of the trustees convinced him that the organization's mission was being compromised. Regardless of the merits of the case, the fact that such a legal action was threatened indicated the troubling aspects of the executive director's plan in the minds of some trustees. In the end, there was no right decision because "right" depended on each person's point of view. In spite of this, there was a correct and responsible course of action, which was the decision to debate the executive director's plan in an open and informed manner. The trustees considered the question of mission on the one hand and organizational security on the other. They weighed their options and came down in favor of a recommitment to the original mission. Those who disagreed (the executive director, some of the staff, and some of the board members), left the organization, and although they were disappointed with the decision, all believed in the integrity of the decision-making process. The organization had successfully met the challenge of risk/survival analysis.

HOW LARGE AND DIVERSE A PUBLIC?

The mission of every nonprofit organization centers around serving the public. But what precisely does that mean? The public, in the broadest sense, is everyone; yet few nonprofit organizations see themselves as offering their services to everyone. Unlike public agencies, they do not operate under any such implied or stated obligation. Therefore, every nonprofit organization must decide how broadly to define its constituency and how large or diverse a public to serve.

This decision is not simply a theoretical one. It is practical. The decision has ramifications for programs and activities, fund raising, budget planning, and staff size and structure. It touches on questions of constituency representation on the board. It is a question that cannot be finessed through a mission statement that refers in a general sort of way to the fact that the organization "serves the public." The organization must demonstrate the scope of its service and interests through its governance, its staffing, its programs, and its activities.

The contrast with profit-sector organizations sharpens our understanding of this special characteristic of nonprofits. In the profit sector, an organization's public is determined by its need to sell products and services. Therefore, its public consists of those who have either a direct or indirect effect on profitability: its customers and clients, its employees, and those significant others who can either promote or hamper the organization's ability to carry out its activities. Significant others, in the case of a soft drink company, might include a senator considering bottle bill legislation; for a major armaments manufacturer, it might include a group of newspaper writers who regularly cover defense issues.

Each of these constituency groups—customers and clients, employees, and significant others—are important to a profit-making entity to the extent that they can influence the business enterprise, and the primary strategy for dealing with each group is determined from a business perspective. For example, a profit-making company may survey the attitudes and predilections of its customers and clients, adjust its products and services accordingly, and then adopt marketing strategies to promote an image of service. It might offer its employees a generous benefits package or a bonus to promote good management/employee relations. In some cases, it might decide to make certain kinds of investments to promote a positive public image among those whose opinions can affect the conduct of business and, ultimately, profitability. The business may make contributions to political candidates to try to influence legislation or it may make charitable contributions to promote an image of a "caring" organization. When these decisions are explained to the organization's owners or investors, they can be justified on the basis that they promote the business's own interests. In all cases, service to and involvement of various constituency groups is seen as a strategy, and in no case is involvement of the constituency in the decision-making process seen as essential.

In the nonprofit world, the situation is completely reversed. Service to the public is not seen as a strategy; it is an end in itself. While a nonprofit organization can engage in many of the same activities that were described for the profit-making business—surveying its constituency to adjust products and services, promoting harmony among employees, and even, occasionally, making contributions to other charities—it does so out of a conviction that these activities further the organization's service mission. In order to be effective, the organization cannot keep its public at arm's length. Broad involvement of its public at all levels of operation is absolutely necessary to achieve effective nonprofit administration.

Yet, the nonprofit organization does not have the same kind of public mandate that the government (or public) agency does. The public agency, because it is tax based in its support, theoretically must offer its services to anyone. In many cases, "anyone" is restricted to people or organizations meeting certain eligibility requirements. But there are two significant points here. First, eligibility is always defined precisely, usually in quantitative terms (for example, people over sixty-five, people who earn less than $6,000 per year, organizations with budgets of less than $100,000 per year, or nonprofit 501[c][3] organizations). Second, once eligibility criteria are set, anyone who meets those criteria can expect to be served. Not so with the nonprofit organization. Such an organization has the luxury of picking and choosing who it wishes to serve. But this very flexibility is also a challenge. Defining the constituency too narrowly or failing to include representatives of that constituency in the operation of a nonprofit organization may have negative consequences.

Indeed, this is the third major challenge for a nonprofit organization, the challenge of constituency identification and involvement. A nonprofit organization must identify clearly those it intends to serve, and once it does so it must work toward an organizational structure—through board, staff, and activities—that reinforces its commitment to that group. The various decisions that follow the identification of an organization's constituents establish its specific image in the community, provide a clue to potential funders concerning its public commitment, and either attract or repel the people the organization wishes to serve.

Why is this issue so important? Consider the following situations:

☐ An art museum fails to secure a grant from its state arts agency because its programs "serve only an elitist and affluent audience." It is encouraged to find ways to reach out to a broader public.

☐ A health clinic based in an urban ghetto claims to be serving its community that is composed of 80 percent black residents. Yet, despite efforts to attract blacks to the clinic, nearly all of the clinic's patients are white. Significantly, so are its entire board and staff.

☐ The board of directors of a community recreation center is mystified by the low attendance at a newly planned series of events. The problem stems from the fact that the events were planned by a consultant who failed to seek community input.

☐ The IRS challenges the tax-exempt status of a nonprofit literary marketing service on the grounds that membership is open only to a select few who derive clear financial benefits from the association.

Each of these organizations finds itself in a dilemma. In each case, the concept of public involvement has been defined too narrowly:

☐ In the case of the art museum, the director of the funding agency that dispenses public tax dollars says her grants committee is unwilling to "see the taxes of poor people going to pay for the pleasures of the rich." She claims that her agency might feel very differently if the museum offered subsidized admissions for senior citizens, attempted to make the facility accessible to the handicapped, provided informal concerts in community locations, or offered an educational program for local schoolchildren.

☐ In the case of the health center, the organization's mission statement speaks about service to the community, but the organization's all-white board and staff transmit a different message to the black people in that community. It is an example of actions speaking louder than words.

☐ In the case of the recreation center, the organization appears to have alienated its primary community constituency by placing too much confidence in the abilities of a consultant. Perhaps if community representatives had been involved in the planning process from the start, there would have been a greater sense of ownership once the programs were established.

☐ Finally, the literary organization offers a chilling preview of what can happen when an organization defines its membership and services too narrowly. The consequences of ambiguity about the nonprofit intent of the organization are possible loss of funding and ultimately of tax-exempt status as well.

For a nonprofit organization, then, defining its service to the public involves the following components:

- A well-defined understanding of an organization's constituency
- Involvement of this constituency at all levels of the organization, but particularly at the trustee level
- Programs and activities that demonstrate a strong commitment to the constituency

THE TEST FOR ORGANIZED ABANDONMENT

One of the greatest challenges for a nonprofit organization, as we have seen, is to determine its mission, but it is equally difficult to decide at what point the mission is no longer appropriate or there are other organizations that can achieve it more effectively. A so-called test for organized abandonment is so difficult to apply that many nonprofit organizations simply struggle along year after year without ever facing up to the fact that their existence is of very little consequence to anyone outside of the organization itself.

Consider the organization whose mission centers on the eradication of a particular disease. What should happen to that organization when a cure for the disease is discovered, medicine made available, and the disease eliminated? At first glance, it would seem obvious that the organization should disband. But should it? It has over the years built up a loyal constituency. Might that constituency be encouraged to join the fight to eliminate another disease?

Or consider the organization that has been allowed to atrophy over the years and now finds itself surrounded by a number of younger, more vital organizations that appear to be carrying out its mission more effectively. This would appear to be a clear case where the organization should disband. But again, one should not jump quickly to conclusions. By whose standards is the organization judged moribund and by what criteria is it determined that others are carrying out its mission more effectively?

The concept of organized abandonment is central to our understanding of nonprofit organizations and illustrates one of the principal difficulties in responsible governance and management. *Organized abandonment* refers to the planned phasing out of an organization's operation. The word *organized* is used to characterize a kind of disbanding that is the result of careful deliberation rather than of unwelcome and unexpected financial reversals, management upheaval, or other external or internal crises. One of the major problems in the nonprofit world is that the test for organized abandonment is difficult to apply because the criteria by which judgments are made are relative and subjective.

Once again, the contrast with the profit and public sectors is clear. In the profit sector, when an organization loses money for any length of time and the future does not promise a turnaround, it is usually a signal that something must change. Investors move in to cut their losses and the organization may be sold, disbanded, or reorganized. There are two essential differences in the nonprofit sector. The first is that it is not nearly as obvious when things should change because there is not a single, objective criterion by which to measure success or failure. Second, there is no predictable outside pressure to reorganize or disband. There is no voting group moving quickly to protect its investments and the governing group and staff can continue operating for years without a real sense of purpose or standard of excellence.

In the public sector, there is also a clear difference in knowing when to cease operations. For a government agency, publicly elected individuals hold the purse strings and review the agency's achievements and plans, usually on an annual basis. The agency must perform to the elected individuals' satisfaction or its funding, and sometimes its continued existence, is threatened. Periodically, the agency may be further subjected to some form of "sunset review" that requires a formal justification of its continued existence before it is authorized to continue operating. No such external pressures are brought to bear on private nonprofit organizations.

We have arrived, then, at the final critical challenge for a nonprofit organization—the challenge of testing for organized abandonment. This challenge requires that the organization:

- Has defined its mission clearly
- Has established success criteria by which it can evaluate the relevance and effectiveness of its mission
- Has set up a formal system by which it can determine whether the mission is still relevant and whether it is carrying out the mission effectively

The following case may provide insight into how this can be accomplished.

THE REGIONAL HEALTH NETWORK

In the late 1970s, a federal agency, in partnership with three state agencies from northern New England and with the help of several area corporations, put together a funding package to promote exemplary health education programs in rural Maine, New Hampshire, and Vermont. A new private nonprofit organization—The Regional Health Network—was established in New Hampshire. Its mission was twofold: first, to improve the quality and quantity of health education in the three northern New England states through workshops, seminars, classes, and community events and second, to upgrade the expertise of schools and community groups in establishing permanent ongoing programs at the local level.

For ten years, the Regional Health Network thrived. Its budget increased, its staff grew to ten people, it was given a home within a large university, and its program was cited as a national model. By the late 1970s, things had begun to change. The funding of the Regional Health Network became more precarious because the federal agency had changed its funding priorities and state agencies had followed suit. The funding crisis was the result of a policy shift for which the Network was not to blame and over which it had no control. The Network's federal and state funders had decided to establish regional health education organizations, but the definition of a region was six states. The Network, because it served only three states, was not considered an appropriate recipient of funding. Hence, through a technicality in federal and state policy, continued funding for the Network appeared to be uncertain.

Money was not the Regional Health Network's only problem. From its inception in 1978, the Network's constituency had been composed largely of volunteers with little experience in health education. Initially, teachers, parents, and other volunteers continually praised the technical assistance provided by the Regional Exchange staff stating that "we never could have done these programs without you." But ten years later, the Network's constituency was becoming far more sophisticated. Many of the local programs were staffed by professionals and these people were demanding either that the Network provide better and more extensive services or simply turn the scarce federal and state money directly over to them.

It is fortunate that the Regional Health Network had defined its mission clearly, set up evaluation criteria, and was willing to engage in the test for organized abandonment. By doing so, it was able to provide improved services to its constituents, preserve all of its important programs, find challenging jobs for its staff members, and, ultimately, to disband.

The organization went through the following steps to determine whether organized abandonment was appropriate. An evaluation was done to determine how well the organization had fulfilled or was fulfilling its mission. Through the evaluation, it was discovered that the ten years of developmental work in rural northern New England had spawned a large number of ongoing, self-sufficient programs in both the schools and community organizations—a discovery that pleased the board but indicated that the need for developmental work had diminished. The evaluation also revealed that while the need for health education, technical assistance, and resources was still great, the Network's constituents were looking to larger and better-funded organizations to provide these resources and the Network was becoming less important to them.

Subsequent to the evaluation, the board and staff of the Network talked to funders in both the public and private sectors to analyze the financial prospects for the future. While most of the funders said that they would be willing to help the organization by making small gifts toward its programmatic activities, no funder was willing to underwrite basic administrative costs. Because the federal and state agencies that had originally provided the administrative underwriting were in the process of designating another organization (which serviced six states) to be the official regional organization and because federal policy required that only one organization per region could receive basic administrative underwriting, the Network's financial future did not look good.

The board and the staff of the Regional Health Network met for several months to consider the situation. Could the organization change its mission in order to secure basic administrative funding? Should the organization charge for its services? Should the staff be cut to one or two people so that the organization could continue to run a token program, hoping for a better future later? Each of these alternatives and many others were considered. But each was rejected. The original mission of the organization had been right for its time. Much of what the organization had set out to do had been accomplished. Now there were other organizations that were carrying out the balance of the mission with greater effectiveness and financial viability.

The board voted to disband, but set up a nine-month timetable to make sure that every significant program of the Network was placed in another organization, that each member of the staff had another place to go, and that a history of the organization and its accomplishments could be written to become a part of the public record. Several of the programs were absorbed by the new six-state regional organization, based in Massachusetts, and to ensure continuity through the first year of transition, that organization hired the Network's executive director as a full-time consultant/coordinator for program implementation in the three northern New England states. In January 1990, the Network closed its doors. It did so after a champagne reception to celebrate its accomplishments and the future of its programs.

The history of the Regional Health Network is a success story in nonprofit administration. Its success is represented not only by what it accomplished during its eleven years of existence but also what it accomplished in disbanding at the right time and in the right way. There are many nonprofit organizations that would benefit from a close analysis of the history of the Network, particularly the events of the final two years. This history demonstrates how one nonprofit organization met the challenge of accountability to its mission.

The purpose of this chapter has been to describe some of the more important characteristics of nonprofit organizations and the consequent challenges that face those who govern and manage them. Nonprofit organizations are private-sector organizations with public purposes. This combination gives them great flexibility in their operation. However, flexibility is a double-edged sword. It offers opportunities yet poses certain dangers. Most particularly, it can cause ambiguity and uncertainty in the areas of mission, constituency, and activities. A nonprofit organization must address these dangers by:

1. Articulating its mission clearly
2. Engaging in ongoing planning with an eye toward careful consideration of the risks and benefits of every proposed course of action and the relation of these actions to the organization's mission
3. Identifying its constituency and involving representatives of that constituency in all phases of the organization's operation
4. Testing for organized abandonment in order to ensure that the organization remains needed and wanted

These challenges, when properly met, provide a basic framework for responsible governance and management in nonprofit organizations.

CHECKLIST QUESTIONS FOR CHAPTER 1

1. Has the mission statement of your organization been reviewed within the last five years?
2. Does the mission statement contain both a broad statement of purpose and a more detailed framework from which your organization can develop a coherent set of activities?
3. Has a planning process been developed that balances the need for organizational and program development with long-term financial security?
4. Who are your organization's constituents? Are they well represented in the organization? Are they well served by the organization's activities?
5. Has there been a formal test for organized abandonment in your organization within the last decade?
6. What criteria have been developed to evaluate the continued relevance and appropriateness of your organization's mission and activities?

2
The Board

Mary Clarke founded the Compton Community Center eleven years ago. Had she known then what she knows now, she would have done things differently. Who could have imagined back then, when the center was just an idea in her head, that the idea would become a reality, that within ten years the community center would be serving more than 15,000 people every year, that it would own a building (a former schoolhouse that was purchased from the town for $1), and that it would have a paid staff of twenty-two people and a budget in excess of $1 million? Had she known all these things were possible, she might have taken the advice of people who told her to go more slowly and carefully. But, at the time, she felt she had to move quickly and decisively. She had to garner support from anyone who would help. She had to show confidence even when she was not sure she was doing the right thing. Her philosophy was that enthusiasm is contagious, and it is enthusiasm that builds community organizations.

Mary Clarke's biggest regret is that she did not exercise greater care in assembling a board of trustees. Her mistake is completely understandable given the circumstances. The community center had operated for two years as a project of the local YMCA and had not needed to incorporate. It was a convenient relationship. The YMCA provided space, took care of all of the necessary bookkeeping, and lent its tax-exempt status to the center so that Mary could go out and fund raise. Eventually, she knew, she would have to worry about separate corporate status but many people advised her to wait until the program was well established. However, something unexpected happened that required a change in her timetable. When Compton's school board decided to close one of the local elementary schools, several influential people in town felt that it should become the new home for the Compton Community Center. The idea was the fulfillment of Mary Clarke's dream and she was not about to claim that the organization was not ready for such a step.

After that, things moved quickly. There was a special town referendum in which the voters agreed that the school should be sold to the Compton Community Center for $1. Lawyers for the town met with lawyers representing the YMCA and Mary Clarke's committee. All agreed that under these new circumstances Mary Clarke's project had gone beyond the point

27

at which the YMCA could assume a fiscal agent status and that separate incorporation for the Compton Community Center would be a necessity. It was further agreed that Mary needed an official nonprofit corporation to which the property could be deeded.

It was at this point that Mary Clarke made her first serious mistake. In her haste to get the corporation together, she asked a group of her friends to serve as the trustees. "It is just to satisfy the lawyers," she said, "and to put some names on the incorporation papers. I promise that you won't really have to do anything." These were words that she soon came to regret. She regretted them when the Compton Community Center needed to begin serious fund raising, when she needed to mobilize support in the community for a zoning change, and when she came to realize that one person could not single-handedly assume responsibility for an organization as large and complex as the Compton Community Center. Like many nonprofit organizations, Mary's was incorporated in haste and a governing group was thrown together that knew nothing about the considerable responsibilities of trusteeship. This was to haunt Mary Clarke for the next five years.

Perhaps all of this would have been clearer if Mary Clarke herself had understood the specific role that the law has carved out for trustees[1] in connection with the governance of a legally constituted nonprofit organization. Chapter 1 indicated that nonprofit organizations are granted several very lucrative concessions and immunities by the federal and state governments, especially after they have received permission to operate as tax-exempt corporations. Once the organizations are declared tax-exempt, several governmental authorities at the federal, state, and, in some cases, the local level give up their right to tax. Furthermore, the IRS generally agrees to allow individuals and institutional donors to claim tax deductions when they make gifts to these organizations. This is no less than a generous public subsidy. In making this concession, the government is assuming that the organizations are somehow serving the public and not operating for anyone's private financial gain.

By giving up the power to tax, and granting the status of tax deductibility on gifts, government taxing authorities are making tremendous concessions and in many cases bestowing a great deal of indirect financial assistance on nonprofit organizations. For example, in a particular organization that is receiving $500,000 in individual contributions each year, we can assume that at least $100,000 of that is indirectly provided by the government through taxes not paid to the U.S. Treasury. For the nonprofit field as a whole, foregone taxes from individuals alone may be as high as $13 billion.[2] For this reason, there needs to be some protection built into the system so that the government can feel that the public purposes of nonprofit organizations are in fact being carried out. It requires that a group of people act as guardians of the public trust—individuals who have the public's interest at heart. These people are trustees. It is their task to act as stewards, accountable to the state government that granted the organizations their respective charters, accountable to the federal government that granted tax-exempt status, and ultimately accountable to the public itself.

In order to ensure that trustees of nonprofit organizations have the public's interest at heart, the individuals should not serve in order to derive financial benefits from trusteeship, as would be the case in a profit-making organization. They may not personally own stock in nonprofit organizations nor have an owner's equity in any of its assets. For the most part, they are expected to serve without compensation (except reasonable reimbursement for out-of-pocket expenses).[3] Indeed, instead of serving as trustees for the financial benefits that might accrue to them, they are expected to carry out their duties as volunteers, for the public good, and to exercise, on behalf of the public, a legal and fiduciary responsibility. They must make sure that the organizations they serve are carrying out their missions as articulated in the articles of incorporation and that their financial activities are both legal and proper given federal and state requirements.

In this context, trusteeship is a serious business carrying extensive legal obligations. It is not simply an honor. Nor is it simply attendance at luncheons and tea parties, as trustees who have been sued have learned to their dismay. It is an activity that requires knowledge, commitment, and time. In selecting trustees, Mary Clarke should have found people who understood this; she should have searched out people with proper legal and financial skills. Most important, she should have looked for people who understood something about the responsibilities and duties of trusteeship.

THE RESPONSIBILITIES AND DUTIES OF TRUSTEES
There are six principal areas of responsibility for trustees. Trustees should:

- Determine the organization's mission and set policies for its operation, ensuring that the provisions of the organization's charter and the law are being followed
- Set the organization's overall program from year to year and engage in longer range planning to establish its general course for the future
- Establish fiscal policy and boundaries, with budgets and financial controls
- Provide adequate resources for the activities of the organization through direct financial contributions and a commitment to fund raising

- Select, evaluate, and, if necessary, terminate the appointment of the chief executive
- Develop and maintain a communication link to the community, promoting the work of the organization

Important as it is to understand what the duties of trustees include, it is equally important to understand what they do not include. Trustees should not:

- Engage in the day-to-day operation of the organization
- Hire staff other than the chief executive
- Make detailed programmatic decisions without consulting staff

Let us look in more detail at the six responsibility areas of trustees.

POLICY MAKING

By law, the board of trustees is responsible for setting policy for a nonprofit organization. This begins with drafting (and amending when necessary) two documents that set out various rules, regulations, and procedures. These are the *articles of incorporation* (sometimes called the *articles of organization*) and the *bylaws.* In addition, the trustees may wish to develop other documents such as a personnel manual and a trustee manual to further clarify roles, responsibilities, duties, and general policies. In many nonprofit organizations, additional policies are drafted in the areas of conflict of interest, use of organizational funds by board and staff (for such things as travel and entertainment), and other matters pertaining to the particular activities of the organization they serve.

Developing policies for the smooth operation of a nonprofit organization has two advantages. From a very practical point of view, a set of rules, regulations, and operating procedures ensures that there is a standard against which to measure employee and trustee actions and that the standards provide grounds for dismissal when individuals do not conform to them. More broadly, fully documented policies partially protect the trustees from liability as will be described later in this chapter. Lawsuits are far less likely when the trustees have taken the trouble to develop, debate, revise, and adopt policies that demonstrate their involvement in the affairs of the organization.

The first document that the trustees must concern themselves with is the organization's *charter* referred to in some states as the *articles of incorporation* and in others as the *articles of organization.* The articles are initially submitted at the time the organization petitions the state for corporate status and they are reviewed in the state office that maintains corporate records (e.g., Department of Corporations or the Secretary of State's office). That portion of the articles that sets out the basic operating framework of the organization is almost always drafted with the assistance of an attorney to ensure conformity with the laws governing nonprofit corporations, although the portion containing the corporate purpose should be drafted with the input of the trustees.

Once the articles of incorporation are approved, the original copy remains in the state office and serves as official documentation of the corporation's structure, purpose, fiscal year, and so on. Because so much of the organization's character and reason for being are contained in the articles of organization, the trustees should review it at least once every three years. Changes should be stated as amendments, approved by the trustees, and subsequently filed with the state. It is important to remind the trustees that part of their legal obligation is to make sure that the corporation is carrying out its activities and fulfilling its mission as specified in the charter. Thus the trustees should be supplied with a copy of the charter at the time they join the organization.

The board of trustees is also responsible for drafting a second document, called the *bylaws,* which serves as the organization's operating constitution. Bylaws go beyond the general material contained in the charter and discuss more detailed and specific procedures affecting the trustees themselves. For example, the bylaws set out the number, tenure, and election procedure for trustees, discuss how and when meetings are called, how officers (president, treasurer, clerk, and so on) are elected and what their powers are, how votes are taken, how board vacancies are filled, and a host of other small details essential to the smooth operation of the organization.

Bylaws, like articles of organization, must be reviewed periodically and updated. Furthermore, it is the responsibility of the trustees to see that the provisions are followed in order to avoid legal complications. Consider the following case.

PETERSON PARK ZOO

The executive director of the Peterson Park Zoo, a nonprofit organization with a budget of $10 million, had been warned several times by the president of the board that the trustees were unhappy with his performance. After six months, the president held a special meeting of the executive committee and a vote was taken to terminate the appointment of the executive director with two months' notice. The executive director was informed of the decision and, unbeknownst to the trustees, secured the services of a lawyer. Meanwhile, a search committee was formed and a new executive director was hired.

When the time came for the first executive director to leave, he stated that he had not been legally removed from his job and was therefore still the executive director. He pointed out that according to the bylaws, the executive committee was not empowered to terminate him because he was an officer of the corporation and that such an action required a majority vote of the entire board at a full board meeting. Furthermore, according to his contract, three months' notice was required between the official vote to terminate and actual termination of services.

The Peterson Park Zoo now had two executive directors each threatening a law suit and the trustees were in a quandary. Three weeks elapsed before the full board could meet to discuss the problem and take a vote on the first executive director's job. During that time, the executive director mobilized considerable support from disgruntled trustees who were angry at the incompetence of the executive committee. During the board meeting, the lawyer for the executive director successfully convinced a majority of trustees to provide two years of severance pay for his client, an expense that the Peterson Park Zoo could ill afford and that could have been avoided had the board given proper attention to the bylaws.

Subsequently, a group of trustees who had not been part of the executive committee and had not been consulted in the original decision to fire the executive director threatened to bring suit against members of the executive committee (as was their legal right under state law). In order to avoid the potential financial consequences of legal action, the executive committee members voluntarily resigned from the board in exchange for having the suit dropped.

In addition to the articles of organization and the bylaws, some organizations develop two rule books, one primarily for staff and the other for the board. The staff rule book is called a *personnel manual* and is discussed in detail in chapter 4. It provides information about hiring and firing, vacation and sick days, leaves, performance and salary reviews, working hours and conditions, and benefits. The board rule book, or *trustee manual,* is discussed later in this chapter. It provides a more detailed account of the roles and responsibilities of trustees.

Either included in both the personnel and trustee manuals or developed as a separate document, many organizations develop a set of *conflict-of-interest* policies. The potential for conflict of interest arises when members of the board or staff might find themselves in a position to benefit themselves, family members, or other organizations with which they are associated by virtue of their position with the nonprofit organization. It should be pointed out that in many cases the action by the nonprofit organization might be entirely appropriate—as, for example, when the organization chooses to engage the law firm of one of its trustees to undertake a complex real estate transaction or defend the organization against a lawsuit. However, in all cases, conflict-of-interest policies should suggest:

1. That an individual with a conflict fully disclose his or her relationship to the individual or organization benefiting from the decision
2. That the individual with a conflict not participate in the decision in which the conflict exists, which might mean:

   - Not participating in the vote
   - Not entering into the discussion prior to the vote
   - Absenting himself or herself from the room during the discussion and the vote

The documents just described provide the trustees with a mechanism for setting broad policy on the internal structure and operation of their organization and they can develop other policies from time to time that further help bring clarity to these areas. By developing these policies, they also protect the organization and themselves considerably from legal exposure because they demonstrate that the group took reasonable care to ensure that the organization would operate in a manner that would appear reasonable to "an ordinary prudent person in a like position" (the standard that most states' attorneys general would by law adopt in judging the actions of trustees).

PLANNING

The second major responsibility of the trustees is to engage in planning both for the short term (the next year), the medium term (the next five years), and the long term (the next decade). Planning involves the setting of broadly stated goals and specific objectives. To establish goals, the board must decide on directions for the organization and determine what they want to see accomplished. For example, a goal of the Compton Community Center might be to provide a rich variety of sports-related opportunities for disadvantaged schoolchildren in the city. To establish objectives, the board must be much more specific. Objectives are time bound, usually quantitative, and measurable. Thus for the goal of providing a rich variety of sports-related opportunities for disadvantaged schoolchildren in the city, an objective might be to provide at least one hour a week of supervised physical activities to 850 children, aged eight to eighteen, from low-income families.

Objectives, once set, allow for two additional activities to take place. One is the drafting of an action or implementation plan by which the objectives will be achieved. Generally, the implementation plan is developed primarily by staff and is reviewed by the board. It lays out the actual schedule of activities, use of resources (both human and financial), and logistics. The second activity that should follow the development of objectives is the establishment of an evaluation process to determine whether the organization actually achieves the objectives in the time allotted. Unfortunately, evaluation is one area that is often neglected by trustees. But it should not be. The trustees are responsible for keeping the organization on track. They should do so partially by tracking the effectiveness with which plans are actually carried out and objectives met.

Although planning will be discussed in more depth in chapter 9, it is important to outline at least some activities that a board should generally consider in the planning area. These include:

- Appointing a planning committee to develop the planning agenda for the organization
- Holding periodic planning retreats at least once every two years (and more frequently during the development of a long-range plan)
- Developing a written plan at least once every five years
- Establishing goals and objectives in advance of every new year
- Reviewing the operational and financial consequences of these goals and objectives

FISCAL RESPONSIBILITIES

The executive director really knows about the budget. Let's let him develop the numbers, and we will simply approve what he comes up with.

The staff is honest; let's not make their life complicated by insisting on cumbersome check-signing and cash-handling procedures.

Many trustees either make statements like these or make decisions that indicate that they believe them. In doing so, they are not only abrogating their responsibility to preserve the public trust by neglecting a fiduciary (or fiscal/financial) responsibility, but they are making themselves personally liable for legal action. Many trustees are under the mistaken notion that while a corporation can be sued, an individual who serves on its board is immune and cannot be sued. This is not the case. Corporations do offer certain protections, but if it can be proven that the trustees showed negligence in financial matters, they can be held personally liable. It is very unusual that creditors would have standing to sue trustees if the organization failed to pay them.[4] However, the federal government has standing to sue for the nonpayment of withholding taxes and there are other cases where the personal assets of the trustees could be at risk. For example, in a trustee dispute, one group of trustees could, on behalf of the organization, hold another group liable if it could be demonstrated that they provided inaccurate financial information in the case of an important financial decision that adversely affected the organization. Even if the case had no merit and the judgment was for those accused, the defending trustees might find themselves bearing heavy legal costs.

The best way for trustees to avoid such situations is to exercise financial responsibility. This involves developing and monitoring budgets on the one hand and establishing fiscal controls on the other. In the area of budgets, the trustees perform several functions. One is a planning function. The preparation of the annual budget must be accomplished with the involvement of board members (a finance committee is often assembled for this purpose) and these individuals must satisfy themselves that revenues will be adequate to meet projected expenses. If there is a deficit at the end of the year, the trustees should share the responsibility with the staff. It is simply not sufficient to say, "The executive director was incorrect in his projections." The trustees must also admit, "We did not ask enough probing questions." (Chapter 6 details the steps involved in the budgeting process.)

Preparation of the budget is only part of the trustee's oversight responsibility in this area. The two additional trustee functions are approval and monitoring. The approval step, which must be completed before the budget period begins, is an official action on the part of the trustees that carries the force of an endorsement. It says to the staff, "We have reviewed this budget and are satisfied that revenues and expenditures appear reasonable and achievable. We will take responsibility in helping you meet your revenue targets." Obviously, if such a statement indicates that there are projected revenues based on fund raising, the trustees have implicitly made a commitment to assist in this area.

Approving a budget is not enough. The trustees are responsible for monitoring and, if necessary, amending the budget throughout the year. Financial statements must be prepared for every board meeting that show how the actual revenue and expense figures compare with what has been budgeted (see figure 2.1). The example in figure 2.1 was taken from the first year's operation of the Compton Community Center as an independent corporation. The move to the new building had not yet taken place, and the budget was still modest. In spite of these factors, the trustees of the

FIGURE 2.1.   Compton Community Center Three-Month Financial Statement
(September 1, 1989–November 30, 1989)

	Budget	Year to Date	Balance
Revenues			
Membership	$22,500	$ 6,212	$ 16,288
Admissions	6,500	2,431	4,069
Contributions	5,000	1,100	3,900
Grants	10,000	1,000	9,000
Total	$44,000	$ 10,743	$33,257
Expenses			
Salaries	$21,000	$ 5,250	$ 15,750
Fees/honoraria	5,000	2,000	3,000
Rent	4,000	1,000	3,000
Telephone	1,000	512	488
Utilities	500	333	167
Office supplies	800	612	188
Sports equipment	2,200	1,000	1,200
Benefit expense	2,000	0	2,000
Educational program	7,500	3,333	4,167
Total	$44,000	$ 14,040	$29,960
Net income (or loss)	0	($3,297)	

Source: Compiled by the author.

Compton Community Center received some surprises when they reviewed
the financial statement for the first three months of the fiscal year.

The left-hand column of figure 2.1 shows the actual approved annual
budget figures, the center column shows receipts and expenditures up to
the closing date on the statement, and the right-hand column shows the
difference between the first two columns for each budget category. At this
point in the year, the trustees had an opportunity to assess the various
budget estimates and adjust the original budget based on the up-to-date
information given in the financial statement.

The trustees were not pleased with what they saw on this statement. For
example, the revenue category called Grants showed only $1,000 of income
after three months even though $10,000 had been budgeted for the year.
One trustee asked whether the original figure was realistic. If not, she
suggested that a more modest projection of income be inserted into the
original budget; expenditures would then have to be adjusted downward
as well. Similarly, the expense categories of Telephone, Utilities, and Office
supplies appear to have been considerably underbudgeted given the fact
that nine months remained in the fiscal year. To her surprise, the board
asked Mary Clarke to make adjustments.

Monitoring the budget is an important responsibility of the trustees, one
that establishes certain important financial controls. Other controls can be

set through financial policy development. The board must determine such things as:

☐ Who will approve invoices and sign checks?
☐ Will individual staff members who are responsible for finances be bonded? Will the treasurer be bonded?
☐ Will there be a petty cash account and what controls will be put on its use?
☐ Should the organization allow first person checks that are not counter-signed?
☐ Should the books be audited by an outside examiner? If so, a group of board members must assist in the selection of this individual, review his or her report, and address any deficiencies that are revealed by the examination (or audit) itself?

More information in each of these areas is given in chapter 7. It is sufficient to say at this point that there are standard fiscal operating procedures for nonprofit organizations. These are generally known by most accountants and thus it is appropriate that such an individual should serve on the board so that he or she can assist in developing appropriate fiscal policies. In this way, the trustees can assure themselves that the organization's financial house is in order.

FUND RAISING

No group of people should display a greater commitment to a nonprofit organization than its trustees. These individuals, who have agreed to serve the organization in a variety of ways, must set the tone for others—people in the community, funders, constituents, audience members, and clients. Trustees must support the organization in spirit, encouraging others to be as enthusiastic about its programs and activities as they are and they must support the organization more tangibly with money, demonstrating that those closest to the organization, its trustees, are 100 percent committed to it. Put quite simply, everyone who serves on a board of trustees must contribute some cash every year to his or her organization. How much they contribute is another matter, but there should be no ambiguity about the requirement of some sort of annual cash gift.

It is not unusual for a potential funder to ask, "What percentage of your trustees contribute to your organization?" This question is a quick way for a donor to garner information on board commitment. If 100 percent of the trustees are contributing and if 20 percent of the total monies raised from individuals are coming from the board, then the donor sees a level of commitment that allows him or her to say, "I see there is support from the core group, which gives me confidence to invest in the effort." On the other hand, minimal support can make a donor somewhat suspicious. "If the board is not contributing, why should I? What do they know that I don't?"

In some organizations, the matter of trustee donations is controversial because the trustees are recruited from community groups representing the lower end of the economic scale. The statement that "some people cannot afford to make a donation" is generally a ruse to avoid tackling the issue of required trustee donations head on. There is practically no one sitting on a board of trustees who cannot afford to come up with $10 once a year, and most people can probably come up with $50. If special exceptions have to be made from time to time, they can be considered on a case-by-case basis; this should be no excuse for the absence of a stated policy on board contributions.

How much should trustees be required to give? There is no correct amount and each organization must try to arrive at a formula that seems right and fair. In some organizations, there is no minimum contribution, people simply give what they can but everyone must give something. In other organizations, a guideline rather than a requirement is offered. For example, "This year, our twenty-member board will be expected to contribute $10,000, or an average of $500 per trustee." In still others, a minimum level is set, anywhere from $100 to $10,000 per person. Finally, some organizations set a minimum level, say $300 per person, and state that only half or a third must be contributed in cash and the rest may be contributed in some other form such as help in the office, donated equipment or food, or other forms of volunteer assistance. Keep in mind, though, that trustees are already expected to contribute time to the organization and if volunteer hours are to be counted toward a donation, these should very clearly be "over-and-above" hours.

In addition to giving money, trustees must help raise money. Each trustee, in fact, should assist in some way with the fund-raising effort. Some will feel uncomfortable doing direct solicitation; however, as we will see in chapter 8, there are many other tasks involved in fund raising—prospect identification, list development and maintenance, letter writing, planning of events, and proposal writing—and every member of the board should be assigned some task related to one of these activities.

In selecting trustees, it is important to recruit people who have contacts in the funding community such as businesspeople, wealthy individuals, and prominent citizens. Some of these people will recoil from the idea of fund raising. "I couldn't possibly ask my friends for money," is a typical refrain. However, these same people may be willing to do other things that are equally valuable. For example, while they may not want to ask their friends for money directly, they may be willing to make appointments for other people in the organization to do it. Or it is likely that they will at least share their knowledge of these friends' philanthropic interests, which is valuable information as the organization plans how and when to ask them for money. Trustees from the business community may not be willing to solicit their peers but may be willing to give a lunch on the organization's behalf at which contacts can be made, or they may be willing to make a phone call to set up an appointment for the executive director, which will ensure that the request gets past the secretary. Trustees who can open doors in this way can be as valuable as those who actually do the fund raising.

Ultimately, an organization's list of trustees can itself be part of a fund-raising strategy. While people should not be selected for name value alone—a blue-ribbon name list can be put together as an advisory committee if window dressing is called for—a well-balanced group of influential trustees says something to funders about the importance of the organization in the community. If Mabel, John, and Sam (all prominent citizens) are willing to give their time and their names to this organization, it must be worthy of attention. If, in addition, they are willing to solicit funds on the organization's behalf, it must be worthy of support.

HIRING AND WORKING WITH THE CHIEF EXECUTIVE

The character of almost every nonprofit organization is set in large measure by its chief executive. This is because the chief executive not only speaks for the organization publicly but he or she also hires the staff that deals on a day-to-day basis with the organization's constituency. Thus the public's impression of the organization is very much in the chief executive's hands. Consequently, the selection of this person is a very great responsibility. In selecting the chief executive, the following rules should be followed:

☐ Trustees should agree on what their expectations are. They should decide what kind of person they are looking for and what special qualifications the person should possess before they look at a single résumé.

☐ Trustees should document what the job entails. There should be a clear job description (see chapter 4) that lists both general responsibilities and specific tasks.

☐ In talking to serious candidates, trustees should be honest about organizational problems. They should not pretend things are fine when they are not. If there are financial problems, staff problems, or even trustee problems, there is nothing to gain in the long run by hiding them.

☐ Trustees should be clear about how the chief executive's performance is going to be evaluated. If there is a formal review process, it should be described. If there is not, the person should be told what criteria will be used to determine how successfully he or she is doing the job.

☐ In many cases, trustees may wish to utilize the professional experience, expertise, and contacts of an executive search firm. Although there may be substantial costs involved, the trustees may decide that such an investment is worthwhile in order to find, recruit, and select the best person for the job.

Evaluation. Regular evaluation of a chief executive is also an important responsibility of the trustees. It is an excellent way to foster good communication about perceived successes, failures, and expectations for the future. Evaluation should take place at least once a year, at some time immediately prior to the negotiation over salary for the upcoming year. Although chapter 4 gives general advice on personnel evaluations, one special feature of the chief executive's review should be mentioned here. Unlike most staff members, the chief executive works for more than one person. He or she works for all of the trustees. Thus the evaluation of a chief executive is not quite as straightforward as regular staff evaluations. Whatever system is set up, there should be some way for the full board to have input into the process.

One system that seems to work well is for the president of the board to circulate a questionnaire to trustees asking specific questions about the chief executive's performance during the past year. After the responses are collected, the board president can then summarize these responses for the chief executive, soliciting his or her reaction. Once the performance review is completed and general job performance objectives are set for the following year, the results are summarized and circulated to the full board for review. After the process is completed, salary negotiation can begin.

Sometimes a board of trustees is faced with the unpleasant task of having to fire a chief executive. Occasionally, although the occasions are few, the individual has done something illegal or so blatantly offensive that immediate termination is the only alternative. More often, the situation is a judgment call, which makes the decision particularly sensitive and difficult. In spite of this fact, it is always better to bite the bullet and address the problem directly rather than to let it fester and hope it will go away. Trustees should never feel guilty about initiating a process of evaluation that may lead to termination. Those who resist doing so are not exercising their responsibility to the organization they are serving.

The *performance review* is a convenient first opportunity to alert the chief executive that the trustees are dissatisfied with his or her performance. The more specific the criticisms at this stage, the easier it will be for the board president to communicate them and to develop a procedure whereby the executive is given some time to try to improve job performance. At the time that the board president speaks to the chief executive, board concerns should be communicated in writing and written performance objectives should be set for a fixed probationary time period (preferably not more than three months). For example, the board may be concerned that fiscal management is sloppy and that financial statements are always late and inaccurate. A specific performance objective might be that the chief executive provide monthly financial statements to the board no later than two weeks after the close of each month. These statements can be checked by the board's treasurer. Along with specific job objectives such as this, the president should outline the criteria that will be used to judge whether the executive has been able to improve his or her performance on the job. After all of this is explained, the chief executive is given time to evaluate the situation, to try to improve, and to explore other employment opportunities. If, at the end of the period, the executive has not resigned, and the board is still unhappy with job performance, a final opportunity for a resignation should be offered before the board resorts to the more extreme measure of formal termination.

Developing a Good Working Relationship. The relationship between the board and staff of a nonprofit organization is critical to its successful operation. Much of the tone of that relationship is set by the chief executive and the board president. When these two individuals work well together, many potential problems between staff and board can be averted. When the working relationship is strained, a "we/they" atmosphere can permeate the internal operations of the organization.

Many of the problems in this area result from a fundamental misunderstanding of the limits of trusteeship on the part of particular board members. Some examples are:

☐ Board members may attempt to involve themselves in detailed administrative tasks that are the responsibility of staff. For example, a board member might visit the site of an activity sponsored by the organization and take it upon himself or herself to correct or try to supervise a staff person when this task is the responsibility of the chief executive.

☐ Board members may make programmatic decisions without consulting staff in areas where staff expertise would have been helpful. For example, a group of board members might decide to proceed with a fund-raising event without consulting the chief executive and the staff fund-raiser.

☐ Board members may interfere in personnel issues. For example, they might invite unhappy staff members to bring complaints directly to them rather than to work through the chief executive.

These kinds of problems can surface in any organization but they are most common in newer ones, especially those that are just beginning to hire professional staff. Board members who performed many stafflike functions on a volunteer basis as the organization was being formed often find it difficult to give up some of their authority. It is not uncommon for these individuals to continue to want to play an active role in the administration of the organization even after it is no longer appropriate to do so.

But this overstepping of board role undermines the authority of the chief executive and can lead to an untenable working relationship with the board. Because chief executives are hired by their boards and must report to them, they are not in a position to reprimand those trustees who are out of line and they must rely on the president of the board to do so.

THE COMMUNICATIONS LINK

Many nonprofit organizations are the best kept secret in town. Others go about their business without the benefit of any input from those they are supposed to be serving. In both cases, the fault lies partly with trustees who do not understand that part of their responsibility is to promote their organization's activities widely and to seek opinions and observations about the organization from a variety of people. Trustees should make regular appearances on behalf of the organization, speaking to community and business groups as well as to friends and associates. Some trustees may be better public speakers than others, but every trustee should take the responsibility to tell people about the organization's activities and its importance to the community. At both formal functions and informal get-togethers, trustees should attempt to set up the two-way communications link with the public, they should provide free publicity and advocacy on behalf of the organization, and they should also get feedback from people to find out how others feel about what the organization is doing. Consider the following case.

CONCERTS FOR SCHOOLS, INC.

During a Rotary Club luncheon, a trustee of Concerts for Schools, Inc., a local music education organization, gave a short talk about the upcoming activities for the year, gently suggesting that the Rotarians might wish to make a modest contribution to the program. During the question and answer period, several members of her audience chided her about the seemingly elitist attitude of her program. Why did the group present only classical music? Wasn't jazz an art form too? Why were all the performers from out of state? Didn't their state have any good musicians? After hearing the reactions of the Rotarians, the trustee discussed the experience with her board. Several substantive changes were made in the program. The following year, the trustee went back to the Rotarians to thank them for their suggestions that had resulted in major changes in the program. The result was a $1,000 donation from the Rotary Club.

Because part of the responsibility of trustees is to provide a communications link with the community, it should be clear why it is so important that a diversity of backgrounds be represented on the board. When all segments of the community are represented, each group sees the organization as its own and this increases support in many tangible and intangible ways.

BOARD COMPOSITION

The responsibilities of trustees suggest those skills and areas of knowledge that a board must collectively possess. A practical listing might include the following areas of expertise:

- Nonprofit trusteeship
- Organizational planning
- Financial/accounting
- Fund raising (including business/corporate, individual, public agency, and foundation)
- Personnel management
- Legal matters especially relating to nonprofit corporations, contracts, and personnel
- Public relations

Various trustees should also be familiar with the programs and activities that the organization sponsors, and all trustees should support the organization's mission. They should represent a variety of backgrounds as well as various segments of the community, including different minority and ethnic groups that will give the board a broad vision and understanding of the true meaning of community and public service. In addition, specific nonprofits may require trustees with other types of expertise and representation. For example, if a nonprofit corporation owns a facility, operates a building, or maintains extensive grounds, it may be desirable to have an architect or a contractor on the board.

The purpose of having trustees with specific expertise is not to encourage encroachment on day-to-day activities that are staff responsibility but to provide a monitoring capability for the board. Such trustee expertise helps the board in formulating policy, reacting to staff recommendations, and choosing between alternative courses of action.

When choosing fellow trustees, the tendency is to say, "My friend John is interested in what we do, and he has served on the governing board of our church. I think he would be excellent." But this approach is not systematic enough and does not give enough consideration to the kinds of specific expertise that the board requires. An interest in an organization is not sufficient. For this reason, the development of a skills inventory chart is an excellent and simple mechanism for forcing the board (through its nominating committee, and with the staff, when appropriate) to analyze its needs. A skills inventory chart lists specific skills down the left-hand margin and lists existing and potential board members along the top axis.

Figure 2.2 is an example of a skills inventory chart. In this specific case, it is clear, first, that none of the existing trustees (Jones, Smith, Brown, Fox, and Evans) bring expertise in the legal field, in corporate fund raising, or in personnel. As the organization looks for new trustees, people with skills and experience in these areas should be sought. Second, we can see that Jones does not appear to be pulling his weight according to the skill areas listed. He may be on the board for other valid reasons, but the organization should analyze carefully what these reasons are. Third, while Smith (the organization's treasurer and a certified public accountant) brings considerable expertise in the financial/accounting area, her term is

	Jones	Smith	Brown	Fox	Evans	etc.
legal						
accounting		X				
corporate fund raising						
public relations			X			
music performance				X		
personnel						
facility management					X	

Figure 2.2. Skills Inventory Chart

due to expire. If she is not reelected to the board, it will be necessary to find someone with similar skills to replace her.

THE DEADWOOD PROBLEM

Regardless of how hard a nominating committee may work, there will always be some board members who are not pulling their weight, are not active, and are not contributing either financially or otherwise to the organization. While this *deadwood problem* will almost always exist to a certain extent, there are things that can be done to minimize it.

Limiting Terms of Office

No trustee should assume that he or she is going to serve the organization indefinitely. Limits should be placed on terms of office and on the number of times a trustee can be reelected. One system that seems to work well is to have a three-year term with one opportunity for reelection. After three years, a trustee comes up for reelection; after six, he or she must go off the board for at least one year before being invited to serve again. Trustee rotation offers a process for replacing weak board members with enthusiastic and committed trustees. Because continuity on the board is important, though, it is desirable to stagger the terms of trustees so that only one-third of the board members should be reaching the end of their terms in any one year.

Attendance

Nothing undermines the effectiveness of a board more than absence from meetings. Indeed, regular attendance at meetings is one criterion that could be used in a legal case to judge whether a board member had exercised reasonable care and diligence in exercising his or her trustee responsibilities. Participation by everyone is necessary if the board is going to operate effectively. Thus it should be a stated policy of the organization that attendance at board meetings is required. Beyond this, the board might adopt a policy that two unexcused absences in a year constitute an automatic resignation. If a trustee has a legitimate problem, such as an illness or a death in the family, the president can excuse that trustee from a meeting. However, without such a legitimate excuse (and without approval of the president), the policy should be clear that the trustee is expected to be at all board meetings. A slightly more liberal policy might be developed for attendance at committee meetings.

Financial Commitment

Previously it was pointed out that a nonprofit organization should insist that every trustee make an annual cash contribution. This contribution requirement, as well as the other obligations of trusteeship, must be clearly articulated to potential trustees as part of the recruitment and invitation process. The *pocketbook test* is, in fact, one excellent way to separate those trustees who will demonstrate commitment to the organization from those who will not.

The Trustee Manual

The deadwood problem is most prevalent when trustees lack a thorough understanding of the responsibilities of trusteeship and when they have the impression that serving on a board is more of a social function than a business function. To combat this problem, every organization should develop a trustee manual. Such a manual should be presented in loose-leaf form so that it can be updated regularly. The manual should include the following sections:

☐ Articles of incorporation with mission statement (the actual incorporation papers are less critical than the language that defines the nature and function of the organization).

☐ Bylaws (usually divided into sections; each of which should begin on a new page to facilitate scanning for specific information).

☐ List of current trustees with business affiliations, business and home addresses, phone numbers, and term expiration dates.

☐ List of committees and their respective members.

☐ List of staff members with titles and areas of responsibility.

☐ Brief (two- to three-page) history of the organization.

☐ Description of roles, responsibilities, and requirements of trustees (a summary of the kind of information contained in this chapter relating to general trustee responsibilities as well as the specific requirements—attendance, financial contribution, and committee responsibility—that will be expected of everyone).

☐ Minutes of current fiscal year meetings.

☐ Specific planning documents if available (a series of goal statements is often included here).

☐ The annual report from the last completed fiscal year (generally includes the audited financial statement; in lieu of an annual report, a promotional booklet can be submitted along with the financial statements for the most recently completed fiscal year).

Recruitment and Orientation

Related to the need for a trustee manual is a complementary need for both a clear recruitment procedure (which spells out the roles and responsibilities of trustees) and an orientation session for individuals who have agreed to join the board. The process follows:

1. A nominating committee is set up (with members either elected by the board or appointed by the president).
2. The committee analyzes board needs, evaluates the performance of trustees up for reelection, solicits names of other prospective trustees, and reviews a prospective slate with the full board.
3. After tentative and initial approval of the slate, appointments are made with prospective trustees. Each individual is visited by at least one member of the board (often the president) who is sometimes accompanied by the executive director. At the meeting, the roles, responsibilities, and requirements of trusteeship are described. A copy of the trustee manual is left with the person so that he or she may study it in detail before making his or her decision. (If the person elects not to serve on the board, the trustee manual should be returned.)
4. No more than one week after the visit, the prospective trustee should be asked for a final decision. If the answer is yes, then the individual will have to be officially elected to the board according to the process set out in the bylaws.
5. Once a year, the board should hold an orientation session. If held at the organization's office, the session can provide new trustees with the opportunity to meet the staff and observe the daily operations. The president, executive director, and committee chairs often give a series of short and informal speeches and, in some cases, an outside expert provides a pep talk on trustee roles and responsibilities. An orientation session is sometimes arranged to coincide with an event sponsored by the organization.

Evaluation and Dismissal

Some organizations have a formal review period at the end of each year at which time trustees evaluate one another's performance. It is usually the president who determines the evaluation process. Among the options available are informal discussions with each trustee or anonymous written statements. Whatever the process, the objective is the same: to identify ineffective trustees. If the president discovers that a trustee consistently receives poor evaluations from fellow board members, it is time to take action. Dismissal, through a majority vote of the board or some other procedure, is an action that should only be taken in the case of gross misconduct. However, other more moderate methods may lead to the same outcome. For example, a strong president can often counsel a trustee to resign by suggesting that he or she is overcommitted or seems to have lost interest.

It should be remembered that a good rotation policy through limited terms of office often makes the issue of trustee dismissal and forced resignation moot. Because terms are limited, most boards can live with a do-nothing trustee for a year, or two, or even three. On self-perpetuating boards, however, where terms are not fixed, evaluation, dismissal, and resignation become more critical.

COMMITTEES

When a nonprofit organization reaches a certain size and its operation becomes more complex, the board usually finds that it is difficult to carry out all of its responsibilities efficiently without dividing up into smaller groups. These groups, or committees, allow for a detailed analysis of specific areas such as fund raising, planning, budgeting, or programs, before they are discussed by the full board. A committee structure offers several advantages. First, it allows for a division of the workload. Second, it promotes a more informal discussion of the pros and cons of various issues before they come to the board for a formal resolution. Third, it allows an organization to bring experts into the deliberation process without putting them on the board. For example, a fund-raising committee might include representatives from the business community willing to help on an occasional basis but does not have the time or the inclination to be a trustee. In general, a committee should be chaired by a trustee and the majority of committee members should be board members, but outside resource people and staff members can and should be included because they are often an asset. The following committees are common in nonprofit organizations:

Executive. This committee is generally empowered to act for the full board in matters that require immediate action or do not involve major questions of policy or funding. It is also the chief coordinating committee for the board, mapping out how the board's business should be conducted, setting agendas, and organizing the activity of other committees. The executive director will often use the executive committee as a troubleshooting group, bringing to it problems needing rapid resolution. Generally the corporation's officers serve on this committee along with a few other members of the board, some of whom may be chairs of other committees. The executive committee should be small enough to function effectively (seven or eight members is common) and it should be made up of individuals who do not live or work so far away from the organization's home base that they are unable to come to meetings on short notice.

Finance. This committee is usually headed by the treasurer. It is empowered to study and make recommendations regarding all financial procedures and controls, assist in the preparation and presentation of budgets, and review all financial statements. This committee reviews audit results and recommends the retention of the auditor. An accountant is invaluable on this committee. In some large organizations there are separate committees for finance and audit.

Development. This committee, sometimes called the fund-raising committee, oversees the planning and coordination of fund-raising efforts. This will certainly include ongoing annual fund-raising for operations and solicitations of larger gifts. It may also include planning for fund-raising events and for capital campaigns, although these are sometimes handled by separate committees in larger organizations.

Nominating. This committee identifies, screens, and recommends prospective trustees. Members of this committee can also assist in the recruitment and orientation of the trustees.

Planning. This committee coordinates long-range planning. Its function is described in detail in chapter 9.

Buildings and grounds. For organizations that own or manage facilities or property, this committee will monitor their condition, recommend maintenance and repairs, and plan renovation projects. It is advisable to have an architect, contractor, or someone with similar expertise on this committee.

Marketing/public relations. Many nonprofit organizations have not developed a well-conceived approach to marketing or public relations and find themselves relatively unknown in the community. For those organizations and for others that sell a service or a product, it may be important to have a committee that can develop a marketing strategy and plan and oversee a public relations approach. On such a committee, it is often useful to have someone from the media or from a public relations firm.

Events or benefit. Organizations planning special events generally delegate responsibility for them to a special committee. Fund-raising events, such as benefits, should be handled by this committee if they are not handled by the development committee.

Program. This committee is organized to review the program activities of the organization and plan for the future. Because this committee has to work very closely with staff, its members must take care not to meddle in areas better left to staff management.

Personnel. This committee develops personnel policies (see chapter 4), recommends salary ranges to the board, may evaluate the executive director and recommend a specific salary level for that individual, reviews benefits packages, and handles grievances when board involvement is necessary.

Investment. For organizations that own significant assets that require investment (such as endowment funds), a special committee oversees the management of these funds. This may involve the evaluation of investment managers (with subsequent recommendation to the full board about which managers to retain), or it may involve investment decisions by the committee itself. Because of the fiduciary responsibilities associated with management of the organization's assets, the committee (and the full board) should make sure that there is adequate expertise on this committee and that its decisions seem prudent and do not involve excessive risk of the corporation's assets.

Few organizations will have all of these committees, and some organizations will have committees not listed here. Committees should only be formed if and when there is a need for them. Committee meetings, like board meetings, should have tight agendas and should not waste people's time.

OFFICERS

State laws vary but most generally require that a nonprofit corporation's board of trustees include at least three officers: a president (or chairperson), a treasurer, and a clerk (or secretary). Some organizations include additional officers, such as a vice-president or an assistant treasurer. The organization's bylaws will specify how many officers there must be, their titles, powers, and duties. The bylaws will also state the process by which they are elected and the frequency of the elections. (In this connection, it is common practice for the board to elect officers from among its ranks at the annual meeting of the corporation.) The selection of the right people to fill officer positions is an important task. Only the most qualified trustees should be considered for the regular officer positions. No one should be appointed to any of the three crucial positions (president, treasurer, and clerk) simply as an honor. It is an acceptable practice for an organization to create honorary officer positions such as "honorary chairperson" or "president emeritus" (to honor a past president who is no longer active), so long as it is clear that these people have no special powers.

President. The president should be a person of authority who is respected by the board, the staff, the community, and has plenty of time to devote to the job. He or she should serve on the executive committee for at least a year before assuming the presidency in order to become thoroughly familiar with the operation of the organization. A good president can set the work standard for the board that keeps the deadwood problem to a minimum and keeps the trustees on track with their tasks in board and committee work. A good president can serve as a buffer between disgruntled trustees and the executive director, mediating tensions and resolving differences. A weak president, on the other hand, may allow various factions to secure for themselves too much authority and control. Personal agendas may then take precedence over organizational priorities. No one should be appointed to the presidency who is afraid to deal firmly with those who are getting out of line.

In some organizations, there is both a chairperson and a president. This structure is borrowed from the profit sector but makes much less sense in the nonprofit environment. In a nonprofit organization, neither officer has any owner's equity and, generally, neither is a member of the staff. The main function in the nonprofit sector is to be the head of the voluntary board. Under this set of circumstances, it seems more reasonable and less confusing to have either a president or a chair but not both. Sometimes the motivation in creating the chair's slot in addition to the president's on a nonprofit board is honorific rather than functional. However, in the nonprofit sector this is generally accomplished more effectively, and with less confusion, by creating a slot for an honorary president or honorary chairperson who does not have any special powers beyond that of an ordinary board member.

Treasurer. The treasurer must be someone with a good deal of financial experience, preferably related to the operation of nonprofit organizations. Accountants and businesspeople are generally preferred for this job; however, many of these individuals who have only profit-sector experience are not sufficiently sensitive to the special characteristics of financial management in the nonprofit sector, which are discussed in chapters 6 and 7. It is advantageous to find a person with some board experience in another nonprofit organization who also has financial expertise to fill the role of treasurer and head a finance committee.

Clerk. The clerk (or secretary) must be well organized and have the ability to record information accurately. The clerk's task is important to the extent that he or she is responsible for maintaining the official records of meetings. For each meeting, the clerk must send out the agenda and keep the minutes. Unless meetings are tape-recorded, the minutes will be the only official record of board deliberation, and consequently they must reproduce the actual words of motions, who made and seconded them, and how they were voted. It is less important to keep a record of extended discussion on any particular issue, and the clerk should focus primarily on the decisions themselves. Once minutes are written, they should be circulated so that the trustees have a chance to review them in preparation for approval at the subsequent board meeting. If corrections are needed, a board member makes a motion to amend a certain section. After all the corrections are complete, the trustees vote to accept the minutes. With this vote, the minutes become part of the corporate records. The importance of the minutes cannot be overstated. Once they are approved, no board or staff member can claim that "things really did not happen that way at the meeting." They constitute the official and binding record of board decisions.

BOARD LIABILITY [5]

Accountability is an important concept in trusteeship and many board members ask, quite properly, whether they are legally liable for their actions and whether the corporation should carry liability insurance for itself and for the trustees individually. The issue is of particular concern to individual board members who worry that their own financial assets might be at risk in cases where there was proven negligence on their part.

The subject of board liability is complex, particularly because it involves state laws, which vary from state to state. Legal advice should be sought, particularly by those who sit on the boards of organizations engaged in hazardous activities or close care services where risk may be higher. Some generalizations can be made, however, to give general guidance in this area:

☐ The standards that are established for the actions of trustees of nonprofit organizations are found in the area of corporate law, not trust law. What this means is that the requirements governing trustee behavior are much less stringent and allow considerable opportunity to delegate authority and decision making and to rely on the expertise of others. Effectively, trustees are only liable for gross negligence and, according to the language of many statutes, need only exhibit "such care as an ordinary prudent person in a like position would use under similar circumstances."

☐ In general, trustees cannot be held liable for business judgments or financial decisions if these are informed, show no conflict of interest, and do not appear highly irrational. A financial decision that has an undesirable outcome or one that involves a high degree of risk is not sufficient grounds to hold trustees liable. Nevertheless, if trustees never attend meetings, if they approve major decisions involving the corporation's funds without soliciting any background financial information, or if they engage in any illegal financial activity, they can be held liable.

☐ Trustees are liable when conflict of interest is involved—especially where a trustee's personal financial interest is put ahead of that of the corporation. Using corporate property for personal purposes, taking advantage of a financial opportunity at the expense of the corporation, or any kind of self-dealing without proper disclosure is generally not permitted by law.

☐ The trustees are liable for making sure that the corporation is carrying out its mission as articulated to both the state and federal governments. Donors, in particular, should be able to expect that their funds are used for the purposes for which the organization is established.

☐ Trustees can be held personally liable for damages in the case of personal injury cases. Although it is generally the corporation that will be sued, trustees can also be sued if it can be demonstrated that the injury resulted from gross negligence on their part.

☐ Trustees of nonprofit organizations are expected to make sure that their organizations comply with the rules and regulations set by federal, state, and local governments. They must file financial reports with the IRS and with the state office handling public charities. They must fill out tax forms for employees, deduct taxes from paychecks, and deposit these funds periodically (trustees can be held personally and financially liable for noncompliance with tax requirements). In some cases, trustees can be held responsible for the organization's compliance with laws limiting lobbying activities; where a building is involved, they can be held responsible for making sure the organization is complying with building codes. It is essential to remember that as stewards of the public trust, the trustees are responsible for overseeing compliance with legal requirements.

Even though the instance of lawsuits is relatively infrequent in the nonprofit world, trustees do get sued and, to a much greater extent, they become involved in threatened lawsuits that are settled before they ever get to court. Thus board members are rightly concerned about the risks associated with trusteeship. While laws generally favor trustees of nonprofit organizations, the cost of mounting a successful defense in a lawsuit can be very high. This is why many states are enacting laws to limit the kinds of cases that can come to court in this area. Nevertheless, the exposure to risk will never be reduced completely by state or federal statutes because trustees, in the end, must be held somewhat accountable for their actions.

Securing Protection
There are several ways that trustees of nonprofit organizations can be protected from legal exposure:

☐ Nonprofit organizations can indemnify their trustees. *This does not protect the trustees from legal action.* But it does means that the organization will pay for all costs associated with such action directed against the trustees including the cost of settlement. The problem of indemnification is that it transfers risk from the trustees to the organization and puts the organization's assets at risk. Another problem is that in certain cases, the organization may sue one of its trustees and, if successful, would not be responsible for paying the costs associated with indemnification.

☐ Indemnification insurance reimburses the corporation for expenses associated with the costs of indemnification as outlined above.

☐ Directors and officers (D & O) insurance protects both against indemnification costs and any other costs incurred by trustees that would not be covered by the corporation.

☐ Because all of these measures protect only the trustees themselves, the corporation should carry sufficient liability insurance to protect itself in the case of a lawsuit.

Should organizations take any or all of the steps outlined above? In the case of most nonprofit organizations, failure to carry liability insurance for the corporation is a mistake. When legal action is contemplated, it is well known that the law will greatly favor actions taken against the corporation over actions taken against the trustees. Thus it is the corporation that needs the greatest protection.

How much protection to afford the trustees is less clear. Indemnifying trustees may be an important step in recruiting prominent people to boards of directors. Nevertheless, such an action represents a major commitment of the corporation's assets and, without proper insurance to back it up, could put some organizations out of business. In other cases, where the organization had few assets to begin with, indemnification would be fairly meaningless because there would be little money to reimburse the expenses associated with legal action.

This leaves the question of insurance. There are those who contend that in many nonprofit industries the chance of a lawsuit against the trustees is so small and the cost of insurance so high that it is not worth purchasing a policy. In the case of nonprofit organizations engaged in hazardous services or those involving the care of patients, students, or infants, the same experts often advise that insurance coverage for trustees is a necessity. Insurance protection has become very expensive in recent years, however, and this has become a particularly acute problem for smaller organizations. An increasing number of states, recognizing this problem, have been enacting laws protecting both nonprofit organizations and their trustees from lawsuits. Over time, it may be that more and more nonprofit organizations will forego many kinds of insurance coverage that explicitly protect the trustees.

Five years after Mary Clarke had assembled her first board of trustees, she decided to find out why she was having such problems with the group. She went to one of her mentors, an experienced trustee from another organization, and asked for his views on trusteeship. After getting a long briefing on the roles and responsibilities of trustees, their various obligations, the commitment of time and money they should be expected to make, and the legal risks associated with trusteeship, Mary asked, "Why would anyone want to serve on a board?"

The answer to Mary's question is that trusteeship is a form of public service that often carries with it status in the community. Many established nonprofit organizations find people vying for the chance to become trustees. These are the lucky ones. For many of the newer, less prestigious organizations, finding committed trustees is more difficult. Nevertheless, these organizations should not compromise and turn the board into a social group with minimal responsibilities because eventually, as the organization grows in prominence and importance, weak trustees become a tremendous drawback. It is better to take great care and to move slowly and carefully, even if it takes several years to achieve the full complement of trustees. In the long run, the safe and prudent course is to build soundly for the organization's future.

CHECKLIST QUESTIONS FOR CHAPTER 2

1. Have the articles of incorporation and the bylaws of your organization been reviewed by the board within the last five years? If changes are appropriate, has the board formally voted on amendments?

2. Has your board engaged in a comprehensive long-range planning process within the last five years? Does your board approve specific goals and objectives each year?

3. Is your board (or a subcommittee of the board) involved in the process of developing the annual budget? Do the trustees formally approve the budget? Do they compare financial performance to budgeted figures throughout the year?

4. Has your board developed and approved proper financial controls that meet generally accepted practices for nonprofit organizations?

5. Are all board members required to make a financial contribution? Is there a system that ensures that they will do so?

6. How active is your board in raising money? Are all trustees active in fund raising?

7. Has your board developed a process for evaluating the performance of the chief executive? Have your trustees given some thought to how they will recruit and hire a new chief executive when the time comes?

8. Does your board play a leadership role in promoting your organization in the community?

9. Is the process for identifying and recruiting new trustees effective; that is, does it result in a collection of trustees with the necessary skills and diversity of backgrounds? Is there a proper orientation process for new trustees?

10. Is there a trustee manual in your organization that spells out the requirements of trusteeship? Is there a clearly documented conflict-of-interest policy?

11. Have sufficient numbers of committees been developed in your organization to accomplish the work of the board effectively?

12. Is there a process that ensures that appropriately qualified people become officers in your organization?

13. Has your board considered the question of trustee liability? If appropriate, has your organization secured proper protection for the trustees including insurance protection?

3
Assembling the Work Force

Sandra Harris is the executive director of Parent/Child Stress Services, a nonprofit organization whose mission is to prevent child abuse through parental counseling. The organization was founded in 1970, grew substantially during the 1980s, and is undergoing a shift toward increased professionalism. Sandra Harris finds herself facing several dilemmas. One is that she needs to decide on the types of people to hire for particular jobs. Her own background leads her to favor those who have a strong empathy for the field of child abuse but many of her board members are urging her to hire individuals with specific management expertise. A second dilemma she faces is that she does not want to lose the loyalty of her volunteers, although increasingly she finds it necessary to replace many of them with professional staff.

The purpose of this chapter and the next one is to analyze the challenges associated with assembling a work force. These include putting together the right mix of people who can provide maximum productivity and at the same time utilizing organizational resources most effectively. This chapter will discuss the philosophical principles that should dictate the hiring of staff and it will suggest how organizations should combine salaried staff members, volunteers, and other kinds of workers most effectively. Chapter 4 will analyze how nonprofit organizations can clarify their personnel policies in order to develop a positive work environment for their work force.

HIRING THE RIGHT PERSON FOR THE JOB
Sandra Harris's first dilemma has to do with hiring the right person for a new job. The board has authorized the hiring of a new director of resource development to oversee organizational fund-raising efforts. After an extensive search, she has narrowed her choice to two candidates. The first is a man who has worked for ten years in fund raising at a private school. His references are excellent. In his previous job, he was credited with working effectively both with the headmaster and the trustees, coordinating the annual fund drive and running a small capital drive. He writes well and has experience writing foundation proposals. However, he has no background in the child abuse field. The other candidate has worked in child

abuse organizations for twenty years. Originally attracted to the field because she herself was a victim, she has been primarily a counselor working directly with parents. She is personable and has excellent references.

In the interviews, Sandra finds herself leaning toward the second candidate. Although the woman has never been involved in fund raising (or in any management-level position), she says she is willing to accept a lower wage until she has proven herself. She understands the basic needs of Parent/Child Stress Services and talks easily and familiarly with Sandra about mutual acquaintances. She knows the acronyms associated with other service providers, government agencies, and national organizations. While the first candidate brings an appropriate set of skills to the job, Sandra is concerned that he lacks adequate familiarity with child abuse and prevention. Sandra likes him, feels he is talented and energetic, but worries about his ability to be credible to others in the field.

The dilemma faced by Sandra Harris is not unusual in the nonprofit environment and like many of her peers, she is naturally gravitating toward hiring someone who is creative, enthusiastic, and has considerable training and background in her organization's field. But this training is not related to the task that the candidate will be asked to perform. Like many people with an abiding interest in the field, the candidate is willing to accept low wages and learn a new skill on the job. Unfortunately, what this prospective employee may bring in enthusiasm, creativity, and the willingness to learn, she lacks in key management skills that can help her succeed in the job. Like any nonprofit organization, Parent/Child Stress Services needs experienced managers with business, financial, marketing, fund-raising, and even legal skills; it needs clerical workers and data processing professionals who are familiar with the workings of an office and the needs of administrators.

For people like Sandra Harris attempting to fill staff positions, there are some basic questions that need to be addressed:

☐ Should they favor candidates who are bright and may be able to learn quickly on the job, even if they're inexperienced?

☐ Should they hire people who have experience in the field in which the organization is active, even if it is not related to the job to be filled?

☐ Should they lean toward individuals with a strong educational background (a Ph.D., perhaps), even if the training is in an unrelated field?

☐ Should they give serious consideration to an individual for a management job if the person's training and experience does not include administration?

In order to answer these questions, it is first necessary to distinguish between program personnel and management personnel. Obviously, if a mental health center is hiring a psychiatrist, it will look for one who is well trained and knowledgeable in psychology; if a theater troupe is hiring actors for a stage production, the people selected must have dramatic talent; if a school is hiring a teacher, a strong educational background is a primary prerequisite if not the paramount consideration. In staffing the programmatic side of a nonprofit organization, direct training, experience, and skill in the field of activity is the sine qua non by which people should initially be judged.

However, on the management side, the issue is not so clear. Might we speculate that an accountant with a knowledge of biology will do a better job of keeping the books for a hospital than someone without such knowledge? Will a clerk-typist who is also a painter be expected to perform better than an ordinary secretary if the employer happens to run an art gallery? More generally, should recruitment procedures in nonprofit organizations give preference to those whose backgrounds are somehow related to the programmatic activity of the organization? *The answer to all these questions is probably no.* If Sandra Harris is looking for a fund-raiser, she should hire a fund-raiser. Unless she is prepared to spend many months teaching someone without proper background and unless she is willing to take the risk that that person may not have the proper aptitude for the task, she should hire someone with an appropriate set of skills.

Similarly, when looking for a bookkeeper or a secretary, the most important consideration is the person's skill *at that job.* In some cases, at the clerical level, it may even be preferable to hire someone without a special interest in the organization's field of activity because there is less likelihood that the individual will feel frustrated in performing menial tasks. It is also less likely that the employee will possess a driving ambition to move up or out to a more interesting, program-related job. The controversy surrounding this point among nonprofit administrators is keen. But more often than not, experienced executives tend to favor entry-level and middle-management personnel with strong backgrounds in administrative areas.

Hierarchies and Expectations

There are other, more subtle reasons why people with management backgrounds may be preferable choices for administrative tasks in nonprofit organizations. Many people who consider working in nonprofit fields think of the organizations they might work for as places full of interesting people who work in a loose administrative structure. While this may attract creative people, it also tends to attract those who are less comfortable with organizational hierarchies. Individuals who come from management backgrounds, on the other hand, tend to be more familiar and comfortable with hierarchically arranged organizations. Often they have worked for profit-making concerns where pyramidal authority chains are firmly established.

As nonprofit organizations grow in complexity and size, they must also move toward increasingly hierarchical structures. If they are staffed primarily by people who believe in collective decision making, or who feel that all supervision should be informal and unstructured, then dissension, frustration, and unhappiness can quickly set in.

Another major misconception about nonprofit organizations is that administrative jobs within them tend to be more interesting than comparable jobs in the profit sector. By and large, this is not the case. An unsuccessful candidate for political office should not look to a bookkeeping job in a university's public administration graduate school as a way to work off his or her disappointment and frustration. An unemployed musician or painter who looks to an arts organization as a way to satisfy his or her creative needs is likely to be equally unhappy. "Administration," says one nonprofit executive, "is the art of pushing paper. If you enjoy doing that task well, if you like inventing better systems for making the paper pushing more efficient, you can get great satisfaction from your job."

Finally, it is not true that a nonprofit organization is a haven from the real workaday world dominated by profit-motivated corporations, big government, and a largely impersonal, insensitive, and inflexible work environment. While there is a grain of truth here, it is remarkable how rapidly nonprofit organizations have become integrated into the world they are supposed to be unlike. Nonprofits that find themselves competing to sell a service or a product, to influence public policy, or to secure funding, find the going very competitive and the pressure at times tremendous. Nonprofit organizations must work with government agencies at the local, state, and federal levels to preserve tax exemptions, secure funding, and handle personnel issues, to name just a few such interactions. Nonprofit organizations are very much a part of the corporate/government structure as some employees discover to their unhappiness.

Creativity/Flexibility

It would be misleading to suggest that the best nonprofit employees are nose-to-the-grindstone management types without any sensitivity or interest in their organization's activities and without any imagination. Obviously, all other things being equal, an executive should certainly give preference to an applicant who, along with management skills, brings a knowledge, aptitude, or interest in other fields, particularly those related to the organization's mission. Even more important, however, may be the quality of imagination and flexibility that the person brings to the organization that allows him or her to grow in the job and help shape it and make it more productive.

Unlike large corporations that are highly structured and in which roles are carefully defined and largely unchanging, the nonprofit organization is usually small enough and sufficiently understaffed that a single person may be called on to fill a number of roles and perform a variety of tasks. In addition, because the administrative needs of the organization can change quickly through rapid growth or equally rapid constriction, a person hired to perform one constellation of tasks may be asked to consider a reassignment of responsibilities. Volatility and change is common among nonprofits and, as a consequence, flexibility in employees is an asset. Nonprofit organizations, with the exception of the oldest and most established, are not places for people who want to know that the job that they are taking today will be the same job ten years hence. Rather, they are good places for people who see organizational change as an opportunity to learn new skills and possibly to secure rapid job advancement.

It is here, in the area of creativity and flexibility, that someone with a broader educational background and varied experience may have a substantial advantage over someone with fairly narrow training and experience in management. In many instances, it will be advantageous to have a person who has, in addition to some administrative skills, an interest in growing with a job and shaping that job into something exciting and challenging. This is not true in every case, of course, because many jobs in nonprofits are routine. However, the nonprofit executive should consider searching out people who appear to have the special spark of curiosity, energy, and creativity even when their management skills are not fully developed.

To summarize, the nonprofit executive must look for several qualities in prospective employees. In order of importance, these may be summarized as follows:

1. Management skills related to the job to be performed
2. Character traits that reflect creativity, flexibility, an enthusiasm for solving problems, and an ability to work with others
3. An understanding of the need for authority in an organizational structure
4. A knowledge, sensitivity, and enjoyment of the nonprofit field in which they will be employed

SETTING THE ORGANIZATIONAL PARAMETERS

Many organizations are anxious to begin recruiting and hiring staff before they have set basic organizational parameters. Both new organizations filling positions for the first time, and older organizations replacing departing staff, should not rush into the hiring process. Whether it is the trustees hiring the executive director, or the director hiring other staff,[1] organizational parameters have to be set in two areas by:

- Determining specific tasks
- Distributing those tasks among salaried employees, volunteers, independent contractors, and outside organization service providers

Determining Tasks

At least annually, or more often if there are significant changes requiring a reshuffling of personnel, the executive director (with the assistance of the board) must systematically outline everything that needs to get done in the organization. Objectivity is important and those working on this effort should not simply be guided by the way things have been in the past. Rather, they should ask themselves the following series of questions:

☐ What tasks are being performed now and are they absolutely necessary?
☐ What tasks are not being performed that should be?
☐ What new activities are being added that will require additional work?
☐ What specific tasks are associated with the new activities?
☐ Do existing tasks need to be redefined or reshuffled in order to address staff concerns over job assignments?

In large organizations, this step, together with the ones that follow, may be carried out more effectively with the help of an outside consultant. The consultant brings a kind of objectivity to the process that can be refreshing. Whether or not a consultant is used, employees should be interviewed throughout this process because they have the most expertise about the jobs they perform.

Distributing Tasks among Salaried Staff, Volunteers, Independent Contractors, and Outside Organization Service Providers

Many people make the mistake of assuming that all of the important tasks in a nonprofit organization need to be done by salaried staff. Often this is the most expensive way of getting jobs done and is not always the most efficient. There are actually four groups that make up a nonprofit organization's work force—salaried staff, volunteers, independent contractors, and outside organization service providers.

Salaried staff members answer an organization's need for people who will provide ongoing services for important tasks and functions. Because they are on salary, an organization can expect them to meet high standards in their work and can subject them to more careful supervision and evaluation than other kinds of workers. Because they have a continuing relationship with an organization, state and federal laws require that they be provided with various kinds of protection—unemployment coverage, social security protection, and various other benefits. In many nonprofit organizations, salaried staff form the core of the work force, promoting a sense of accountability and stability both internally and externally.

Volunteers are a source of free labor and can be of great value to nonprofit organizations. However, because they do not get paid, an organization has to devise other kinds of rewards that will keep them motivated and interested in offering their services. This may mean finding challenging tasks for volunteers when what the organization really needs is help with more mundane jobs. Furthermore, the process of recruiting, training, and retaining volunteers is not always easy and their interaction with paid staff must be carefully orchestrated. Nevertheless, without volunteers, many nonprofit organizations would simply not be able to function and they are an important component of the work force mix.

Independent contractors are individuals who are not members of the regular staff but who are hired for a specified period of time or on an occasional basis, often to perform a discrete set of tasks. A nonprofit organization pays them a flat rate for the job, does not withhold taxes from their salary, and does not extend employee benefits to them. When an organization is looking for special expertise to handle a particular job or is looking for an individual to offer a service for which there is not a continuing need, independent contractors often provide the most cost-effective solution.

Outside organization service providers also provide a discrete service on a fee basis and in many respects are the organizational versions of independent contractors. Many of these organizations specialize in a single functional area and can offer their services at very competitive rates. Efficiencies of scale or access to special equipment or trained personnel often gives them a competitive edge. Organizational service providers are especially common in areas where routine functions are the norm—financial management, data processing, equipment maintenance, cleaning, food services, and so on.

In assigning tasks between staff, volunteers, independent contractors, and outside organization service providers, there are generally a variety of options, each with its particular set of advantages and disadvantages. For example, consider three nonprofit organizations of roughly comparable size that are faced with the need to maintain their fiscal records:

☐ Organization A has put a bookkeeper on staff, at a salary of $20,000, who records all transactions, reconciles the bank statement, prepares financial statements for the board, computes all withholding taxes, issues the payroll checks, and prepares W-2 forms for employees and 1099 forms for indpendent contractors. This employee is costing the organization a good deal more than $20,000. In addition to her salary, the organization is paying its share of her social security taxes as well as her medical and disability benefits, sick time, holidays and vacation days, workmen's compensation, and state unemployment insurance. Finally, it provides her with office space and furniture. Thus the real cost of this employee is close to $26,000.

☐ Organization B has hired a bookkeeping service at $20,000 a year. The service not only completes all the tasks that Organization A's bookkeeper performs, but it also computerizes all the records and makes available various kinds of reports that the executive director and the board can use for budgeting and reporting purposes. The service constantly monitors all changes in tax laws, updates its accounting procedures as the laws change, and provides free advice that is quite useful. The service requires no office space—payroll records and other reports are picked up and delivered—requires no employee benefits, and is entitled to no unemployment benefits (hence Organization B is not liable for unemployment insurance). The work of the bookkeeping service is reviewed by Organization B's treasurer who is a volunteer.

☐ Organization C has taken care of its fiscal operation in still a different way. One of the trustees, a retired accountant, has agreed to serve as treasurer. He volunteers his time to the organization, writing checks, preparing financial statements, and helping the executive director with budgets. A staff member, who costs the organization $26,000 a year ($20,000 in salary and $6,000 in benefits, allocated office space, and so on), spends about 20 percent of his time assisting the treasurer with the paperwork, filing, and record keeping. Finally, at the treasurer's request, the organization has contracted a payroll service at a local bank. The service handles all of the payroll-related activity including the collecting of W-4 forms, the computation of deductions, the issuing of checks (as well as automatic depositing into employee accounts where this is requested), and the preparation of W-2 forms at the end of the year. Organization C's total cost is approximately $13,000.

As can be readily seen, Organization A, by opting to assign a full-time staff member to the bookkeeping tasks, chose the most expensive alternative. Under certain circumstances, this choice might have been justified if people felt that it was desirable to have someone in the office all the time who was fully conversant with financial matters. Nevertheless, in other cases it probably would have been desirable for the board of trustees and the executive director to have chosen other alternatives. Some combination of outside organization service bureaus, volunteers, or independent contractors would certainly have been less expensive and might have provided greater expertise.

Special Issues Relating to Independent Contractors

Many organizations are tempted to hire individuals as independent contractors because it is simpler and less expensive than hiring regular employees. It is true that there is far less paperwork associated with independent contractors. No withholding taxes are required, independent contractors receive no benefits, and organizations are only required to file forms with the IRS at the end of the calendar year, and that only if the individual earns over $600.

But it is not legal to hire people as independent contractors when their working patterns indicate that they should really be categorized as members of the regular staff. Someone who works in the office on a continuing basis should be treated as a salaried employee even if he or she works only part time. Indeed, several governmental agencies including the IRS and the state's Division of Employment Security can, and sometimes do, apply a test to determine whether independent contractors should have been categorized as salaried employees. If the work they do is short-term and if the individuals enjoy more independence than other regular employees, the agencies are usually satisfied. If the individuals do not meet these criteria and do not fit the definition of an independent contractor, the nonprofit organization can be forced to pay back taxes as well as unemployment compensation. For this reason, the advice of an accountant or a lawyer in the hiring of independent contractors is desirable.

It is always desirable to have a written contract (or work agreement) with an independent contractor that specifies the task to be accomplished, the start date, the end date, and the compensation level. The contract usually does not specify the place where the work will be performed, unless this is crucial to a description of the task, nor does it describe the work hours or any other conditions that would suggest that this person is being treated like a regular employee. A sample work agreement is given in figure 3.1 below.

FIGURE 3.1. Sample Independent Contractor Work Agreement

This work agreement, dated March 21, 1990, is between Parent/Child Stress Services (hereinafter the organization) and John Doe of 25 Compton Road, Compton, California, whose social security number is 000–00–0000 (hereinafter the contractor). The period covered by this contract is from May 1, 1990, to December 31, 1990.

The contractor agrees to collaborate on a research project being carried out by the organization under contract to the State Department of Youth Services. The contractor agrees to provide up to ten working days to the project. His task will be to provide advice and guidance in the area of data analysis. Specifically, the consultant will:

- Review software documentation and capabilities
- Design data analysis procedure
- Check final data analysis
- Write the statistical section of the final report

The total compensation is fixed at $575 per day and will not exceed $5,750 for the ten days. This is the total financial obligation under this contract. Payment will be made by the organization within fifteen days of receipt of invoices from the contractor, which may be submitted once each month. It is understood that the contractor is not an employee of the organization but is serving as an independent contractor and is liable for all taxes in conjunction with his fee.

The work agreement must be executed by both parties before April 15, 1990, or it is null and void. Changes to this work agreement will require an amendment signed by the consultant and by an authorized official of the organization. The work agreement may be canceled by either party provided forty-five days' notice is given in writing. The organization will be obligated to pay for all completed work prior to termination.

This contract shall meet all standards specified in the State Department of Youth Services' General Provisions dealing with Fixed-Price Contracts, a copy of which is on file with the organization.

Agreed: _____ Date: _____
                   (Consultant signature)

Agreed: _____ Date: _____
              (for Parent/Child Stress Services)

The work agreement shown in Figure 3.1 grew out of Sandra Harris's need to find someone to work on a short-term project at Parent/Child Stress Services. The organization had received funds from the State Department of Youth Services to analyze phone calls associated with its counseling program. The analysis required the creation of categories of calls and callers, types of caller problems, times of calls (by day of the week, time of day, holidays, etc.), and it also required looking for correlations between these various pieces of information.

It was clear to Sandra Harris that some specialized expertise and help would be needed and that it wasn't necessary or even desirable to add someone to the permanent staff. She considered using a volunteer to assist on the project; but in the end, she could not find anyone she could count on who had the proper set of skills and who could guarantee the time and help when it was needed. Wisely, she chose an independent contractor, hiring an individual for a specified number of days at the specific time when the project needed him.

After Sandra Harris had the work agreement drawn up and checked over by the organization's lawyer, she sent two copies to the independent contractor so that he could sign and date them first. This is the preferred procedure because an organization wants to withhold its final signed commitment to an agreement until after the independent contractor has reviewed the agreement and accepted its terms in writing. Once the two forms were returned by the contractor with his signature, Sandra Harris signed and dated the documents, which made them fully executed and legally binding copies of the work agreement. One copy was returned to the independent contractor; the other was retained as the organization's copy.

VOLUNTEERS

By the fifth year of Sandra Harris's tenure as executive director of Parent/Child Stress Services she had assembled an excellent team of staff, independent contractors, and outside organization service providers. She and her board were pleased. But now there was a new set of challenges that she had not anticipated and it concerned her volunteers. Parent/Child Stress Services had been established by a group of individuals and in the early days they contributed their time in running the organization. Many of these original founders continued to provide their services to the organization for free. But as Parent/Child Stress Services grew, some of these people had to relinquish their jobs to paid workers and the transition was not always handled gracefully. A number of the volunteers who had worked in the office were not happy about being displaced by paid staff (many of whom they found arrogant and uninformed about the organization's history) or by independent contractors (who, they believed, brought no new skills to the organization). They resented the fact that all of these people were now being paid for what the volunteers had always done for free. Deep down, some wondered whether their many years of volunteer efforts had been appreciated.

At the same time, Sandra Harris had identified many new kinds of activities for which volunteers were needed—fund raising, phone counseling, and basic data collection for research projects. But many of these areas required people with particular abilities or specialized interests and she did not know whether to try to convince the existing volunteers to undergo some retraining or to attempt to locate other individuals who were already sufficiently motivated and knowledgeable to move into these areas.

Part of the problem was that Sandra Harris had been so focused on the needs of her organization that she had not thought about the volunteers themselves. If she had done so, she might have been better prepared to handle the psychological needs of her existing volunteers and she might also have been better equipped to recruit and retain new people who would be enthusiastic about working for her organization for no money.

Why do people volunteer? Volunteers themselves have provided a host of reasons:

☐ *Sense of self-satisfaction.* Many people like to use their free time in ways that bring them personal satisfaction and allow them to develop a positive self-image. Some volunteer because they want to feel needed, others like to keep busy in a way that is useful, and still others want to earn the respect of their peers and friends while doing something useful for the community.

☐ *Altruism.* Many people from all economic strata believe that helping others is a necessary part of a complete and good life. Often this impulse grows out of religious beliefs or family traditions and upbringing. In some cases, where individuals have little cash to spare, volunteering provides the only way to express such altruism. In others, volunteering may be combined with the giving of cash.

☐ *Companionship/meeting people.* Another important reason why individuals volunteer is to meet and mix with other people. Volunteering can allow them to widen their circle of acquaintances and develop personal bonds that can spill over into other parts of their life. Individuals who move to new communities, older people who have lost a spouse, even adolescents and young professionals looking for a more active social life, may all look to volunteerism as a way to widen their circle of friends.

☐ *Learning about a field.* Some individuals who have an interest in a particular field see volunteering as an excellent way to learn more about it, particularly if training and learning opportunities are built into an organization's volunteer program. Those who want to learn about foreign countries, current events, religious traditions, the arts, or a host of other fields can do so through volunteerism.

☐ *Creating/maintaining an organization.* Some volunteers are entrepreneurs who devote their energies to creating nonprofit organizations and helping them grow and thrive. Pride in their organizations' success and continued expansion is often a prime motivating factor in their volunteer activities.

☐ *Developing professional contacts.* In some organizations, volunteering can put one in touch with important members of the community. Some people use volunteer jobs as a way to make contacts that may lead them to clients or other kinds of business or professional associations and opportunities.

☐ *Getting ahead in the corporation.* Many profit sector corporations view employee volunteer service as an important way for the company to make a contribution to the community. Young executives and other company representatives are encouraged to volunteer; those wanting to move up the corporate ladder know that a volunteer position can be a real asset on a résumé.

☐ *Getting training/experience.* For some individuals, a volunteer position is a route to finding a paying job. Young people, people who have been out of the labor force for some time, or people wishing to change professions will sometimes use volunteer opportunities as a way to further these personal goals. They may learn a task, gain a marketable skill, or secure a recommendation for future employment.

☐ *Providing entry to a particular organization.* For some people who have a strong interest in working or serving on the board of a particular nonprofit organization, volunteering provides an important entry point to becoming involved. Volunteering may be the necessary first step on a ladder which eventually leads to a paying job or a seat on the board.

☐ *Social panache.* There is much prestige associated with certain organizations and their volunteers represent an elite group within the community. Associating with these volunteers carries a certain degree of status and marks a person as being part of a desirable social group.

Meeting the Needs of Volunteers

Board members and staff of nonprofit organizations must consider the motivations of prospective volunteers if they want their help. Unfortunately, both are often too focused on their organizations' needs. "We need door-to-door fund-raising volunteers." "We need someone to donate legal help." "We need volunteers to read the newspaper to patients." "We need people who will help learning disabled children with their reading." This identification of volunteer jobs is important, of course, and a detailed description of what is involved in each task will make the actual assignment of volunteers a great deal easier when the appropriate time comes. What is lacking however, is an understanding of volunteer needs and a clear concept of how particular tasks can fulfill those needs.

Why should an organization focus on the needs of volunteers? Very simply, if it wants to be able to recruit and retain people to work for no money, it must figure out another means of providing them with satisfaction and fulfillment. In the case of Parent/Child Stress Services, Sandra Harris failed to think about this and she was chided by one of her trustees who told her, "Volunteerism is a quid pro quo business. The organization gets something, but we don't get it for nothing—we have to give something back. A volunteer wants meaningful responsibility and wants to be taken seriously. The minute we take a volunteer for granted, we are in trouble."

Sandra Harris had been so focused on the needs of her organization that she failed even to provide recognition to those volunteers who had worked so long and so hard and whose jobs were now being taken by paid staff and independent contractors. Awards luncheons, mention in the organization's annual report and press releases, framed certificates of merit, or other clear indications of the organization's appreciation would have gone a long way toward meeting these individuals' need to feel appreciated.

Other nonprofit organizations have found a variety of ways to meet the needs of volunteers. Two interesting examples show how diverse the approach can be:

THE ART MUSEUM

An art museum in a large city needed volunteers to serve as guides for two special visitor groups—deaf visitors (who required guides who could use sign language) and foreign visitors (who required guides fluent in their language). At first, the volunteer coordinator had a difficult time finding volunteers. As she recalled, "I put ads in specialized publications and printed up some brochures that were distributed at professional conferences where there were many individuals who had the signing skills or the foreign language skills. Some of the inquiries I got as a result of these recruitment efforts were from people who were interested in paying jobs, but few wanted to volunteer. Those who did had work schedules that prevented them from giving us the required number of hours. Some balked at the amount of time they would have to commit to learning about the collection.

"Then, after talking to some of my other volunteer guides, I realized that I had been using the wrong approach. My most loyal volunteers told me that their original motivation for getting involved had been to learn about the incredible collection we have here at the museum. For people with the slightest interest in art, our volunteer training program is a wonderful opportunity to learn from recognized experts—curators, conservators, artists. So, I changed the way I went about recruiting volunteers and I even dropped the word 'volunteer' from my pitch entirely. Instead, I said that the museum was starting a series of free seminars on the collection taught by noted authorities. The seminars would have extremely limited enrollments and would only be open to those who had the necessary skills to serve as guides for the hearing impaired or for foreign visitors. I set fairly rigorous eligibility requirements, including a minimum number of hours required per month. Of course, this just happened to be the same number of hours we require of all our volunteers but I didn't say anything about that.

"Within three weeks, we had more volunteers than we could use and I had to start a waiting list. And those we got were extremely motivated by the seminar. The irony is that we have always required that our guides go through this training because you cannot be a guide unless you know a great deal about the collection. But this was the first time that we referred to the training program as a 'seminar' and promoted our staff as the 'faculty' in our recruitment efforts. Now instead of people complaining about the requirements that we impose on them, they respond with enthusiasm because this is clearly meeting their desire to learn about art. The lesson is that it is extremely important to think about the motivations of potential volunteers before you try to recruit them and it is equally important to meet their expectations once they have agreed to come on board."

HIGH SCHOOL HEALTH CORPS

The High School Health Corps is a United States–based nonprofit organization that sends high-school volunteers to Central America during the summer to assist on public health projects in rural areas. The organization is not affiliated with any religious group and it attempts to stay apolitical in offering volunteer assistance to countries where young Americans will be welcome and safe. According to one of the volunteer recruiters for the program, meeting the needs of the countries is essential but meeting the needs of the young volunteers is just as critical. Not only is it an important strategy in recruitment but it becomes an even more important strategy in retaining volunteers once the rigorous six-month training phase begins.

"Our initial recruitment is done through schools and churches. We have a large group of ministers and principals who know the High School Health Corps and support it. They urge students to consider our program and to come to an informational meeting to find out more about it. They talk positively to the kids about our program. It is described as an exciting challenge and an adventure, a trip to exotic lands, an alternative to a boring summer. But the adults describing the High School Health Corps also say that the program meets the needs of young people in other ways. Kids can develop language skills, they can learn about the health field by actually working beside healthcare professionals, they can involve themselves in an extracurricular activity that may help them with college admissions. By the time kids come to one of our informational meetings with their parents to learn more about the program, they are usually convinced that volunteering will do a lot for them.

"Even so, we do not leave anything to chance. We constantly emphasize the good points of the program but begin to shift our emphasis somewhat. We understand that the parents usually need some convincing too. They are concerned first and foremost about safety and we have a good track record there. But we develop a pitch that will convince both parents and kids that the program will meet the most basic need of a young person—the need to be taken seriously and treated as an adult.

"In fact, at this meeting, we tend to talk less about the fun of world travel and more about the rigor and long-lasting impact of our training, the challenge of working in a foreign land with a different culture and language, and the genuine discomforts of living in a third world country. In a way, we are doing two things. We want to discourage those who are not serious and never will be. But for the others, we want to convey the message that the challenges of this program are precisely the reason that many young people should want to participate. The program gives them more responsibility than they have ever had before. We tell them that it will not be easy but that they will get tremendous positive reinforcement when they meet the challenge. Often, the person who conveys this message is another young person who has already served in the program."

The Volunteer Coordinator

At Parent/Child Stress Services, Sandra Harris admitted to her board that she had failed to address the needs of her volunteers. But she had a valid excuse. She simply had too many other things to do. She also had to confess that in her own mind volunteers were a lower priority in organizing the work force than other groups—paid staff, independent contractors, outside organization service providers.

Sandra Harris's attitude is not unusual and this is one reason that in many nonprofit organizations there is someone who serves as an advocate for volunteers and helps the chief executive understand their importance. In larger organizations or in organizations where volunteers constitute a large proportion of the work force, the individual in this position is a member of the paid staff and may go by various titles such as volunteer coordinator or director of volunteers. In smaller organizations or ones requiring fewer volunteers, the volunteer coordinator may be uncompensated. In either case, a volunteer coordinator—whether paid or not—should have access to the chief executive because a significant part of his or her job has to do with shaping the director's attitude toward the role of volunteers in the organization.

Indeed, a volunteer coordinator must be integrated into the operation of the organization at the highest levels and must be given the full cooperation of any department or staff person who will be working with volunteers. When the volunteer coordinator is a member of the staff, it is important to consider where he or she should be placed in the organizational structure. In the art museum described earlier, the volunteer coordinator was placed in the department of education because 90 percent of the volunteers worked in that area. Altogether the department had eighteen staff members but the volunteer coordinator was one of only three who reported directly to the director of the department and periodically met with the chief executive of the museum itself. In the High School Health Corps, which had a full-time staff of only seven, the volunteer coordinator reported to the executive director of the organization.

While the volunteer coordinator plays an important advocacy and educational role, sensitizing senior staff to the important place of volunteers in the organization, he or she has many other responsibilities. The volunteer coordinator is to the volunteers what a personnel director is to the paid staff. He or she has the overall responsibility for finding and placing volunteers and mediating between their needs and the needs of the organization. The full range of responsibilities in the job generally includes oversight of the following tasks:

- Establishing and constantly updating written policies on volunteer procedures, responsibilities, supervision, placement, restrictions, reporting, evaluation, recognition, and termination
- Developing volunteer benefits including free or low-cost use of organizational facilities or programs, access to organizational resources (e.g., library and dining facilities), opportunities to attend conferences, cash for travel and other expenses, letters of recommendation for subsequent job searches, etc.
- Determining where volunteers can be used most effectively in the organization
- Creating job descriptions for volunteers
- Developing recruitment procedures including identifying organizations and individuals who will promote the volunteer opportunities, maintaining contacts with the media, using existing volunteers and staff for informational meetings, and designing appropriate printed material
- Interviewing, selecting, and placing volunteers in appropriate jobs
- Developing orientation and training programs for volunteers
- Evaluating the performance of volunteers and reassigning or terminating a volunteer in cases of unsatisfactory performance
- Organizing recognition events and opportunities to honor volunteers
- Helping to formulate and evaluate the structure and function of separate volunteer groups such as guilds or friend organizations

- Responding to the needs of designated representatives and officers of these volunteer groups
- Acting as an advocate of volunteer needs and interests with staff and others in the organization
- Training staff in how to work with volunteers, including supervision, evaluation, and recognition
- Responding to problems and complaints from or about volunteers and mediating conflicts among volunteers or between volunteers and staff

It should be noted that one of the most important responsibilities of the volunteer coordinator has to do with the termination of an unsuccessful volunteer placement. The old adage that a volunteer is someone who works for no pay and therefore can't be fired is not true. What is true is that the situation has to be handled with great finesse. The first step is for the volunteer coordinator to get all the facts and quietly evaluate the complaints. Sometimes the volunteer in question was not properly trained, did not receive adequate supervision, or was not told early enough that there was a problem. In such cases, it may be appropriate for the volunteer coordinator to remedy these problems and give the volunteer another chance. Alternatively, the volunteer can be reassigned to a less demanding or more appropriate position. In extreme cases, the job can be eliminated for a time or the volunteer can simply be told that his or her services are no longer needed. Such actions are difficult, but a skilled volunteer coordinator cannot shirk this responsibility.

It is obvious that in large organizations, no one person can be expected to actually carry out each and every task associated with the volunteer coordinator responsibilities listed above. In some cases, the volunteer coordinator may supervise several other paid staff members who will collectively attend to these tasks or he or she may work with a formal volunteer organization to help with the various aspects of organizing the volunteer program.

Volunteer Organizations
In some nonprofit organizations, volunteers have created separate formal organizational structures with their own boards, officers, and committees. These groups can help formulate volunteer policy, they can be active in recruitment, training, and supervision of volunteers, and they can be responsible for specific fund-raising projects or other kinds of special events. Often, the president of the volunteer organization sits on the parent organization's board of directors and represents the interests and needs of the volunteers at that level. The volunteer organization may have its own paid

staff; however, more commonly, it interacts with the staff of the parent organization, especially with the volunteer coordinator.

The structural relationship between a nonprofit organization and its volunteer organization can vary. In some cases, the volunteer organization is called a committee and its operation is strictly controlled by the parent organization's board. At the other extreme, volunteer organizations are legally and structurally distinct. They are separately incorporated, file their own financial reports to the federal government, and have boards of directors who are not accountable to the parent organization's board.

There is much to be said in favor of volunteer organizations. They give the volunteers their own sense of place and allow them a chance to advance within the volunteer structure itself—serving on a committee, on the board, or as an officer. Just as important, volunteer organizations ensure that there is a formal vehicle by which the volunteers have a voice in policy development as it affects their ranks. Indeed, in most organizations that rely heavily on volunteers, such organizations are considered a necessity.

Nevertheless, from the parent organization's vantage point, tensions can arise over the issue of control. Particularly when a volunteer organization is separately incorporated, very clear rules have to be established to ensure that the goals of the two organizations are consistent. Where fund raising is involved, tensions can become particularly acute. If the volunteer organization has the legal right to dictate how its money is spent, much time can be wasted haggling over the transfer of funds. For this reason, most nonprofit organizations require that volunteer organizations are maintained as part of their own corporate structures.

Interviewing Potential Volunteers

Volunteers as well as paid staff may be involved in recruiting prospective volunteers. Once recruitment activities have begun, prospects have to be screened and placed. In most cases, interviews are the best way to accomplish this task. An interview has several purposes. First, it assures the prospective volunteer that the organization wishes to meet his or her needs and expectations. Second, it allows the interviewer to clarify the organization's expectations—often some kind of volunteer handbook is shared with prospects that outlines the goals, policies, and procedures of the organization's volunteer program. Finally, the interview provides an opportunity to assess a prospective volunteer's skills, temperament, and motivations and to begin to determine where that individual might fit into the organization.

Often the prospective volunteer is asked to fill out a form that provides basic information and can be a starting off place for the interview. It might include some or all of the following information:

- Name, address, phone number, date of interview
- Name and phone number of two references
- Previous volunteer experience, including names of organizations, dates of affiliation, responsibilities, and contact persons
- Time availability
- What the volunteer hopes to get out of the assignment
- Special areas of interest that might be relevant to job assignment
- Paid work experience, including present employer
- Specialized skills, including languages, clerical/typing, and computer
- Education
- Health status

In order to maintain consistency in the interviews, some organizations find it desirable to have a prepared set of questions. In addition, they may require that the interviewer keep a written summary of the conversation that, together with the information form filled out by the prospective volunteer, goes into a file and is maintained with other records by the volunteer coordinator. These records are invaluable.

Orientation and Training

Once volunteers are selected, they must be oriented and trained. Generally, orientation consists of all or some of the following:

☐ *An organizational packet.* It might include the organization's annual report, newspaper articles, brochures, flyers, reports, a list of board members, staff organization chart, and organization chart of volunteer organization (if one exists) together with its charter and bylaws.

☐ *Background reading material.* In some cases, it is important to gather additional information about the volunteer assignment and responsibilities. In the High School Health Corps, described earlier, young people are required to read several books and pamphlets about the history and culture of the country they will be working in, healthcare in third world countries, and case studies based on the experiences of other volunteers.

☐ *A tour of the facility where the volunteers will work.* In some organizations, it is helpful for volunteers to actually tour the facility where volunteer services will be provided. For example, a church in a major city offers daily meals to the homeless. It recruits volunteers to cook, to set up tables, to serve, to clean up, to greet and seat the homeless, and so on. New volunteers are required to come to the facility when it is empty and to walk and talk through the various tasks before being given an actual assignment.

☐ *A tour of the office and a meeting with the staff.* Where volunteers will be interacting regularly with staff, new recruits are often required to spend some time in the office before being given a specific assignment. They are introduced to staff members, shown where office equipment is located, and told how they are expected to fit into the general office work flow.

☐ *Films, slide shows, and demonstrations.* Often films or slide shows are the best way for volunteers to get a sense of the place where they will be volunteering before they get there. For example, the High School Health Corps shows films and slides of the countries where volunteers will be assigned so that they will be better prepared once they arrive. In other cases, films and slide shows are an excellent way to provide background on the organization, its history, and its volunteer activities. Films, slide shows, and demonstrations can also be used to show how particular volunteer tasks are carried out.

☐ *Group meetings and discussions.* Particularly in organizations where groups of volunteers come into an organization at the same time, group meetings provide an excellent way for basic orientation tasks to get accomplished. They also allow new volunteers to get acquainted with one another and to get basic questions answered.

After the completion of general orientation (or sometimes combined with it), comes the training for the particular job the volunteer will be doing. Training varies depending on the complexity of the job and the background and experience of the volunteer. However, it should always begin with a discussion of the written job (task) description, which provides answers to some key questions:

☐ What is the job?
☐ Why is it necessary, what is its purpose, and how does it contribute to the overall operation of the organization?
☐ How is it done, what special equipment or expertise is involved, and what are the steps necessary for completion?
☐ With whom does the volunteer have to work and to whom is the volunteer accountable?
☐ How much time is involved, how many hours (or days or months) is the volunteer expected to work, and when is the job to be completed?

Training should also involve at least one preliminary meeting with the people with whom the volunteer will have to interact and, often, some practice or on-the-job training by a supervisor. Field trips, guided observations, and role-playing sessions may also be desirable in cases where the task is complicated or involves new skills.

It has been said that the single most important defining characteristic of any nonprofit organization is the people who work within it. The staff, volunteers, and other workers in the organization establish a tone, help to define its image, and determine the effectiveness with which the organization carries out its mission, its programs, and its activities.

Yet many nonprofit organizations operate under severe financial constraints, which makes it difficult to get enough good people in their work force. They cannot simply hire more employees whenever there is another job to be done. They cannot always pay more money to get the most qualified people for particular jobs. Instead, they have to maximize and stretch their scant resources. They must find committed workers who will work hard, often for modest pay, sometimes for no pay at all. They must make sure that everyone's skills are utilized to the fullest extent possible. And, perhaps most important, nonprofit organizations must create an environment where workers—whether paid or volunteer—know that their work is appreciated. For in the end, individuals are most likely to make the required extra effort when they feel their work is valued and contributes to the overall good of the organization.

CHECKLIST QUESTIONS FOR CHAPTER 3

1. Is the chief executive in your organization skilled in personnel work? Has he or she developed a system that ensures that each job will be filled by the best possible candidate?
2. Do employees come to your organization with the proper management skills related to the jobs they will perform? Do they seem to work well with others?
3. Has a proper assessment been made of all the tasks that need to get done in your organization? Has it been documented?
4. Are tasks in your organization appropriately distributed among salaried staff members, volunteers, independent contractors, and outside organization service providers?
5. Has your organization found effective ways to identify, recruit, orient, motivate, and recognize the work of volunteers?
6. Is there a volunteer coordinator in your organization? Are the coordinator's responsibilities clearly spelled out? Are this person's activities well integrated into the operation of your organization?
7. Is there a separate volunteer organization that is affiliated with your organization? Are issues of control and authority clearly resolved and documented?

4
Personnel Policy

When John Sims of the Compton Community Center was hired as executive director, he was one of only five employees. The president of the board that hired him explained that there were no job descriptions for any of the staff positions because things were a bit "fluid"; it would be up to him to decide how to allocate tasks among the employees. Five years later, the Compton Community Center had a salaried staff of fifteen along with several teachers, coaches, and artists who were independent contractors. In order for the organization to run smoothly, there had to be very clear definitions of roles, responsibilities, and chains of command. The employees also had to know what they could expect from the organization in terms of compensation, job advancement, and other aspects of employer/employee relations.

Fortunately, John Sims had taken care of three things immediately on assuming the role of executive director:

- Preparing an organization chart showing chains of command and lines of responsibility
- Writing job descriptions
- Deciding on compensation levels and specific benefits[1]

Preparing the Organization Chart
As John Sims found, small nonprofit organizations such as the Compton Community Center often resist preparing an organization chart. This is probably acceptable when there are only two or three employees. But with five or more, an organization chart is a necessity. It establishes lines of authority and of reporting as well as chains of accountability.

In a large organization, an organization chart is particularly important. Chief executives must delegate some of their supervising authority because supervision of each and every employee is not possible. In delegating authority, chief executives must also delegate some accountability. The organization chart in figure 4.1, for example, tells us to whom the executive director has delegated supervisory authority and who must be spoken to if things go awry.

Consider what would happen in this organization if John Sims, the

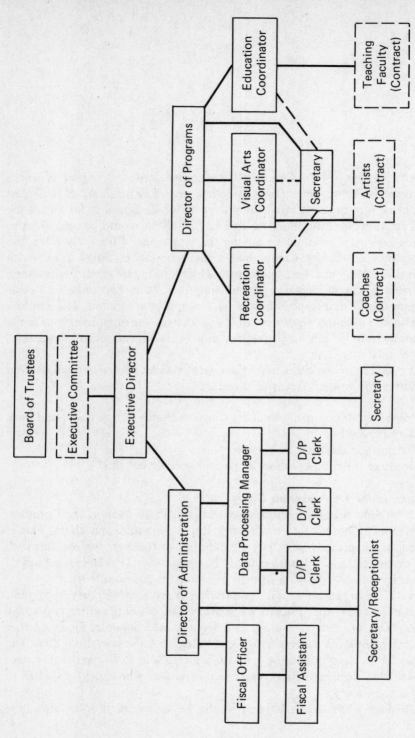

Figure 4.1. Organizational Structure for the Compton Community Center

executive director, received a computer printout that was full of incorrect information. The director of administration would be called in to discuss the problem. The director of administration, in turn, would take up the problem with the data processing manager who would call in the appropriate data processing (D/P) clerk responsible for the incorrect input. What the executive director should not do (unless the supervisor has been informed and approves) is to deal directly with the D/P clerk in trying to find out why the printout was incorrect. This undermines the authority both of the data processing manager and the director of administration and leaves them uninformed about the problem. The executive director may wish to be in attendance when the director of administration talks to the data processing manager or when the manager talks to the D/P clerk. Or the executive director may request a meeting in which all are present. In no case should the authority lines be bypassed.

Given the fact that reporting and authority lines must be respected, they must be set up carefully. Supervisors must be capable of supervision; employees should not be expected to report to people who are incompetent. In addition, multiple supervisors should be avoided whenever possible. If an employee must report to two bosses and the two do not agree, this puts the employee in an awkward position. In the organization chart in figure 4.1, for example, the third secretary carries out work for four people—the director of programs and the three coordinators (as indicated by the dotted lines). However, the principal reporting line is to the director of programs. This means that in instances where it is unclear whose work needs to get done, the secretary can ask the director of programs to establish priorities.

Finally, when contracted personnel are employed by the organization on a regular basis, it is sometimes advantageous to place them on the organization chart so it is clear to whom they report. They are generally shown in boxes with broken rather than solid lines and are indicated as contractual. Figure 4.1 shows three groups of contractors all reporting to the appropriate staff coordinator.

Writing Job Descriptions
A job description typically includes three components:

- A general description of the job
- A statement about who the person holding the job reports to and who he or she will supervise
- A list of specific responsibilities and functions

A sample job description is shown in figure 4.2.

FIGURE 4.2. Sample Job Description

DATA PROCESSING AND FISCAL ASSISTANT

The data processing and fiscal assistant is responsible for the thorough and accurate maintenance of the program and fiscal computer files of the Compton Community Center. He/she
is also responsible for the preparation of certain fiscal documents and forms and for the
maintenance of related paper files.

The data processing and fiscal assistant reports to the director of administration. He/she
supervises a part-time clerk who is a regular part-time employee.

RESPONSIBILITIES AND FUNCTIONS

Programs

- Reviews and codes all information questionnaires
- Updates and maintains all information through preparation of appropriate input forms
- Codes report forms for computer input
- Prepares and maintains all evaluation reports
- Reviews computer edit reports and documents all necessary changes
- Maintains master file code records, paper files for questionnaires, office copies of
  computer edits, master file printouts and reports

Fiscal

- Prepares receipt and disbursement reports and general ledgers for all cost centers and
  accounts; prepares related computer input forms
- Reconciles monthly checking and savings account balances with bank statement
- Processes payables and receivables and generates checks following assignment of
  accounting codes by the director of administration
- Maintains paper files for all current and historic payable and receivable items
- Maintains computerized cost center, chart of accounts, and vendor files
- Maintains paper files for contracts, insurance policies, and other material pertinent to
  the fiscal administration of the Compton Community Center

Occasionally, particularly in large organizations, job descriptions contain
a fourth element: Performance criteria that detail the minimum performance level expected of the employee for each task. For example, if the task
is described as "Reconciles monthly checking and savings account balances with bank statement," the corresponding performance criterion
might be "minimum performance standards will have been met if employee
presents reconciled statements to supervisor within two weeks of receipt
of monthly bank statements."

Although performance criteria may be useful in very large organizations
in which there are routine jobs with predictable tasks, they are usually
cumbersome for smaller organizations. Unless it is difficult to evaluate
employee performance without them or unless the situation requires that

specific performance criteria be developed while an employee is on proba-
tion, doing without them may be preferable.

Why have job descriptions at all? There are many arguments against
them. They often take a long time to write and require extensive discussions with staff and several drafts. Furthermore, every time there is a staff
reorganization with a shifting of responsibilities, the job descriptions have
to be redrafted. Why not spend the time on something more productive and
just explain to new staff what they are expected to do when they are hired?
There are three reasons why it is important to have job descriptions.

First, the very process of writing job descriptions often reveals that the
job responsibilities envisioned for a single person are unrealistic. For example, the executive director and the trustees may agree that one person
should staff the development and public relations areas but once each and
every task is detailed in the job description, it may become apparent that
no one person could possibly do all of them. In addition, once all the tasks
are written down, it becomes easier to juggle responsibilities with a clearer
sense of the total work needs of the organization and the time commitments of each staff member.

Second, job descriptions protect the organization's employees. Employees are able to refer to a document that outlines what is expected of them
and provides the basis for an evaluation of their job performance. They
cannot be dismissed for not performing a task not mentioned in the job
description. Commonly, an employee can expect to be consulted before
changes are made in a job description, particularly if the change involves
the carrying out of additional tasks. Similarly, the employee's supervisor
owes him or her an explanation when tasks detailed in the job description
are taken away and given to others. Finally, the employee can expect any
job review, particularly one leading to salary adjustments, to be based on
an assessment of performance of the tasks listed in the job description.

Third, job descriptions protect the organization. Like contracts, a job
description outlines certain expectations in writing that, if not lived up to,
offer grounds for dismissal. Without a job description, an employee can
always say, "But no one ever told me I was supposed to do that." With
the written document, there can be no disputing that the responsibilities
were spelled out clearly. Similarly, as the supervisor assesses the job performance of an employee at the time of a performance review, he or she
has a clear set of tasks and responsibilities on which to exercise valuative
judgment. It helps the supervisor to be objective and to resist the temptation of giving a good evaluation to an employee simply because he or she
is quiet or pleasant and a negative evaluation to a less personable or less
friendly member of the staff.

Many organizations have job descriptions. However, they are often out-of-date. Typically, an organization will write job descriptions (or hire a consultant to do it) and then forget that the descriptions need to be updated as new tasks and jobs are added and responsibilities change. Updating does not have to be difficult and should be done regularly. A certain time can be set aside, at least once a year, for the executive director (or his or her assistant) to review all job descriptions and, in the case of those job descriptions requiring board approval, recommend changes to the trustees.

Deciding on Compensation Levels

Deciding on salary levels and benefits for employees of nonprofit organizations often leads to controversy. On one side, there are many arguments to keep salaries low. Commonly nonprofit organizations are faced with difficult financial obstacles because there is a limit to the amount of money that can be earned and raised. Furthermore, it is well known that many people may be willing to make financial sacrifices in order to work in the nonprofit sector—many have emotional investments in the organization's mission and activities—so it seems good business sense to take advantage of this situation. Finally, in the special case of a nonprofit organization setting the salary of a staff member who also sits on the board (often the chief executive), there may be arguments that an excessively high salary appears to circumvent the principles of nonprofit trusteeship discussed in chapter 2.

Up until the 1950s, many nonprofit organizations were staffed largely with volunteers and independently affluent people who were paid modest salaries. With increased professionalization, conditions have changed, but nonprofit administrators are still, on average, underpaid for the kinds of jobs they do. In some ways this is good for the organizations and their boards. Many organizations find themselves with plenty of applicants for jobs that pay far less than would comparable jobs in industry. But in other ways the situation is problematic. As large nonprofits have discovered over the years, organized labor has made significant inroads in nonprofit organizations where collective bargaining is probably not the best way to negotiate wages and working conditions. The unions' successes grew principally out of workers' frustrations with inadequate wage scales. In addition, even where employees are unable or unwilling to bargain for better wages, talented people will generally work for inadequate pay for only so long. Eventually, they are lured by other opportunities offering new challenges and more money. While the nonprofit organization is usually able to find young, enthusiastic people to fill the places of departing staff, retaining the experienced employee is more difficult.

Nonprofit organizations are notorious for practicing false economy when it comes to staff salaries. For example, one organization may set the executive director's salary so low that it cannot afford someone with the kind of credentials and experience necessary to raise money and make the rest of the staff productive. The organization that pays its executive director $60,000 may be able to attract someone who can raise at least two times that in fund-raising efforts while a $35,000 executive director may be unable to raise any money at all. Similarly, there is false economy practiced in hiring untrained or unqualified people. It is not unusual to find an organization with two secretaries who have no clerical skills when a single, well-trained secretary would cost far less, be more productive, and could supervise a couple of volunteers or work-study students for routine filing, typing, and errand running.

How much to pay? The setting of compensation levels is a difficult task, yet there are certain things an organization can do to make it easier. The first is to look for salary surveys of nonprofit industries that show the range of salaries paid for comparable positions. The second is to locate a number of similar organizations, then call or write them seeking information on employee compensation as well as the type and cost of benefits provided. This information should be summarized for the board showing the lowest, highest, and average salary level for each staff position, together with the range of offered benefits. This helps establish norms for the industry (although local cost-of-living adjustments may be appropriate before compensation levels are set).

Next, the organization's budget should be studied for answers to the following questions:

☐ How much can realistically be expended on personnel?
☐ How much is necessary for nonpersonnel-related administrative costs (rent, telephone, postage, office supplies, and so on)?
☐ Is there enough left over for the organization to carry out its programs and activities or is the ratio of administrative costs to total budget too high?

If it turns out that administrative costs are too high, the organization may face some difficult choices. Can the staff structure be reworked without compromising the level of service provided? Can some work be done by volunteers, by consultants, by work-study students, or by other organizations? Can more money be raised?

There will probably not be enough money to pay people what they ought to be earning. Yet, because compensation levels are so crucial in determining the kind of people who will ultimately work for the organization, the board should know what the ideal salary and benefit packages look like for each position. Some organizations prepare an ideal budget showing personnel costs at proper levels. The resulting deficit figure is called the staff contribution to the organization and it is the trustees' responsibility to reduce that number as quickly as possible.

Before any final decisions are made about compensation levels, consideration must be given to whether the organization needs an especially qualified and talented person for a particular job. If a good fund-raiser is a priority, the trustees may decide to favor a high salary in the development area. If someone with computer experience is necessary and there is a shortage of data processing professionals in the area, it may be necessary to bring the salary of this individual up to a level more closely comparable to the level in the profit sector. Keep in mind, though, that when two individuals on the same level on the organization chart are earning substantially different amounts, this can undermine morale.

High salaries are controversial in nonprofit organizations, but they may be necessary to attract top-flight people. One device that some organizations use to justify the cost of expensive employees is to contract them out to other institutions on a time-available basis at a cost that earns substantial dollars for the organization. The employees must be willing, of course, and the employer should be careful that the organization's own needs are not compromised. Once the arrangement is finalized, it should be fully documented in the employee's job description. An example of how the arrangement might work follows:

The executive director of the Compton Hospital is an expert in the use of computers in hospital administration. His total annual compensation (salary plus benefits) is $88,000. Taking into account holidays, weekends, vacation days, and so on, the actual number of working days per year is 220, thus the director costs the hospital $400 per day. Yet it turns out that other organizations are willing to pay a fee of $1,200 per day plus expenses for the director to come consult with them about computer use in hospital administration. The hospital and the director have come to an agreement that he will consult on hospital time for fifteen days a year at a rate of $1,200 per day. The hospital takes in $18,000 for these fifteen release days, reducing the $88,000 compensation package to $70,000.

Once salary and benefits discussions have been completed, the trustees must set a salary range for each class of positions—executive director, assistant directors, program directors, coordinators, program assistants, clerical–secretarial, and so on. The top dollar figure in a range should be 15 to 30 percent higher than the bottom figure. If someone with relatively little experience is offered a job, he or she will probably be offered a salary near the bottom of the range but will be able to receive annual merit increases with more experience. Someone coming to the job with plenty of credentials and lots of experience will be offered a salary at a level nearer the top of the range.

Benefits. Today it is not uncommon for prospective employees to look as carefully at benefits packages offered by nonprofit organizations as at salary ranges. This is not surprising. With medical costs rising at a rate far higher than the inflation rate and with inflation itself making retirement seem more like a curse than a blessing, people want to know what the employer will do in these areas. Individual medical plans are expensive so prospective employees will want to know whether there is a group plan available through the employer and what percentage of the cost the employer will pay. There will be questions about disability insurance, life insurance, and tax-sheltered annuity plans. More prosaic benefits such as paid holidays, personal days, sick days, paid vacation, and so on will also need to be decided on by the board and documented for the employees.

In determining benefits, the first thing the trustees might do is set a target percentage-of-total-salaries figure on which to base the benefits package. For example, suppose the organization says that an amount equal to 15 percent of the total annual payroll will be paid to the employees in the form of extras. With that figure as a target, they can then determine which combination of benefits is best and how they should be allocated. In some cases, every employee will receive the same percentage of his or her salary in benefits. In other cases, the amount and percentage will vary depending on salary level, years of service, and other variables. Surveying similar organizations may be useful in attempting to come up with the best combination of benefits (published salary surveys that contain benefits information may be available from national service organizations). Keep in mind that nonprofit organizations have been slow to introduce adequate benefits packages and newer organizations may want to err on the side of generosity in this area.

In budgeting benefits, it is important to leave some unallocated dollars for such employee-related expenses as workmen's compensation and state unemployment insurance,[2] which are technically not considered part of the benefits package. Also, a percentage of the benefits package may be held in escrow for discretionary extras such as attendance at conferences, tuition assistance for work-related special courses, or other activities that may be made available to certain employees when they are requested and approved by a supervisor.

In addition to querying other organizations, expertise about benefits options may be available from independent insurance agents, the organization's accountant, or from a consultant specializing in this area. Expertise may also be available on the board of trustees, particularly from business-people. Because of the complexity of the subject and the plethora of choices, it may be desirable to make a special effort to recruit a trustee with relevant experience in this area. This same trustee might also chair a personnel committee, if the board decides to have one.

SETTING POLICIES AND PROCEDURES

After an organization has set the three basic parameters for personnel just discussed, the most important work is done. However, it is desirable to establish additional policies and procedures as follows:

- Employment and pay procedures
- Staff evaluation procedures
- Conflict-of-interest policies
- Termination and grievance procedures
- General office practices and procedures

The clearer the policies in each of these areas, the less chance there is for misunderstandings. In addition, organizations that have documented policies in each of these areas are more favorably regarded by government enforcing agencies, prospective trustees, employees, and funders.

Employment and Pay Procedures

Most employees are interested in knowing as much as they can about an organization's hiring policy.

☐ How are employees hired and is there a formal process with public notice required?
☐ Are current employees given first preference for a job vacancy?
☐ Is there an affirmative action policy?
☐ Is hiring done solely on the basis of competence and qualifications?
☐ Is every prospective employee allowed to see a job description?

There is also interest in the question of what happens to an employee once he or she is hired.

☐ Is there an official probationary period?
☐ Do temporary or permanent part-time employees enjoy the same rights and benefits as full-time employees?
☐ How often are salary ranges and job classifications reviewed and by whom?

Another series of questions focuses on pay procedures.

☐ How often and in what form are employees paid?
☐ What opportunity is there for merit raises and are there annual cost-of-living increases?
☐ Is extra pay available for overtime or extra work?

There are no right answers to these questions, but they do provide a kind of checklist of items that the board may wish to discuss and resolve. There are always a number of options and points of view. On the question of promotion from within, for example, organizational loyalty tends to be developed when employees view advancement as the reward for good work. Thus promotion from within can be a goal that the board and executive director decide to make into an explicit policy. On the other hand, a desire for fresh vision by top management may suggest that, in the case of the executive director's position and positions of senior staff, outsiders be given preference.

Documenting each and every policy once it is decided on is important. If the organization is vigorously attempting to attract minorities and other special constituencies onto the staff, for example, it is important to state this and have a clearly written affirmative action policy. The morale of employees can be badly bruised when such practices and preferences of the board are not made explicit. On the matter of probationary periods for new employees, many organizations find them useful. During this period the organization or the employee can sever an untenable working relationship without having to resort to the more cumbersome termination or resignation procedures that have been developed for regular employees. Once again, such a practice should be made explicit in a written policy statement that is given to new employees when they are hired.

Staff Evaluation Procedures

A prospective employee should be made aware of the process by which his or her performance will be evaluated, by whom, how often, and whether salary increases depend on a formal review process. In many organizations, an employee's supervisor meets with the employee once a year for a formal evaluation (the executive director's review, described in chapter 2, is conducted by the president of the board). A series of questions relating to the job description, performance, employee satisfaction, supervisor satisfaction, and so on can be drawn up. For example:

☐ Which aspects of your job do you consider to be of highest priority and of lowest priority?

☐ Are there tasks that you are having to perform that are not in your job description and if so, do you feel they should be added to the description or given to someone else?

☐ Are the demands on your time reasonable?

☐ Have there been aspects of your job that you have had to neglect for lack of time?

☐ How well do you feel you are getting along with your coworkers?

☐ What suggestions do you have about how you could be more productive?

☐ Do you get enough supervision or too much?

☐ Is this the right job for you, which areas are most appealing, and which are least appealing?

☐ Which aspects of your job have you completed most successfully in the last six months and which aspects least successfully?

☐ What do you hope to accomplish in the next six months in your job?

☐ Other comments, complaints, observations, and questions?

In addition to asking these questions, the supervisor gives his or her impressions of the strengths and weaknesses of the employee's performance and discusses job objectives for the coming year.

After the meeting, the employee writes a summary of the meeting that is submitted to the supervisor. Specific job objectives, agreed on by both employee and supervisor, are listed. The supervisor reviews the document, adds his or her comments, and both sign it. The executive director reviews the document and may decide to intervene if a problem seems to be brewing. Otherwise, the document becomes the basis for a decision regarding a merit increase in salary and ultimately becomes a part of the organization's personnel records.

Conflict-of-Interest Policies

Conflict of interest was discussed in chapter 2 in connection with trustees of nonprofit organizations and it is also relevant in this chapter on staff. Like trustees, if staff members are involved in a decision that could substantially benefit themselves, their family members, or others close to them, there can be an appearance that the decision was not arrived at objectively, that there was conflict of interest. In most cases, the benefit will be a financial one, though not always. If a staff person of a university sits on the university's admissions committee, he or she has a conflict of interest if involved in a committee decision to admit a child or relative.

Because nonprofit organizations are so clearly mandated to have a broad public purpose and not to serve the parochial interests of board and staff, conflict of interest can have particularly negative connotations. For that reason, conflict-of-interest policies should be developed that state clearly how the organization will handle such sensitive situations.

The key to sound policies in this area is what is called *disclosure.* This is because it is not always inappropriate for people to be involved in decisions that may benefit them or a member of their family so long as the nature of the situation is clear to everyone else voting on the matter. Consider, for example, Joan Simons, the data processing supervisor of the Compton Community Center. She has decided to purchase computer supplies from her husband's company. The company is extending a 35 percent discount, which is a better deal for the center than any other vendor in the city will offer. Thus no one questions the propriety of the decision. Nevertheless, it is important for Joan Simons to disclose the nature of her conflict of interest to her supervisor and seek approval before proceeding. In some cases, it may be appropriate for the supervisor to get the approval of the executive director or the board itself, particularly when large sums of money are involved. Conflict-of-interest policies do not necessarily prevent a financial transaction or any other kind of action from taking place, but they do ensure an objective review and decision on the issue based on a disclosure of all the facts.

There are times when a conflict situation can have a blatant appearance of self-interest. Suppose an organization had to decide whether to buy a piece of property from the executive director, who himself had purchased the property only one year before. In this situation, it is unclear whether the executive director acted in good faith in purchasing the property or whether his decision was based on knowledge that the organization would be interested in purchasing it later on. In such a situation, it may be appropriate for the organization's conflict-of-interest policies to indicate that an outside impartial review of such situations will always precede any kind of legal action. Because conflict-of-interest situations can vary so greatly in nature and because the appropriate response to them is not uniform, it is advantageous to secure the help of an attorney in drafting appropriate language for conflict-of-interest policies.

Termination and Grievance Procedures

Almost every organization is beset at one time or another with an employee who simply does not work out. As unpleasant as it is to ask someone to leave, sometimes it is necessary for the good of the organization, the other employees, and the individual in question. By the same token, in any hierarchical organization, employees are somewhat at the mercy of their supervisors and there must be organizational safeguards to protect them.

There are some offenses an employee may commit that are grounds for immediate dismissal. These include falsification of information given for personnel records, drug use during working hours, indecent behavior, theft, pretending illness to avoid work, and gross insubordination. In most cases where a supervisor is unhappy with an employee's performance, however, the situation requires a more moderate response because the problem is not as clear-cut. As soon as there are any grounds for concern, the supervisor *must* begin to keep detailed written records of problems, offenses, and discussions that include dates, times, and places. Without such a record, it becomes much more difficult to justify termination of an employee and, in some cases, such action may actually be illegal.

In addition to keeping written documentation, it is generally a good idea for a supervisor to ask for a preliminary meeting with an employee once it is clear that there is a problem. A record of the meeting should be prepared, signed by both parties, and placed in the personnel file of the employee. The document should summarize the nature of the supervisor's criticism, the employee's response, and the specific job objectives and performance criteria to be used to evaluate that employee's performance in the future. A date should also be set for another meeting to review the employee's progress in the job. In cases where the performance of the employee is so poor that the supervisor thinks termination is a real possibility, the period between the first meeting and the second should be called probationary with the understanding that if performance does not improve, the employee will be asked to resign or be fired.

If an employee has a grievance regarding treatment, working conditions, or other matters, the complaint is usually taken up first with that employee's supervisor. If after an initial meeting, or series of meetings, the employee feels that the matter is not satisfactorily resolved, the employee can request a meeting with the person to whom his or her supervisor reports. (This meeting may or may not be with all three present.) In the case where the employee's complaint is with the executive director, the complaint is referred to the chairman of the personnel committee of the board or the board president. In all cases, it is the third individual consulted, the one with the highest position in the organization, who serves as the final arbiter of the problem.

Once an organization sets its policies on warnings, grievances, dismissals, and so on, it is bound by them. A supervisor cannot simply fire an employee without cause if a termination procedure has been established and not followed. Employees have legal recourse if the organization's own guidelines are not followed. For this reason, it is often preferable to entice an employee into resigning rather than begin what can be a long and unpleasant process leading to termination. A generous severance payment may be all that is required and the resignation (which should be made in writing) prevents the employee from claiming unemployment insurance that, at the very least, would lead to higher premium payments.

General Office Practices and Procedures

There are a host of little details relating to day-to-day work life that should be spelled out for employees. Some relate specifically to in-office procedures; some are more general. For example, there may be:

- Specific rules about how the staff is authorized to make purchases (through purchase orders, petty cash, or on a cash-reimbursable basis)
- Guidelines governing travel (such as per diem limits, times when air travel is permitted, and mileage reimbursement rates)
- Controls on personal use of the telephone or procedures and limits on long distance calls
- Rules governing the use and care of office equipment
- Limits placed on the organization's liability for personal property left on the premises
- Guidelines governing outside work, such as whether the employer has first refusal on publications, and whether the organization permits leaves of absence to do outside jobs
- Policies regarding working hours and conditions that address regular office working hours, flextime or overtime arrangements, and overtime compensation[3]

THE PERSONNEL MANUAL

Once all the organizational parameters and specific policies and procedures have been set and voted on by the board of trustees, they should be collected in one place—put between two covers as it were—and made available to current and prospective employees. A personnel manual is an essential document for any nonprofit organization that has more than seven or eight employees or a budget in excess of $150,000. (Many smaller organizations have personnel manuals as well.) A typical personnel manual table of contents might look something like that in figure 4.3.

FIGURE 4.3. Table of Contents of a Typical Personnel Manual

PERSONNEL POLICIES, PROCEDURES, AND BENEFITS

Foreword—A brief description of the organization, its philosophy, purposes, and programs

Employment
  Basic policies
  Hiring procedures

Interim (probationary) period
Types of employment (full-time, part-time, temporary)
Maintenance of personnel records

Working Hours and Conditions
Office hours
Flexible time
Overtime/Compensatory time
Absence reports

Salaries and Wages
Salary structure through job classification
Paydays
Deductions
Raises (merit and cost-of-living)

Employee Benefits
Leaves and absences
Vacations
Holidays
Sick days
Personal days
Maternity leave
Paternity leave
Leave of absence
Other excused absences

Insurance, Retirement, and Other Benefits
Social security
Medical insurance
Life insurance
Disability insurance
Unemployment insurance
Workmen's compensation
Education fund

General Policies and Procedures
Outside work
Promotions
Office closing
Telephone
Travel
Personal property

General Office Practices and Procedures
Office coverage
Smoking
Use and care of equipment

Performance and Salary Review
Timing
Procedure
Considerations

Problems
  Grievances
  Suggestions
  Warnings

Termination
  Resignation
  Retirement
  Release
  Discharge
  Final pay

Organization Chart

Salary Ranges by Position

Conflict-of-Interest Policies

Personnel Evaluation and Review Procedure

Note: Job descriptions are generally not included in the personnel manual.

Personnel manuals are only useful if they are kept up-to-date. Like job descriptions, they should be reviewed at least annually by the executive director (with help from a trustee or the board's personnel committee if appropriate). A good clear personnel manual contributes to positive staff morale and prevents the kind of procedural ambiguity that often leads to problems. By comparing personnel manuals from well-managed nonprofits, an organization can distill those elements it considers most important before putting together its own. A more detailed example of a personnel manual can be found in figure 4.4.

SPECIAL ISSUES INVOLVING CHIEF EXECUTIVES
The chief executive[4] of a nonprofit organization is often the single most important person in determining the effectiveness and the morale of the staff, establishing the quality of the work environment, and projecting the organization's image in the community. Among the many special challenges that can be faced by nonprofit organizations in connection with chief executives are two that deserve special mention: the issues surrounding a founder/director and the problems associated with codirectors.

Founder/Directors
Nonprofit organizations often encounter special personnel challenges with regard to founders who ultimately become chief executives. The challenges are generally of three kinds.

First, because a founder/director is usually completely committed to the organization he or she has established, there is less likelihood that pressure will be put on the board to provide adequate compensation, staff support, and acceptable working conditions. In this regard, founder/directors generally do not know how to insist on fair treatment and as a result often do not receive it.

Second, as organizations develop, board members are usually content to allow founder/directors to continue their strong leadership. This may turn out to be harmful to the organization in two ways: If the organization is driven primarily by a founder/director, board members may fail to get sufficiently involved in decision making, and such an organization may provide the opportunity for trustees to avoid exerting themselves in critical areas of board responsibility such as fund raising. It may also lead to a crisis if the founder/director resigns.

Third, it is often the case that the individual with the vision, imagination, and entrepreneurial energy to be a founder is not the best person to be an organization's chief executive after a certain number of years. Yet boards are often reluctant to take steps to remove a founder/director.

How should an organization deal with these challenges? In the area of compensation, staff support, and working conditions, a member of the board (or a personnel committee) should regularly interview or survey individuals who are knowledgeable about the organization's industry (representatives from national service organizations, funders, administrators, and trustees from similar organizations). These individuals should be asked what a fair compensation package should include (salary level and benefits) and be asked specific questions about numbers of staff people, job responsibilities of the chief executive, and working conditions that they would expect to see in such an organization.

In the area of defining the appropriate respective roles for the founder/director and the board, it is often useful to bring in an objective outsider who can assess the organization's needs, interview both the director and the trustees, and make recommendations based on the experiences of other organizations. While it may be possible for those involved to redefine their relationship, unfortunately they are often so close to the situation, and the subject is such a sensitive one, that the discussion breaks down and results in hard feelings rather than productive solutions.

Finally, what happens when it becomes clear that the founder/director is not the best person to be the chief executive? In some instances, the solution may be quite straightforward, particularly when the individual in question has a fundamental interest and ability in the programs of the organization and is simply weak as a chief administrator and staff supervisor. In this case, it may be possible to shift the individual to a senior staff position in the organization—a position relating to programs—and bring in another individual to serve as the chief executive. To accomplish such a transition is not easy, but many organizations have pulled it off. To be successful, the founder/director has to welcome the move as an opportunity to focus on his or her area of interest, not as a slap in the face and a demotion. Otherwise, the new chief executive will have a very difficult time and a recalcitrant staff person undermining the effective operation of the organization.

Sometimes it becomes clear to boards of directors of nonprofit organizations that their founder/directors really must move on. This situation is awkward and unenviable. How do board presidents tell founder/directors that their organizations have grown beyond them, that their boards or staffs (or both) are dissatisfied with their performance, that their organizations require chief executives with different skills? And how can these founder/directors be properly rewarded for their substantial contributions even when they are being asked to step down from their positions?

These questions are difficult ones because, in most cases, a founder/director has made a substantial emotional investment in his or her organization. In addition, while the founder/director may or may not have invested cash in the organization, it is almost a certainty that he or she has made a contribution by way of substantial donated time and a compensation package that was not competitive, at least in the earliest days of the organization's history. Board members, taking these things into account, often tolerate an untenable situation for far too long, sometimes putting an organization at risk and almost always undermining the morale of those connected with it.

Given the emotional and financial issues involved, the board should decide on a course that addresses both. First, a great effort should be made to secure a resignation with honor rather than a termination with acknowledgment of failure. Addressing the emotional side of the action, the board should be prepared to take certain steps that will acknowledge the founder/director's accomplishments and importance to the organization. The individual's name (with the title founder) might be listed on all stationery and promotional material above the names of the board members. A special effort might be made with the media to do feature stories celebrating the fine work of the individual (at the very least, press releases should talk about the board's acceptance of the resignation with profound regret and a statement by the president of the board highlighting the important contributions of the founder/director to the organization).

On the financial side, the board should be prepared to offer a generous severance package. From the point of view of organizational self-interest, such a settlement often encourages a speedy and painless resignation by the founder/director. However, in a more generous way, it recognizes the financial sacrifices of the individual over the years. It is also likely that after many years of energetic commitment to a single organization, the individual will need some time to decompress and adjust before seeking other employment and the additional compensation offers this opportunity.

Finally, some organizations take the step of placing a resigning founder/director on the board as a way of rewarding him or her and not severing entirely the connection between the individual and the organization. While this sometimes works well, more often than not it causes problems. The founder/director cannot step back from the day-to-day operational issues and often confounds and frustrates the work of his or her successor. This step, while certainly symbolically advantageous, is usually not practically worthwhile.

Codirectors

A second issue faced by some nonprofit organizations concerns the desire to have more than one chief executive. In some organizations, where there are two staff hierarchies, such a structure makes sense. For example, in a symphony orchestra, there is generally an artistic director (the conductor) and an executive director (who serves as chief of administration). The first makes all personnel decisions regarding musicians while the second hires all other staff. Both individuals report to the board of directors and each has a well-defined area of responsibility. However, in other organizations, the codirector structure causes problems. Consider the following case.

WILDERNESS SERVICE AMERICA

Wilderness Service America (WSA) is a national membership organization whose primary purpose is to provide information, funding, and a national advocacy voice to local organizations in the conservation field. Originally formed at the behest of and with funding from a national foundation, WSA was created through the merger of two national organizations with overlapping activities and mission. The national foundation, which was funding both, threatened to cut off its support unless a merger plan could be worked out. Consequently, the boards of the two organizations agreed to form a single organization and it was further agreed that the two executive directors, who were friendly and had a mutual respect for one another, would serve as codirectors.

Initially the structure worked well and the newly merged board felt itself lucky to have two individuals with such eminence in the field. However, within three years, a consultant's evaluation of the organization revealed several problems with the codirector structure among those he interviewed:

☐ WSA's directors of marketing, fund raising, and programs all complained that they never knew to whom to report. On paper, both of the codirectors were to be consulted on key decisions. But rarely were they both in the office at the same time and when they were, they did not always seem to agree on important matters. Senior staff also confessed that they were beginning to learn how each codirector would react to certain questions and they would go to one or the other depending on what kind of an answer they wanted.

☐ Board members complained that they never knew who was responsible for what. Said one, "Whenever I would ask one codirector for clarification on an important decision or action, I was referred to the other who, inevitably, was out of the office. Sometimes, when I finally reached the second codirector, he claimed that the subject I was interested in really wasn't something he was familiar with. I am losing confidence in the system."

☐ One major foundation representative complained, "Shared accountability is no accountability. If I am giving half a million dollars, I want to know who to call when I need to know about our investment."

In following up on these comments, the consultant found that there was a well-designed organization chart with functions and responsibilities clearly divided. But what existed on paper was not carried out in fact and because the chief executive position was shared, ambiguity and opportunities for misunderstandings crept into the system.

In thinking about Wilderness Service America and other organizations that have experimented with codirectors, it is important to acknowledge that there are organizations that have been successful with various kinds of shared authority arrangements. There are even a few organizations—some that have survived for decades—in which all major decisions are made collectively by the whole staff. But these organizations are rare and the number of instances of shared power arrangements that have failed far outnumber those that have survived. It is generally the case that a conventional hierarchical structure will work best in most nonprofit organizations. When it comes to the chief executive, the outside world and the employees are looking for a single individual whose level of authority and accountability are higher than anyone else's on the staff.

Nonprofit organizations can be very special places to work, and their employees are often especially committed people. Many could earn more money in other kinds of organizations, but they may be attracted to the nonprofit because of what it contributes to the quality of their lives and the lives of others.

Therefore, it is important for the organization to state explicitly in the personnel manual that it regards its employees as one of its most valuable assets. This attitude should also be demonstrated by the interest and compassion that the trustees show toward the staff. It is the trustee's responsibility to set policies that contribute to a harmonious and productive work environment. It is also the trustee's responsibility to praise work that is well done and reward employees who give generously of themselves. Clear and fair personnel policies themselves are only a part of the organization's obligation to the employees. The other part is a positive and caring attitude that reflects the respect and admiration that the employees have earned. In nonprofit organizations particularly, this latter obligation must never be forgotten.

FIGURE 4.4. A Detailed Example of a Personnel Manual

COMPTON COMMUNITY CENTER PERSONNEL POLICIES,
PROCEDURES, AND BENEFITS

Foreword

The Compton Community Center is a nonprofit corporation designated as a 501(c)(3) tax-exempt organization by the United States Internal Revenue Service. It was founded in 1966 to provide recreational opportunities to young people in the Compton community.

The Compton Community Center considers that its staff is its most valuable asset. Furthermore, it believes that a clear understanding of the working agreement between the Compton Community Center and its employees is the basis for a harmonious and productive environment. This document has been developed to explain, in as specific a manner as possible, what the Compton Community Center offers to and asks of its staff.

Policies are not immutable; conditions and attitudes do change. Suggestions are always welcomed. It is, furthermore, an underlying assumption of this manual that special and unique situations may be resolved through the cooperative efforts of all concerned.

Working Hours and Conditions

Overtime/Compensatory time: In most circumstances, the Compton Community Center does not recognize overtime for full-time employees because all such employees are salaried. If staff is required to work on projects or travel after hours and on weekends and holidays, compensatory time off will be offered in half-day increments. All requests for compensatory time must be made in advance to an employee's supervisor.

Absence reports: If, owing to an unforeseen emergency, an employee is unable to be at work, he/she should notify his/her immediate supervisor by 9:30 A.M. on the first day of absence.

If the absence extends beyond one day, the supervisor should be kept informed. An employee should attempt to estimate the likely duration of his/her absence.

Each employee should keep his/her supervisor informed of any planned future absences (vacation, holiday, personal day, leave, and travel). In all instances, provisions should be made to ensure that office deadlines are met and requests from clients are covered.

Salaries and Wages

Payday: Employees are paid by check on the fifteenth and final day of each month. If a payday falls on a weekend or holiday, payment will be made on the preceding workday.

Advance payment of salaries are not made except in the case of a vacation paycheck.

Deductions: The federal and state governments require employers to withhold income tax from each employee's paycheck. Employees, therefore, must complete W-4 forms in order to indicate the number of exemptions claimed and to authorize the Compton Community Center to make the appropriate withholdings. Any changes in an employee's number of exemptions requires the filing of new W-4 forms.

Raises: Each employee is reviewed annually a few weeks before the end of the fiscal year on December 31. Raises will be based on formal and regular review of each employee's performance during the past year.

Employee Benefits

Probationary period: The first month of employment is considered a probationary period. During this time, employees are not eligible for certain benefits. These include the accrual of vacation time and medical insurance. After the interim period, employees are entitled to all the benefits outlined in this section.

Vacation: All full-time employees with less than two years of service will accrue vacation leave at the rate of one day per month up to a total of ten days per year. Vacation leave is credited on the last day of each month worked.

The Compton Community Center believes that vacations serve a purpose and that it is advisable for persons to take vacations regularly. For this reason, no employee may carry forward into any year more than one year's credit of vacation days.

Vacation may be taken at any time following three months of service provided that the timing is approved by the employee's supervisor. Vacations may be taken at any time during the year, but not in advance of being earned. Because, however, all vacation schedules must be approved and coordinated to ensure continued efficient work flow, it may not always be possible for vacations to be taken in a single unbroken period. The Compton Community Center will, however, attempt to meet all requested vacation schedules, but to do so, it is important that employees indicate their vacation preferences as far in advance as possible. Preference will be given on the basis of work schedules and requirements, and employee seniority.

Holidays: The following holidays are customarily observed by the Compton Community Center and the office will be closed on these days:

New Year's Day   January 1
Martin Luther King Day   Third Monday in January
Presidents' Day   Third Monday in February
Memorial Day   Last Monday in May
Independence Day   July 4
Labor Day   First Monday in September
Columbus Day   Second Monday in October
Veteran's Day   November 11
Thanksgiving Day (and day after)   Last Thursday and Friday in November
Christmas Day   December 25
One Floating Holiday   Elective

If any of these holidays falls on a weekend, it will be observed on the Friday before or the Monday after at the discretion of the executive director.

Holidays that fall during an employee's scheduled vacation entitle that employee to another vacation day at his/her discretion.

Sick days: Sick leave is to be used only in the event of actual sickness, and not for personal days. Given this policy, sick leave is available to each employee up to two months' leave, at the discretion of the executive director.

Personal days: Each employee is entitled to three personal day absences per year. A personal day is a planned absence not chargeable to the vacation category. Personal days are available in half-day increments, are credited to each employee at the beginning of his/her working year, and are always subject to prior approval by the employee's supervisor. Personal emergencies, not involving employee illness, may be charged to the personal day category.

Personal days may not be carried forward from one year to the next, nor do they constitute a monetary claim against the Compton Community Center if unused at the termination of an employee's service.

Maternity leave: An employee may be granted up to four weeks' maternity leave with pay and an additional eight weeks of unpaid leave provided that her immediate supervisor is given at least two weeks' notice of the anticipated date of departure. An employee's intention to return to work should also be verified at this time.

An employee may work for as long as she wishes prior to delivery, as long as her health allows her to fulfill her regular duties.

Upon return from maternity leave, an employee will assume whatever position, authority, and level of seniority she held prior to the leave. Regular benefits will continue to accrue during the leave.

After the first four weeks of maternity leave an employee may apply whatever accrued vacation time she may have against the time she is absent. If during any portion of this leave an employee becomes sick or disabled, she will be eligible for regular sickness benefits.

Paternity leave: Under certain circumstances a father may wish to assume family duties following the birth of a child. The Compton Community Center, therefore, offers two weeks' paid and an additional two weeks of unpaid paternity leave. The same conditions apply to paternity leave as to maternity leave.

Leave of absence: A leave of absence is defined as an approved absence, *without pay,* of a limited and specified duration. It does not, therefore, constitute a break in service, although no benefits are accrued during the leave.

A written request for any leave of absence in excess of five working days must be submitted to the executive director at least one month prior to the beginning of the leave. Shorter leaves of absence may be approved verbally by an employee's supervisor.

Unused vacation days may be applied against an approved leave of absence.

Unless expressly stated otherwise in writing by the executive director, a leave of absence in excess of six months will constitute a break in service. A returning employee cannot be guaranteed his/her previous position although every effort will be made to provide a comparable situation. Benefits and seniority will accrue from zero beginning with the date of rehiring.

Other excused absences: Religious holidays are granted with pay. Prior approval of an employee's supervisor must be obtained.

Jury duty leave is granted by the Compton Community Center with the understanding that any employee will clear such leave with his/her supervisor prior to departure. The Compton Community Center will pay the difference between the employee's juror fee and his/her regular rate of pay.

Medical insurance: The Compton Community Center currently participates in the Compton Community Health Plan, a local health maintenance organization. Full medical insurance coverage is part of every full-time employee's benefits. Employees are urged to read the prospectus of the Compton Community Health Plan carefully to learn precisely what coverage is available to them.

Social security: As required by law, the Compton Community Center participates in the social security system. The organization withholds a certain percentage of an employee's salary, which it matches with organizational funds. There are no additional retirement benefits offered to employees.

Unemployment insurance: All staff members are covered by the State Unemployment Insurance Program. Eligibility and waiting periods depend on the reason for termination of employment.

Workmen's Compensation: The Compton Community Center carries compensation insurance in accordance with the requirements of state law. This insurance provides benefit payments to an employee who is injured while working for the Compton Community Center or becomes ill from any occupation-related disease.

General Policies and Procedures

Office closing: If the office is to be closed because of inclement weather or other emergencies, each employee will be notified by telephone as early as possible. The closing decision will be made by the executive director and it is assumed that employees will follow this decision.

Telephones: Compton Community Center telephones are necessary for business purposes. The number of phone lines is limited and it is, therefore, requested that employees keep personal calls to a minimum. Any personal long-distance calls that result in a charge to the

Compton Community Center should be charged to the employee long-distance billing code and paid for when the bill comes in.

Office coverage: It is essential that the office and the telephone be staffed at all times from 9:00 A.M. to 5:00 P.M. Staggered lunch breaks should therefore be arranged among staff. Employees leaving the office should tell the person answering the phones where they will be and when they will return.

Smoking: No smoking is allowed in the Compton Community Center offices.

Performance and Salary Review

Timing: An employee's performance review takes place annually, prior to the end of the fiscal year or more often if it is deemed necessary by the executive director or employee's supervisor. Salary review takes place annually with the performance review.

Procedure: The review process may result in three categories of determination:

1. An employee's work is found to be more than satisfactory and consistent with the objectives for the position. A merit raise will be recommended. All decisions on merit increases are made by the executive director based on a variety of factors such as general economic climate, normal salary range for the job, and so on.

2. An employee's work is found to be generally satisfactory, but not wholly consistent with the objectives set for the position. The employee will be informed as to his/her areas of satisfactory performance and those areas that need strengthening. A specific plan for improving performance in the specified areas will be worked out with the employee's supervisor. A minimum merit raise or no raise may be recommended at the discretion of the employee's immediate supervisor.

3. An employee's performance is found to fall below satisfactory standards and not to approach stated job objectives. The employee will be warned of this situation by his/her supervisor and the specifics of the unsatisfactory performance discussed. No merit raise will be awarded and the employee will be informed that if his/her performance is not raised to acceptable levels within a three-week trial period, the employee may be discharged.

Termination

Resignation: An employee wishing to resign from the Compton Community Center should so indicate to his/her supervisor, in writing, at least two weeks prior to the date of termination. It is requested that an employee who has resigned set aside at least one hour so that the executive director and supervisor of the employee may discuss his/her reasons for leaving.

Discharge: Any employee who has not completed the one-month probationary period may be discharged without a job review. In this case, all payment owed to the employee will be paid on the last day of employment.

Employees who are discharged by the Compton Community Center following the review and warning procedure as outlined under "Performance and Salary Review," employees discharged following warnings for inappropriate behavior, or employees discharged without warnings for serious offenses are not eligible for severance pay. Any employee who is discharged after the probationary period may, on request, receive a written statement giving the reasons for his/her termination.

Final Pay: Prior to the issuance of a final paycheck, an employee must return all keys, books, or other Compton Community Center property.

CHECKLIST QUESTIONS FOR CHAPTER 4

1. Does your organization have an organization chart that clearly and unambiguously shows chains of employee authority and accountability?

2. Are there job descriptions for all employees in your organization? Are they up-to-date?

3. Are compensation scales realistic and fair in your organization? Are employee benefits comparable to those in other nonprofit organizations of similar size? If salaries and benefits are not adequate, is there a plan to address this issue?

4. Has your organization clearly documented its hiring and pay procedures? Is there a formal evaluation procedure for every employee in your organization? Have grievance and termination procedures been developed?

5. Has your organization developed conflict-of-interest policies for employees?

6. Does your organization have a personnel manual? Is it complete and up-to-date?

5
Marketing

Abbott Academy is a prestigious coeducational secondary school in New England. As a college-preparatory day school serving approximately 200 students, Abbott has traditionally been known for several things—its outstanding teachers, its demanding curriculum, its tough grading policy, its urban campus, and its requirement that all students spend a specified amount of time doing some form of public service.

In the early 1970s, the *Simpson Guide to Private Schools* wrote glowingly of Abbott Academy:

> If you care about providing an outstanding education to your child, Abbott Academy should rank high on your list of secondary schools. Its graduates all are admitted to prestigious colleges—one year, almost a third of the class ended up at Harvard or Yale. The tuition is kept considerably below that of comparable institutions thanks to a large endowment and continuing annual support from its founder, Joseph Abbott. As a result of Mr. Abbott's generosity, parents are not asked to make contributions to the school as occurs in most comparable institutions. Some say that when a child is accepted at Abbott, he or she has gained a passport to success in college and later life.
>
> But don't get your hopes up. Abbott accepts only one in eight applicants and the academic accomplishments of those who apply is remarkably high. Abbott boasts the highest "yield" rate of any New England secondary school—that is, once accepted, most applicants happily sign up for the four-year program. Minority students are favored in admission procedures, and because the academic program is so rigorous, the school has instituted a special tutoring program which is geared primarily to those minority students who have not had good academic preparation. Overall, Abbott Academy is among the top institutions of its kind in the country—it is one of those schools that seems to have it all.

At the time it appeared, the *Simpson Guide* article on Abbott Academy greatly pleased the school's trustees, all of whom had been friends of Mr. Abbott himself. For almost a decade, they congratulated themselves on their association with an institution that "had it all." Yet, in the mid-1980s, the school's fortunes began to change. There were fewer applications, and although this reflected the demographics of a smaller applicant pool, the downward trend was even more severe than had been predicted. Of even greater concern was the dropping yield rate (the number of students admitted to Abbott who decided to enroll). In 1975, Abbott's yield rate had been close to 85 percent, but it was below 50 percent only ten years later. Perhaps more alarming, college admissions among Abbott seniors was becoming a much less predictable undertaking. While many students were still going to prestigious colleges, an increasing number of them had to be satisfied with schools that previous Abbott students would not have considered. Finally, there was the problem of the budget. When Mr. Abbott retired as the school's headmaster in 1975, he put the school on notice that his annual contribution would be declining. For the first time, the board had to consider a significant tuition increase, annual fund raising, or both.

At a board meeting in 1985, Charles Mayfield, the school's new headmaster, told the trustees that the situation should not be viewed with alarm. If the number of qualified applicants was dropping, then the school should just make do with fewer students for a year or two. The trends would change and there would be plenty of applicants once the "pendulum swings back as it always does." Tuition could be raised a little to meet the income gap, and affluent parents might want to consider "throwing in a little extra" to help out. Mayfield conceded that the school could do a better job of convincing prospective parents of the superior merits of Abbott Academy once their children had been accepted. But he "eschewed unseemly promotional efforts such as those employed by our competitors" and suggested that sending out a copy of the *Simpson Guide* article was probably the most appropriate public relations effort the school could mount. As to the growing unpredictability of college admissions, Mayfield explained, Abbott's overall record had been very good over the years and no dire predictions should be made based on one or two years of lackluster performance.

By 1989, Abbott Academy's trustees and headmaster could no longer ignore the ominous signs that things were getting worse. Applications were down to such an extent that the school was accepting more than half of the students who applied, a stark contrast to the one in eight applicants that had been reported in the *Simpson Guide* of several years before. Even by admitting such a high percentage of applicants, Abbott could no longer maintain a student body of 200 qualified students because so many of those accepted ended up choosing other schools. With only 178 students in the school, tuition revenue was down, and because fund raising was not very effective, the school was beginning to use principal from its endowment to cover operating shortfalls. The unpleasant and unpredictable trends in college admissions continued—in fact, in 1989, for the first time in the school's history, two seniors were not accepted at any college. Faculty members complained that this was because the quality of students was slipping. Indeed, many of the most experienced teachers were considering alternative employment because their jobs at Abbott "were no longer rewarding." Finally, the percentage of minority students was also declining despite special recruitment efforts in the minority community.

A PROBLEM IN MARKETING

In hindsight, we can see that although the problems of Abbott Academy had been mounting for ten years, they had been misdiagnosed by the headmaster and the trustees. Charles Mayfield had behaved a bit like a doctor telling an elderly woman patient with a ruptured appendix that she was really fine, no examination was necessary, and she might consider taking an indigestion tablet for an upset stomach. By electing not to do a comprehensive diagnosis, and by mistaking symptom for disease, Mayfield and the trustees failed to develop an appropriate strategy for identifying the school's predicament. Like the incompetent doctor, they did not delve beneath the surface to find out what was really wrong. Correct diagnosis, in the case of Abbott Academy, would have required several steps including the following:

1. Accurately identifying the school's multiple constituencies and monitoring their changing characteristics and needs
2. Considering how the school's program could be modified to meet the needs of constituents
3. Conducting appropriate research to determine the school's strengths and weaknesses, its position relative to its competition, and its perceived value in the community
4. Developing a sensible pricing strategy
5. Responding to a changing environment that was making it increasingly difficult for potential clients to take advantage of what the school had to offer
6. Developing a proper image for the school and promoting the institution correctly in the community
7. Promoting the school effectively

In effect, the board did not approach the challenges facing Abbott Academy from a marketing perspective.

What is marketing? Marketing is the continuous diagnosis and analysis of the changing needs of customers, clients, and constituents and devising strategies to meet these needs. Marketing is the creation of an appropriate image for a product, service, or organization. It is the analysis, planning, implementation, and control of decisions in the areas of product offering, distribution, promotion, and pricing.

In the nonprofit sector, marketing is the engineering of *satisfaction* among a variety of groups including users of an organization's services, funders, trustees, regulators, and others who can influence the success of the organization—such as the media and even the general public. In the nonprofit arena, successful marketing strategies allow organizations to accomplish their missions, meet their programmatic goals, and achieve long-term financial stability by focusing on the needs of their constituents and satisfying those needs over time.

As we look at the case of Abbott Academy, we can examine each of these aspects of marketing in some detail and demonstrate how a marketing perspective might have helped the headmaster and trustees correctly diagnose problems and devise strategies to solve them.

THE ISSUE OF MULTIPLE CONSTITUENCIES (MARKET SEGMENTATION)

One of the most important aspects of marketing is called *market segmentation.* In the nonprofit sector, market segmentation refers to the various constituencies whose satisfaction must be addressed. In most cases, different strategies need to be developed for each group, but many nonprofit organizations do not correctly identify all their constituencies in the first place. This was certainly the case with Abbott Academy, which had stated publicly and quite explicitly that the single constituency to which it needed to address itself was its students. The 1985 catalog of the school began with the following words: "Abbott Academy was founded with the express intent of providing an outstanding education to young people. It is to our students, therefore, that we devote our attention, our resources, and our energies."

From a marketing point of view, students were not the only constituency whose needs had to be addressed if Abbott was to be successful. Other groups included:

☐ *Parents.* It was parents, after all, who chose to send their children to the school, judged whether the amount of tuition they were asked to pay was reasonable, and decided whether they might wish to contribute an additional amount voluntarily. Yet, Abbott actively discouraged parents from visiting (except when parents were summoned to a conference with teacher or headmaster). The school had no parent support organization and offered no social events for them. Many parents felt isolated from the school and wondered whether they or their children had done something wrong. Afraid for their children, they never actually complained to the faculty, trustees, or headmaster that they did not feel a part of the school family.

☐ *College representatives.* It was college admissions officers and other officials who decided whether to admit Abbott Academy applicants and, in effect, determined Abbott's reputation as a college preparatory school. Yet, little was done to cultivate this constituency. Mr. Abbott had maintained good contacts at a few Ivy League schools during his tenure. However, once he retired, no new bonds were forged. Furthermore, Abbott Academy had had little or no contact with representatives of "lesser" schools who were given the impression that their campuses were being used as safety applications by the Abbott students. As Abbott students cast a wider and wider net in their applications to colleges, the lack of a strong college network should have become increasingly obvious.

☐ *Potential applicants/prospective students.* By serving its enrolled students well, Abbott administrators felt that they were doing all they could to make the school an enticing place for prospective students. Yet, remarkably, there was little or no opportunity for those enrolled to influence those applying. Prospective students met only with adults (generally in the company of their parents). Their short visits to classes, during which they sat in the back row and were not drawn into discussion, often produced an impression that Abbott was a school only for exceptionally bright kids, not for them. Because Abbott's playing fields were not adjacent to the campus, prospective students never saw them and this confirmed their impression that Abbott consisted primarily of classrooms and hard work.

☐ *Minority representatives.* When Joseph Abbott founded Abbott Academy, he believed that a fundamental tenant of the school should be to offer young people of color an opportunity to gain an outstanding education. He also believed that a critical part of the education of white students was to come into contact with individuals whose backgrounds were substantially different from their own. But the school never really developed a strategy to court this minority constituency. Abbott himself had believed special efforts to be unnecessary inasmuch as the benefits of an Abbott Academy education were an obvious enticement. Gradually the school found itself losing minority candidates to other secondary schools whose faculties included more black, Hispanic, and Asian teachers, whose curricula included works by black and Latin American writers, and whose boards included several nonwhite trustees.

☐ *Alumni.* In most schools, alumni are an important source of dollars and they also promote the institution and help recruit prospective students.

At Abbott, this constituency was never invited to become involved. There was no alumni bulletin to keep them informed of school activities, there were no reunion functions or other opportunities to foster institutional loyalty, and there was no annual appeal for contributions. When Abbott Academy finally launched its first alumni fund-raising activity in 1989, few alumni participated.

☐ *Faculty.* Abbott Academy's faculty, like the employees of many nonprofit organizations, was overworked and underpaid. In the halcyon days of the institution, their satisfaction came from the academy's institutional prestige among secondary schools, the intellectual stimulation that came from working with bright students, and the repeated statement by Joseph Abbott that they were the most talented faculty in secondary education. But as Abbott Academy's problems mounted, the trustees forgot that this constituency was critical to Abbott's success as an institution. They cut the number of faculty members, increased teaching loads, froze salaries, and made the fatal mistake of second-guessing curricula and teaching methods. With the declining quality of the student body, a loss of pride in their work, and no financial incentives, there was very little to keep the best teachers at Abbott.

☐ *Trustees.* Trustees can bring prestige, money, and expertise to the operation of a school or any nonprofit organization. But Abbott Academy's trustees, all of whom were Joseph Abbott's friends, had never been expected or asked to do any of these things. When the school's fortunes began to turn, the new headmaster did not feel comfortable asking the trustees to become more active because, he felt, they were important, busy people who were doing the institution a favor by serving. He was also reluctant to admit that his administration was not as successful as his predecessor's. By not courting this group, he got from them precisely what he asked for: nothing—no support, no money, no commitment.

☐ *Other donors.* Like most nonprofit organizations, Abbott Academy relied on contributed income to balance its budget. Although it had an ongoing source of earned revenue—tuition—it could not charge a high enough price per student to support its expenses. Until 1985, there had been only one donor, Joseph Abbott himself. In this respect, the distinguished founder had been uncharacteristically shortsighted. Unwilling or unable to continue to cover the operating deficit of the school indefinitely, he was forced to put the school on notice that other donors would have to be found. But because they had never been courted, donors were hard to come by. Abbott Academy had never solicited money from alumni, parents, or foundations, and had not appealed to wealthy individuals whose relatives had attended or taught at the school. The school had, in fact, not solicited funds from anyone. As a result, when

Abbott Academy's fortunes began to change, there was no loyal group of donors to turn to for help.

Each of these constituent groups could have been a vital link in helping Abbott Academy solve its problems, achieve its goals, and remain fiscally healthy. Yet, by focusing on only one group—its students—the school's leadership paid a very high price. They were unable to meet one of the great challenges that faces every nonprofit organization—the challenge of identifying each of its constituent groups clearly and accurately and developing separate, appropriate, and effective strategies to satisfy each one.

IMAGE

Choose a nonprofit organization that you know about or work for. Now go out and ask several people to share their impressions of it with you. The responses will give you some sense of that organization's image among those you have interviewed. Image is the sum total of beliefs, ideas and impressions that people have of an organization or the programs, services, or products it offers. In the nonprofit world, a strong, positive image is a critical element in gaining clients, students, or audience. It is also essential in gaining donors and broad community support.

An organization's image can and will change. Sometimes, the change can come about quickly. If a university president resigns after an ethics scandal, if a labor strike at a hospital is described as bitter by a newspaper, if a symphony orchestra receives a spate of negative reviews, a previously good image can be sullied. Trustees often assume under these circumstances that the public will forgive and forget, but this is a dangerous assumption. The proper course is to assume that action should be taken immediately to neutralize any negative events, statements, or impressions. Because image is based on beliefs, it is often not essential for an organization to change its programs, activities, governance or staffing in order to change its image. Rather, it can often change adverse opinion by launching its own carefully designed campaign to create more positive impressions and ideas.

For example, when a precipitous event changes an organization's image, it is fairly simple to diagnose the problem and begin to mount a strategy to address it. If during a political campaign, a candidate for national office suddenly starts branding a nonprofit civil liberties organization as leftist, the organization can mount its own counteroffensive to show that its activities are considered mainstream and it is the candidate who is "out of step with the American people."

What is more difficult is noticing when an organization's positive image is eroding slowly and imperceptibly over time, particularly if this trend occurs during a period in which the trustees and staff believe the organization is flourishing. This is precisely what happened in the case of Abbott Academy. Abbott's image in the early 1970s was reflected by the *Simpson Guide* article that suggested that the institution was among the best of an elite group of private secondary schools. But several things changed that image. As Abbott Academy encountered its first difficulties with college admissions, rumors began to circulate that the school could no longer get its students into college. Although this greatly exaggerated the facts, the rumor worried prospective parents, many of whom began to assume that there was a connection between declining college admissions and the retirement of Joseph Abbott. They wondered what else the founder's retirement might portend. The rumor also had an effect on prospective students. Without a guaranteed passport to college, young people began to question the value of what the *Simpson Guide* had called a "rigorous" academic program. They did not want to attend what one prospective student called an "intellectual boot camp" and another called a "grind farm for turkeys and book lovers." While Abbott Academy could have taken active steps to reverse these assaults on the school's image, the changes occurred so slowly and imperceptibly that no one in the institution clearly understood what was happening.

A second case history provides an even sharper example of how an organization's image can change over time among its various constituencies.

BRIDGE

Jim Richards, Sharon McCabe, and Sam Lindsay met in an advanced counseling class as seniors at a prestigious urban university in the fall of 1968. Each wanted to go on to graduate school in counseling, social work, or psychology. All three had a deep commitment to helping the urban poor and they felt they should not wait until graduate school was finished before they did something tangible. By October 1968, they made two decisions. They would all stay in the city for their graduate training and they would attempt to set up some kind of counseling center in one of the poor neighborhoods in the city.

In December, all three were admitted to graduate school and, by April 1969, they had set up a counseling center, which they called "Bridge," housed in a small storefront surrounded by burned-out houses and boarded-up stores. Using their own savings and modest donations from three local churches, they were able to pay the first three months' rent, install a phone, and purchase some basic equipment. There was no money for chairs and desks so they simply used orange crates and old doors. But the clients, who they started seeing in May, didn't seem to mind. Many were simply lonely, elderly people who wanted to talk. There were also alcoholics, some drug addicts, homeless people, and many who hoped that Jim, Sharon, or Sam could help them find medical attention, fill out welfare forms, or give them advice on how to find a job. Another group of clients included teenagers seeking information on birth control or abortions.

During the first year, Jim, Sharon, and Sam seemed to work around the clock. Between graduate school, seeing clients, making repairs to the building, and staying one step ahead of the bills, they were constantly exhausted. They came to work in messy clothes because they usually had to do some carpentry or painting or had to wash the floor. They were frustrated by the fact that they had to interrupt their counseling sessions to answer the phone because this seemed unprofessional and they were also concerned about the lack of privacy in the large open room. Money was always a problem. Because none of the three were licensed clinicians, public funding agencies and foundations consistently turned down their requests for funds. Most of Bridge's support came from family, friends, church groups, and an occasional modest payment from a grateful client. Yet despite all of this hardship, Jim, Sharon, and Sam became more energized with each sign of increased community respect and acceptance.

In 1971, an event took place that almost led to the end of Bridge. The storefront was torched by five teenagers who, spurred on by alcohol, had been looking for a thrill on a Saturday night. The event was a critical turning point in the organization's history but, ironically, it soon seemed a blessing in disguise. A reporter from a national news magazine visited the burned-out office, interviewed Jim, Sharon, Sam, and their clients and wrote a heartrending story about Bridge's wonderful track record with the truly disenfranchised; he also talked about the organization's imminent demise. Within two months, an outpouring of donations from all over the country provided enough resources for the founders to buy a building, equip it with real furniture, hire a secretary, and, most importantly, put a fully licensed psychologist on the staff, which would allow Bridge to be eligible for third-party payments and grants. It seemed like a dream come true.

Between 1971 and 1975, Bridge changed dramatically. The three young founders all finished graduate school. Their story, which had become a legend in the funding community, helped Bridge become a designated agency in many communitywide appeals. With more money came growth. The organization moved once again, this time to a nicer neighborhood. All of the counseling sessions were now in private offices and there was a pleasant, large waiting area. Psychologists and counselors did not have to interrupt their sessions to answer the phone; the two secretary–receptionists did that for them. Because Jim, Sharon, and Sam were often meeting with funders and public officials, they wore nice clothes to work. They were now fully licensed professionals and gone were the days when they had to worry about painting or carpentry.

But something else was changing at the same time. The client base was shifting. Instead of the elderly urban poor and the pregnant teenagers with virtually nowhere to turn, Bridge found itself serving a more affluent group of working people and housewives. Many of the new clients came in from the suburbs or from their places of work for their counseling sessions. But the old clients, the people for whom Bridge was established, were not coming, and the staff began to worry. Try as they did, they could not figure out how to reverse the trend. On the tenth anniversary of Bridge, the reporter who had done the original 1971 story on Bridge returned to do a flashback feature. He came with a photographer and the two spent a morning at the new office, but the story never appeared. According to rumors, the magazine had decided that Bridge no longer made good copy.

Why did Bridge's original clients stop coming? Why did the organization no longer make good copy? The answer is simple. Bridge had changed in ways that significantly affected the original clients' beliefs, ideas, and impressions of it. To these clients, the first incarnation of the organization had hardly seemed like an organization at all. Their image of Bridge was of three young people, seemingly without pretense, dressed like people they knew, working out of a storefront in their neighborhood. The clients could sympathize with these young people who seemed to be struggling almost as much as they were. Indeed, the whole environment of Bridge was *comfortable*—not necessarily for Jim, Sharon, and Sam and not necessarily for their potential funders, but for the clients they were serving. Bridge's image suggested safety, human warmth, openness, and friendship. There was a sense that everyone understood each other.

Over time, Bridge's image changed. When the office moved, old clients felt abandoned. The move seemed to suggest that the old neighborhood was really no good after all. But that was not the full extent of the image problem. When old clients did travel to the new office, they no longer had direct access to Jim, Sharon, and Sam. Instead, there were two strangers—receptionists with a kind of official demeanor—who greeted them in a waiting room that seemed cold and sterile. After getting inside the counselors' offices, another message was clearly conveyed. "You old clients are still failures, but we have made it. Look at our fancy clothes. Remember those silly orange crates and doors we used for desks? Well, look at our expensive furniture." The new image said to the old clients, "We really don't care about you any more. We have more pressing things to do and to think about. We are part of the establishment. You aren't important and we are."

The experience of Bridge is not unusual. Many nonprofit organizations have suffered the erosion of image with long-time constituents during periods of growth and institutionalization. Many have complained that things were no longer as personal, as smoothly run, or as much fun as they were in the old days. It is important to keep in mind that some of this change in attitude and image may be inevitable and, in some cases, can even be in the best interests of the organization. The critical test becomes whether the change enhances or detracts from the organization's ability to serve its constituents and carry out its mission. In the case of Bridge, the change in the organization and its image actually compromised its ability to do what it was founded to do.

But there is another important lesson in the Bridge story. At the same time that the organization's image was deteriorating with its clients, it was flourishing with its funders. Bridge had become more professional, more corporate, and more establishment, and as this led to a diminished trust level with one constituency, it was enhancing the trust level with another. Herein lies one of the greatest challenges for nonprofit organizations. Because they generally serve multiple constituencies, they must work very hard to develop the proper image for each one. This often involves treading a fine line between competing world views and projecting different aspects of the organization and its programs to different audiences.

A Constituent's Image of Self

There is one other aspect of image that is important to consider. It is the sense of self-image that an organization, its programs, services, or products can create in people about themselves. A feeling of enhanced self-image is often a critical reason why individuals participate in nonprofit organizations, why donors give, and why certain organizations are successful and others are not.

In the profit sector, advertisers have long known that the creation of a positive self-image in a potential customer is one of the most effective ways to sell. A television advertisement for a diet soft drink is usually not trying to sell the merits of the product, rather it is attempting to convince viewers that they can be more beautiful, have more fun, and be liked by more people if they use the product. A collection of thin, lovely, young men and women on a beach, smiling and having a wonderful time says indirectly to the viewer, "This could be you. This is what will happen to you if you drink our soda." The effect is to create a pleasant self-image and an image of the product that speaks to basic desires and needs.

In the nonprofit sector, the creation of image is equally important. A sense of prestige often plays a major role in convincing people to serve on boards. Similarly, donors are often motivated not only by the feeling that they are part of an exclusive group but by being made to feel generous, important, and central to an organization's success or failure. For a volunteer, the self-image of being essential, being needed, and belonging is often what explains why they work hard for no compensation.

Among those who purchase or use a nonprofit organization's products or services, image is also important. In the case of Abbott Academy, the image of the school in the sixties and early seventies spoke to a basic parental need to see their children succeed. At the same time, the school was also able to promote a self-image among students that being admitted to Abbott was itself an indication of accomplishment and bespoke prestige. But as competition for admission declined, so did the prestige factor and the school's image.

In the case of Bridge, there was not only a change in the image of the institution—it no longer met the basic needs of its clients—but a related change in the self-image of its clients. In the early days, they could identify with Jim, Sharon, and Sam and this created a positive self-image, something like "Hey, maybe I am not so bad after all." But once the organization moved and built fancy offices, and once the founders dressed and behaved like regular businesspeople, the negative self-image created in the clients made them avoid seeking services from a cold, impersonal, establishment organization.

THE MARKETING MIX

Why does someone choose to buy a product, purchase services, pay for programs, or even make a contribution to a nonprofit organization? What are the elements that contribute to that individual's decision? From a marketing point of view there are four critical elements, commonly referred to as the four *p*'s, or the marketing mix:

- *Product,* or in the case of most nonprofit organizations, the programs and services offered
- *Promotion* of the product, program, or service
- *Price,* or what it costs to participate
- *Place,* or where the products, programs, and services are available

Product

The most obvious elements in a customer's decision to purchase are the characteristics of the product itself. Very simply, the customer must be satisfied that the product lives up to or exceeds expectations. In the profit sector, many resources are allocated to research and development of new products and product testing. Once a product is developed, the consumer has to be assured that it will deliver on its promise. Thus guarantees and the service accompanying the product are part of the product offering itself. Indeed, some companies have distinguished their products from those of their competition by offering money-back guarantees or a service fleet of trained professionals to keep the product in good working order.

In the nonprofit sector, organizations tend to be much less rigorous in developing and testing new products, programs, and services or updating and modernizing old ones. They also offer few guarantees of program effectiveness to their constituents. This is because nonprofit organizations are not product driven, but mission driven. Whereas an automobile company must develop a popular car to be successful, the most respected theater troupe is not necessarily the one that produces the most popular play, especially if its mission reflects a concern for exploring new and experimental work. Indeed, many nonprofit organizations pride themselves on not designing products for consumers but rather on educating consumers' tastes and preferences.

But this point of view often leads to a lack of rigor in examining and evaluating products, programs, and services in the nonprofit sector and it is shortsighted. Consider, again, the case of Abbott Academy, a school that firmly believed that it knew what was best for its students and would not have considered inquiring about consumer preferences. In 1970, Abbott's product—its academic program—was considered conservative and traditional, but solid. It required students to take, among other things, three years of Latin, a year of Greek, a year of philosophy (including a semester of ethics), a year of ancient history, and a year devoted to the art of the Renaissance. By 1985, such a program was seen to be anachronistic. Abbott offered no course in computers (in fact, there were no computers available to students at the school), it taught no black or Latin American literature, it provided no classes dealing with current events or the politics of the third world. Had Abbott Academy chosen to ask its constituents—prospective parents, college admissions officers, and minority candidates, among others—it would have discovered that its product was no longer competitive in the secondary-school marketplace.

Similarly, Abbott Academy offered nothing in the way of a guarantee of its product to parents concerned about college admission. While no school can guarantee that it will be able to ensure college admission to all of its graduates, Abbott Academy's competition was able to boast about its expanded college advising staff, its special tutoring sessions to prepare students for the college board exam, and its phone call follow-up of student applications by the headmaster in cases where parents and college advisors agreed it might make a difference.

However, other nonprofit organizations can and do offer firmer guarantees of their products, programs, and services and this often makes a good deal of difference to their customers and constituents:

- A shelter for battered women guarantees confidentiality and police protection for its clients
- A third world support organization guarantees that 90 cents of every dollar raised will go directly to people in the third world
- A small liberal arts college guarantees that all of its students will be taught by regular faculty members (not graduate assistants as would be the case in a larger university)

Yet another aspect of the product or service an organization offers includes the manner in which it is packaged. Packaging includes not only the physical container that holds a product but also the aura that surrounds it. Thus, although the color, shape, and design of a box of cereal may influence potential buyers, a brand name may influence them even more. This prestige or name recognition is also important in the nonprofit sector and can enhance marketability. For example, art museums have discovered that blockbuster shows, geared around the name of a famous artist, will draw far more people than shows of comparable quality that feature a mixed group of well-known and less-known artists. The prestige of the sponsoring organization itself may also be an important aspect of packaging the product. Many students who apply to Harvard's graduate schools may be less influenced by the quality of the faculty or the courses and more influenced by the Harvard name.

Promotion

Some nonprofit organizations can be categorized as the best kept secret in town. Their programs and services are largely unknown. If they have an image problem, it is that they have no image at all. By failing to promote themselves and their activities, these organizations sail a dangerous course. For when potential constituents do not know of the existence of an organization or do not really have an impression of what it does, they are reluctant to respond to appeals for participation or support.

Nonprofit organizations can promote themselves in various ways—

through free media coverage, through organized word of mouth campaigns involving their volunteers, through paid advertising, or through a carefully organized series of presentations at conferences, service organizations, clubs, churches, and chambers of commerce. They may be promoting themselves, their image, their products, their programs, or their services. Or they might be advancing a particular political agenda, attempting to influence legislation, or seeking to gain the attention of public and private funders. Whatever the purpose and whatever the techniques, it is essential to remember that few organizations can survive without careful attention to this area.

In a profit-making organization, a great deal of money is spent on promotion. Well-staffed marketing departments allocate large advertising budgets, devise free giveaway campaigns, use mass direct mail, and work with an entire sales force trained to promote products to potential customers. In the nonprofit world, there are generally fewer resources available. Thus those involved in planning promotional campaigns must spend their dollars wisely and use free media and volunteer resources as much as possible. Some examples follow:

☐ News releases should go out regularly to a list of media representatives and other key people on the organization's mailing list.

☐ A newsletter (at least semiannually, if not quarterly) should be distributed to an even larger list of people who should be kept up-to-date on the organization and its activities. If there are significantly distinct constituencies for whom different messages are appropriate, separate newsletters should be developed and sent to each.

☐ The telephone should be used constantly as a public relations vehicle. Major donors should be thanked, constituents should be surveyed for their opinions, board members should be updated regularly, and all complaints should be resolved by someone who projects a positive, pleasant image.

☐ Occasional public relations events should be planned and carried out by volunteers. These can include award ceremonies, involve celebrities, or use any other device to create broader interest.

☐ Displays can be designed for high traffic locations (such as malls) or for offices and institutions whose clientele might have an interest in the material (e.g., hospital weight clinic displays and brochures in doctor's offices and college displays in high-school libraries). When appropriate, these display areas can be manned by volunteers.

☐ Close relationships should be cultivated with local media representatives so that they may be exploited later for placement of feature material, calendar information, and coverage of press conferences and events.

One of the greatest mistakes in promotion is the tendency to oversell a product or service. If customers or constituents have specific expectations about a product or service and these expectations are not met, they will be disappointed. Promotion based on exaggerated claims will generally lead to unfulfilled expectations. When a nonprofit organization oversells a program, the constituents' inevitable disappointment can be doubly dangerous. They will cease supporting the program and they will be critical when they describe it to others.

Indeed, this is precisely what occurred when Abbott Academy chose to send out the *Simpson Guide* article as a promotional piece to prospective parents in 1985. The article, which had been written over a decade earlier, described the Abbott Academy of the 1970s—a school that accepted only one in eight applicants and sent all of its students to prestigious colleges. But that was not a fair description of the school in 1985 and many parents and students felt misled. Many of those who chose the school were disappointed and angry. Some students left the school after one year; parents criticized the school publicly for its false advertising.

Price

Price is also a key element of the marketing mix because it helps establish a perceived value for a product or service. All other things being equal, if two products sit on a grocer's shelf, we will buy the cheaper of the two *if we believe both to be exactly the same.* But two brands of mustard or two kinds of hair spray are rarely seen as the same. The manufacturers go to great pains to make their products appear distinct. And one of the elements that contributes to that distinctiveness is price. We will often buy the more expensive of two products if we think that it offers greater value. Because we usually do not have a well-developed system for assessing value, we will often assume that the more expensive product is the better product.

This close relationship between price and perceived value is nowhere more evident than in the competitive world of nonprofit organizations. It is often difficult to assess the "real" value of the various offerings of hospitals, daycare centers, universities, and theater companies. A consumer, attempting to distinguish between two organizations in the same field, may sometimes conclude that the one whose price is higher actually offers the better product or service.

It was this psychology—the linkage of price and perceived value—that created a major problem for Abbott Academy. Joseph Abbott, the school's founder, had endowed the school heavily in the early years and made significant contributions to keep the tuition affordable for less affluent parents. Yet, over time, as competing schools raised their tuition charges to levels a third or more above those of Abbott, some people began to wonder if there was something wrong with Abbott Academy's academic program. In stark contrast, one of Abbott's competitors, long considered an inferior school academically, decided to price itself higher than any other secondary school in New England hoping that this would create an image of quality. Remarkably, after only three years, this school saw the number of its applicants surpass that of Abbott Academy for the first time. While other factors certainly contributed to this trend—the academic program was revamped and the school increased promotional activities— incoming parents who were interviewed admitted that price played an important role in their determination of quality.

Another important consideration in the area of pricing for nonprofit organizations has to do with the scaling of contribution levels to nonprofit organizations. When asking donors for money, many organizations create a range of giving opportunities. In one organization's annual direct mail appeal, the categories of giving may start at a low of $20 and end at a high of $1,000. A similar organization may scale its categories of giving from $100 to $5,000. Other things being equal, the second organization often will collect more money *from the same group of people* because it has defined itself to be of greater value to donors.

Place

The final element in the marketing mix is place, the location at which the product is made available to the customer. We have already seen an example of the critical role place can play in the provision of a service by a nonprofit organization. When the counseling center Bridge moved its offices from an inner-city neighborhood to a more affluent location, its old clients ceased coming and the organization's mission of serving the poor was significantly compromised.

Place also turned out to play a major role in the decline of Abbott Academy's preeminence in the private secondary school marketplace. In 1970, when the *Simpson Guide* wrote its laudatory article on Abbott, the school's urban campus was an attractive enticement to many young families who had chosen to move back to the city. In those days, downtown real estate was relatively inexpensive and the city itself was going through a kind of renaissance. Abbott catered to a new group of young city families who believed in the importance of education and did not trust the city's public school system. But by 1985, the renaissance of the city had been so successful that downtown real estate prices had escalated tenfold or more. Young families with children could no longer afford to live in the city and were moving closer and closer to Abbott Academy's competition. Whereas the idea of an urban campus had given Abbott an edge in 1970, it put the school at a disadvantage fifteen years later.

Many nonprofit organizations have come to understand that if customers, clients, or constituents cannot or will not come to the organization's headquarters, the organization must take the product or service to them. Indeed, developing a proper *distribution* system for products and services is as important in the nonprofit world as it is among profit-making companies:

☐ A drug treatment center that also provides clean needles to heroin addicts (in order to combat AIDS) found that addicts were reluctant to come to its designated locations for the needles. The organization now uses a mobile van.

☐ A church, whose historic cathedral was located in what had become a major business and industrial center, established two suburban satellite churches for its members who attended weekend services. The downtown cathedral is now used for short midday services during the week.

☐ A major orchestra found that public schools could no longer afford buses to bring schoolchildren to its programs for youth. The orchestra now sends small groups of musicians to the schools.

In each of these examples, the organizations realized that no matter how good the products or services offered, constituents would not make use of them unless they were conveniently available.

MARKET RESEARCH

In order to develop an overall marketing strategy or plan, a nonprofit organization must have the facts on how well it stacks up against its competition, how it is perceived in the community, how its programs, activities, and products are regarded, and how it might command a bigger share of customers, clients, funders, or other constituents. This is accomplished through market research. Market research seeks to:

☐ Analyze the environment in which the organization operates and the leading trends in its industry whether the industry is prevention of child abuse, religious education, care for the terminally ill, or any other.

☐ Analyze threats to the organization according to their potential severity and likely occurrence.

☐ Analyze opportunities for the organization according to their potential and their probability of success.

☐ Understand the perceptions of various constituents in regard to the organization's image, programs, and activities and assess constituent preferences in areas where the organization seeks to be active.

☐ Identify the organization's strengths and weaknesses, both internal (board, staff, and finances) and external (location, level of competition, and public awareness) through a marketing audit.

Some people think that one of the main purposes of market research is to help organizations invent new products or services to satisfy constituents. But this is not usually the case. Nonprofit organizations in particular often need to choose among programs and activities, concentrating on those that most clearly relate to their missions and most appropriately meet the needs of their constituents. Good market research helps organizations to *focus* resources and energies rather than simply to expand activities.

The sequence of steps involved in market research is as follows:

1. *Define research objectives.* Decide very specifically the questions that need to be answered
2. *Do preliminary research.* Collect any information that will help define the objectives more clearly, including existing statistics on the industry or the target constituency, already completed research studies, a general survey of the organization's competition, and an assessment of constituent attitudes that could be revealed through interviews or small group sessions (called focus groups); this preliminary fact-gathering phase could also include a management review or outside assessment of the organization
3. *Design the formal research.* Develop the data-collection instruments (such as questionnaires or interview protocols), decide on how the target group will be sampled (randomly, by zip code, or by occupation), and choose the means of contact (mail, telephone, or in person)
4. *Do fieldwork.* Collect the data, making sure that the procedure is as free of bias as possible
5. *Analyze the data.* Analyze, interpret, and report the results

While nonprofit organizations can conduct market research themselves, it is usually important to have the assistance of an experienced, objective professional in designing the methodology. Unfortunately, it is all too easy for an organization's own representatives unwittingly to design market research that confirms their own prejudices rather than uncovers the facts. Some organizations use their own resources to hire an outside professional to conduct a market study or develop a marketing plan. Others ask outside funders to underwrite the cost. Still others are fortunate to find a member of their own board who has the expertise and skill to design and supervise market research that is largely free of any kind of bias. In the end, whatever resources are used, good market research almost always is a sound investment.

It had never occurred to the headmaster and trustees of Abbott Academy that the institution's problems could be most appropriately analyzed from a marketing perspective. But in 1989, a new board member, who was a marketing consultant, offered to conduct a marketing study for the school free of charge. Ultimately, his fellow trustees declined the offer. They agreed with Headmaster Mayfield, who said that marketing was simply an inappropriate analytical or management tool at a place like Abbott. Mayfield, like so many who work in nonprofit organizations, fundamentally misunderstood what marketing was all about. First, he assumed that marketing was no more than simple promotion and advertising and that the Academy's problems should be solved in ways that were less crass. Second, he felt that marketing was inappropriate because it was oriented toward the idea of buying and selling, customers, and profit. Finally, he was offended by the idea of marketing because he found it so manipulative. He argued that if Abbott was doing a good job and providing services that were genuine and needed, then it should not be necessary to engineer customer satisfaction.

All of these arguments missed the point, of course. Marketing analysis would have allowed the headmaster and trustees of Abbott Academy to look systematically at the school's mission, its image, its constituents, its competitors, its resources, its strengths, and its weaknesses, and then devise strategies to gain a more favorable position in its own competitive marketplace.

CHECKLIST QUESTIONS FOR CHAPTER 5

1. Has your organization accurately identified its various constituencies? Does it have an effective way to determine whether they are well served?
2. Is the organization able to assess its image in the community and among its various constituencies? Is there a strategy for enhancing and improving on the existing image of the organization?
3. Does your organization offer products, services, and programs that are competitive in the marketplace? Are constituents satisfied (i.e., does your organization deliver on its promises)?
4. Does your organization promote itself and its activities to all of its constituencies? Are promotional efforts effectively targeted? Are sufficient dollars budgeted for public relations efforts and are these dollars spent wisely?
5. Are the products, services, and programs of your organization appropriately priced?
6. Has your organization conducted in-depth market research within the last five years? Have you made organizational decisions based on the results of this research?

6
Financial Management

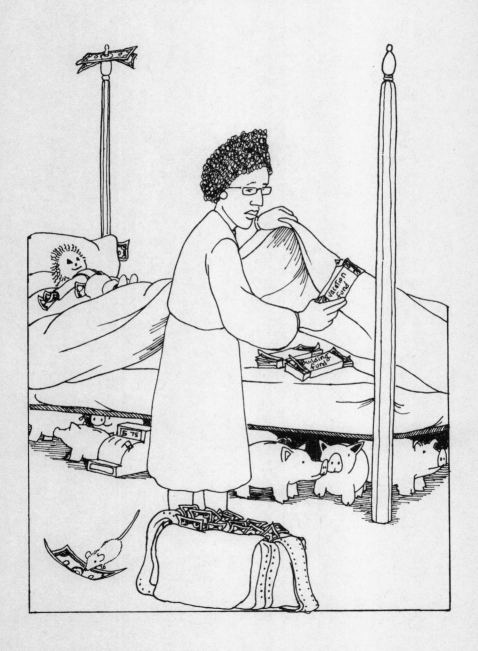

When I am handed a budget or a financial statement, I feel my eyes glazing over. Numbers are just not my thing. Thank goodness there are others in the organization who understand about money.

Financial management is, for many, one of the most forbidding aspects of the administration of nonprofit organizations. This is because they come into nonprofit organizations with no financial background and, in some cases, a numbers phobia. Often they have chosen to work as staff members or serve on boards because of a knowledge and commitment to education, conservation, child abuse, or some other activity. For them, the financial area—budgets, reports, and procedures—seems unrelated and dull, something for the "financial" people to deal with. But unfortunately, finances cannot be left completely to the experts. Budgeting, for example, is a critical part of overall organizational planning and any board member who wants to be involved in setting priorities for the organization must take some interest in the budget. Similarly, analyzing financial statements is an important way to take a measure of an organization's health while at the same time protecting the organization's interests and those of the public. Sound internal financial procedures are necessary to stay within the law and to offer acceptable assurances to donors that their monies are safe.

Part of the reason that people become confused with financial management and draw away from it is because financial experts use a special language. There are many terms that serve as shorthand for basic concepts. The concepts themselves are not difficult; neither is the language, once you know it. However, many people were never taught what the terms mean and some continue their involvement with nonprofit organizations remaining confused about important financial decisions. This chapter and the one that follows introduce some of the financial terms and procedures. It will become clear that financial management is a logical subject. To some, the concepts may seem dull but for the most part they are not difficult. This chapter deals with aspects of planning for the fiscal year, especially developing budgets and cash-flow projections. The following chapter explains how to keep financial records.

THE FINANCIAL, OR FISCAL, YEAR

We all make plans and keep records and we usually have some systematic way of doing so. In financial management, planning and record keeping are set up according to fixed time periods, the most common of which is the fiscal year. Because fiscal is simply another word for financial, the fiscal year is the basic financial record-keeping (or accounting) period of the organization, the time frame in which all financial transactions are grouped together, added up, and reported on.

Individuals also have a fiscal year of sorts. It begins on January 1 and ends on December 31. This is the time period in which individuals group financial transactions for tax purposes. We can say that the fiscal year for individuals is the same as the calendar year. For nonprofit organizations, however, the fiscal year is not always the same as the calendar year. In fact, a nonprofit corporation can specify any dates for its fiscal year. It simply specifies in its articles of incorporation that "the corporation's fiscal year ends on [date] each year." That date could be the executive director's birthday or the anniversary date of the organization's founding, although neither of these choices is likely to be in the best interests of the organization.

How should a nonprofit organization choose a fiscal year? The following three considerations should be kept in mind:

☐ The fiscal year should roughly parallel the organization's program year. That is, one year's program activities should not fall into two fiscal years. If the academic year for a school runs from September to June, for example, it would be unwise to set the fiscal year to run concurrently with the calendar year and end on December 31. The result would be that the academic year would fall into two fiscal years and it would be difficult to prepare budgets and analyze the financial performance of the school on an annual program year basis.

☐ The fiscal year should end, whenever possible, just before a period of relative inactivity. There is a great deal of effort involved in closing the books at the end of the fiscal year. If an audit is involved, and in most organizations it is, an accountant needs to check financial records and review bank statements. Because this places a heavy burden on the staff, the audit should take place when other demands on staff time are minimal.

☐ The fiscal year end may be chosen to coincide with a primary funder's fiscal year end and resulting reporting requirements. For example, if a major portion of an organization's support is from the state government, the organization may select the same fiscal year end as the state to simplify reporting on state grants.

It is an unfortunate fact of life that choosing a fiscal year for a non-profit organization does not guarantee that its financial reports will all conform to the requirements of others to whom it must present its financial statements. The government and other public and private funding sources may require an organization to keep certain records according to *their* accounting periods and often these do not correspond to the organization's fiscal year. For example, payroll records must be kept on a calendar-year basis in order to satisfy federal and state government accounting needs and to give salaried employees and independent contractors their W-2 and 1099 forms, respectively, for tax purposes. A state funding agency, on the other hand, may require financial reports for a year ending June 30 as part of the final report for a grant. However, careful selection of a particular fiscal year end may reduce the number of different financial reports required.

THE BUDGET

A budget is a financial plan. It specifies how much money an organization thinks it will take in and how much it will spend. A budget is generally laid out in two sections that are grouped under two main headings: income (or revenue) and expense (or expenditure) (see figure 6.1). Within the two sections, there is a further subdivision into specific income and expense categories. Each of these categories is placed on its own line with a dollar estimate listed beside it. For this reason, these categories are called *line items.* Another name for a line item is an *account.* Thus when someone refers to the salary account, the reference is to that line item in the budget in which all salary expenditures are grouped. All line items (or accounts) taken together are called the *chart of accounts.* This is the listing of all the budget categories. These categories are generally the same as those on an organization's income statement (see "The Income Statement" in chapter 7).

FIGURE 6.1.   Budget of the Compton School

Income		Expenses	
Tuition	$41,000	Salaries	$38,200
Bookstore sales	10,000	Benefits	4,000
Foundation grant	5,000	Honoraria	2,500
Business scholarships	5,000	Supplies and materials	5,200
Individuals	23,000	Equipment rental	3,400
Total	$84,000	Promotion	6,500
		Facility rental	20,000
		Contingency/reserve	4,200
		Total	$84,000

Source: Compiled by the author.

How does an organization decide what categories to include in its chart of accounts? After all, there are many ways to break down the same financial information. For example, a hospital could decide to lump all salaries under a single line item. Or it could subdivide salaries into many categories such as:

Salaries—physicians
Salaries—nursing staff
Salaries—administrative
Salaries—custodial

Every organization has to decide for itself on an appropriate chart of accounts. It must balance its need for detailed breakdowns of financial projections and records with the need to keep things simple. The best way to develop a chart of accounts is to look at the accounts of similar organizations that are well managed, approximately the same size, and have been around for some time. Compare the various listings of accounts. Look for commonalities and differences. Take into consideration your own special needs. Then begin to develop your chart of accounts based on the collective wisdom you have gained.

PROJECT BUDGETING

Project budgeting (also known as functional accounting or cost center accounting when referring to record-keeping procedures) allows an organization to analyze the income and costs of its various activities on a project-by-project basis. This form of analysis can be useful for organizations evaluating particular programs for cost-effectiveness or for revenue-generating potential. How is the single fund budget (as in figure 6.1) converted to this more complicated format?

☐ Generally, income that is program specific is allocated to the appropriate program categories (or *columns* of the budget). Thus a grant for an education program will be placed in the Education column of the budget as will tuition for educational workshops. Other income that is not tied to a particular program can be spread across the various columns as needed or desired. (A more detailed explanation of income allocation is discussed under "Step 3" of the budgeting process and is shown in figure 6.5, later in this chapter.)

☐ Similarly, program-related expenses are placed in the appropriate columns. The salaries of teachers for the education program are placed in the Education column, as are expenses associated with educational materials.

FIGURE 6.2. Project Budgeting for the Compton Opera Company

VERSION #1
(Note deficit in "Touring" project)

Income	Home Season	Touring	Total
Ticket sales	$62,500	$ 0	$ 62,500
Road fees	0	45,000	45,000
National endowment	0	5,000	5,000
State arts council	10,000	0	10,000
Individual contributions	5,000	5,000	10,000
Total	$77,500	$ 55,000	$ 132,500
Expenses			
Salaries	$56,000	$ 21,500	$ 77,500
Living allowance	0	18,000	18,000
Travel expenses	0	8,000	8,000
Scenery, etc.	8,000	2,000	10,000
Truck	500	4,500	5,000
Promotion	2,000	2,000	4,000
Administration	11,000	4,000	15,000
Total	$77,500	$ 60,000	$ 137,500
Excess (or deficit)	$ 0	($5,000)	($5,000)

VERSION #2
("Individual Contributions" have been shifted from "Home Season" to "Touring" to create a deficit in the "Home Season" budget.)

Income	Home Season	Touring	Total
Ticket sales	$ 62,500	$ 0	$ 62,500
Road fees	0	45,000	45,000
National endowment	0	5,000	5,000
State arts council	10,000	0	10,000
Individual contributions	0	10,000	10,000
Total	$ 72,500	$60,000	$ 132,500
Expenses			
Salaries	$56,000	$21,500	$ 77,500
Living allowance	0	18,000	18,000
Travel expenses	0	8,000	8,000
Scenery, etc.	8,000	2,000	10,000
Truck	500	4,500	5,000
Promotion	2,000	2,000	4,000
Administration	11,000	4,000	15,000
Total	$ 77,500	$60,000	$ 137,500
Excess (or deficit)	($5,000)	$ 0	($5,000)

Source: Compiled by the author.

Note: Project budgets can be summed to one total organizational (or single fund) budget. In this case, while the organizational budget remains constant, the project budgets are quite different in the two versions.

☐ Administrative and fund-raising costs can be isolated in their own columns or allocated among programs (or some combination of both).
Smaller organizations may decide that they do not need to allocate these
costs to analyze the costs of particular programs. Larger organizations
may wish to allocate costs included under fund raising or administration
to particular programs, but there will still be some fund-raising and
administrative costs that may not be attributable to any program and
are isolated in their own columns.

In project budgeting, deciding whether and how to allocate fund-raising
and management and support costs (administration) is often not a simple
matter. Some people feel that the best way to accomplish the allocation of
these costs is some sort of formula basis. They may estimate the percent
of staff time spent on a particular program in order to allocate salaries or
calculate the percent of space used by each program in order to allocate
rent expenses. For example, if the answer to the question "How much of
our director's time will be taken up by the new technical assistance program?" is 10 percent, then 10 percent of his or her salary is allocated to
that program. Or the question might be to determine what percentage of
the photocopier and postage expenses should be allocated to the technical
assistance program. Again, the idea is to find a reasonable figure based on
anticipated demand.

It is unlikely that all fund-raising, management, and support costs can
reasonably be allocated to the various programs; expenses for which no
reasonable basis of allocation exists and should be included under Fund
Raising or Administration (see figure 6.4). There is one cautionary note,
however. Some people take cost allocation much too seriously. They count
stamps, monitor phone calls, and keep logs of people's time. This may be
useful for a day or a week to get a rough approximation on which a
percentage can be developed for each program, but it can be overdone and
can result in much wasted time and frustration.

If one reason to do project budgeting is to determine cost-effectiveness,
another is to offer flexibility in developing budgets for fund-raising purposes. For example, consider the Compton Opera Company's dilemma. It
needs $5,000 to support its touring program activities (figure 6.2), but the
director of the Friendly Foundation of Compton is more interested in
supporting hometown activities, which are currently breaking even. However, $10,000 of unrestricted individual contributions have been split
evenly between Home Season and Touring ($5,000 in each). When the
director of the Friendly Foundation tells the director of the opera company
that he is interested in making a $5,000 contribution to the company's

programs in the local community, the opera company director must find a way to shift the $5,000 shortfall from Touring to Home Season. He can do so by preparing a new budget with all the individual contributions allocated to Touring. In this way, by shifting $5,000 of revenue out of the Home Season category into Touring he creates the required $5,000 income gap in the Home Season.

Now suppose that the opera company director thinks there is a possibility that the foundation might give his organization even more money (perhaps as much as $10,000) if a financial need could be demonstrated in the budget. The director can prepare a budget that includes a Reserve Fund category (see figure 6.3). Income is shifted into the reserve fund thereby creating the appropriate additional shortfall in the Home Season. The opera company director, sensing that the foundation may be prepared to give as much as $10,000 to the Home Season, shows a shortfall of exactly that amount *in that category* (see bottom line of Home Season column in

FIGURE 6.3. Further Adjustments in Project Budgeting for the Compton Opera Company

	Home Season	Touring	Reserve Fund	Total
Income				
Ticket sales	$ 57,500	$ 0	$5,000	$ 62,500
Road fees	0	45,000	0	45,000
National endowment	0	5,000	0	5,000
State arts council	10,000	0	0	10,000
Individuals	0	10,000	0	10,000
Total	$ 67,500	$60,000	$5,000	$132,500
Expenses				
Salaries	$ 56,000	$21,500	0	$ 77,500
Living allowance	0	18,000	0	18,000
Travel expenses	0	8,000	0	8,000
Scenery, etc.	8,000	2,000	0	10,000
Truck	500	4,500	0	5,000
Promotion	2,000	2,000	0	4,000
Administration	11,000	4,000	0	15,000
Total	$ 77,500	$60,000	0	$137,500
Excess (or deficit)	($10,000)	0	$5,000	($5,000)

Source: Compiled by the author.

Note: In this budget, the organization created an even larger deficit position in the Home Season by shifting unrestricted ticket income to its Reserve Fund. Now it can legitimately ask for $10,000 of support for the Home Season budget (bottom line, first column). If a $10,000 grant is not forthcoming, the money allocated to Reserve can be put back into the Home Season and the actual cash requirement is only $5,000. This is why the actual total organizational deficit (as shown on the bottom line of the last column) is only $5,000.

figure 6.3). Meanwhile, the organization banks a healthy surplus for the year (bottom line of Reserve column).

People who work in nonprofit organizations are sometimes nervous about manipulating numbers in this way. They worry that the procedure may not be appropriate or even legal. Some think that nonprofits must lose money—or at best, break even—to meet legal requirements. This is a fundamental misunderstanding of the nonprofit concept. A surplus (that is, an excess of income over expenditure) is not only legal, it is desirable. If it were not, how would it have been possible for the established universities, churches, art museums, and other nonprofits to build such large reserves in the form of endowments over the years?

Although surpluses, reserves, and endowments are legal, profits are not. A profit is another name for *owner's equity.* In a for-profit organization, the organization's owners (or partners or shareholders) benefit directly when the organization makes money. They may take the profit in cash or the distribution may be deferred, but in any case, a direct benefit inures to the people who have the financial interest. Nonprofit organizations do not have owners, of course, and they do not have shareholders. They serve the public, and so any excess of income over expenditure must ultimately be used for a charitable purpose. The word ultimately is important here. The money does not have to be spent right away. It can be put away in some kind of reserve fund or into an endowment (which is simply a reserve fund that has specific restrictions on when and how the assets are to be used). This putting away process is highly desirable and all organizations should strive to put some money away each year.

CONTINGENCY/RESERVE

Generating enough excess income in order to put money away can be facilitated through the budget process. A nonprofit organization should create an account called Contingency/Reserve, which should be listed on the expense side of its budget. The amount budgeted on this line should equal as much as 5 percent of the organization's total income. In figure 6.1, for example, a nonprofit organization that has a budget of $84,000 for the year has budgeted $4,200 (or 5 percent) for contingency/reserve and allocated only $79,800 for its regular ongoing expenses. This contingency/reserve amount may vary in other organizations, however, depending on the following factors:

- The size of the budget (larger organizations can allocate a smaller percentage)
- The predictability of levels and sources of income (the less predictable the income, the larger the contingency/reserve)

- The relative stability of the organization (the more unstable or new the organization is, the larger the contingency/reserve)
- The extent to which expenditures are fixed in advance (the less fixed the expenditures, the greater the contingency/reserve)
- The experience of the current management (the less experienced the management, the greater the contingency/reserve)

What is the contingency/reserve line item used for? First, it can serve as a form of self-insurance in case some unexpected expense comes up during the year. This is the contingency portion. The Compton Opera Company finds that there is a bad storm on the night of the big "Aida" production and single ticket sales come in $2,000 under budget—the contingency/reserve line item takes care of it. Or someone trips on the front stoop of the Compton School and takes legal action, which leads to an unexpected attorney's fee of $1,000. Once again, the organization has a pocket of uncommitted money from which it can draw.

If at the end of the fiscal year there is still money left over after all contingencies have been taken care of, the line item contingency/reserve becomes simply a reserve. In other words, the unallocated money can be put away in some kind of savings instrument—a savings account, money market fund, or stock—as determined by the board of directors on the advice of a financial professional. Each year, funds should be set aside in this way until such time as the organization has 25 to 50 percent of an entire year's budget in reserve.

Why preach such fiscal conservatism? Anyone familiar with the statistics on the plight of nonprofit organizations knows that a great number go bankrupt within the first decade of existence. Ambitious programs get designed with inadequate financial reserves. Inflation and other factors lead to larger and larger cash shortfalls. Prudent planning demands that an organization put away reserves to carry them through tough times.

Another reason to put money in reserve is related to fund raising. Many funders do not wish to be alone in their support of a project or a capital purchase. Others do not like to be the first to contribute. Reserve funds speak to both of these problems in the following way. Suppose a recreation organization wants to buy a new piece of equipment for a town park. It will cost $10,000. The organization wishes to secure ten $1,000 gifts from wealthy individuals in the community. The board knows how difficult it will be to get the first contribution. So, board members agree to guarantee $3,000 of the required amount from the reserve fund. The executive director is now ready to make his first call. He tells the donor that the organization is trying to raise $10,000 and that $3,000 is already in hand. The psychological effect is much more positive than telling the donor that he or she would be making the first contribution. In the end, if the whole $10,000 is raised in contributions, the organization simply does not draw on the reserve funds.

Consider, alternatively, that you wish to embark on an exciting new training program for disadvantaged youth and the U.S. Department of Labor has agreed to give you $25,000 on a matching basis. Because the project is a new one, you cannot find any corporation, foundation, or group of individuals to provide the matching funds. However, you and your board of directors are convinced that the project is important and will ultimately be entirely fundable by outside sources. You decide to draw the matching funds out of your reserve fund. After a year, the project is deemed successful. Now with favorable press material, a positive outside evaluation, and other critical acclaim, you can approach the same funding sources without having to draw on the reserve fund.

Finally, there is another reason why the reserve fund is so important. Most nonprofit organizations experience cash flow problems at some time during the fiscal year, as is discussed later in this chapter. Put another way, these organizations find that they need to pay bills before there is adequate income to do so. Often salaries and programmatic expenditures place heavy cash demands on the budget early in the year while funding sources are slow to come through with the cash (some operate on a reimbursement basis only). It is embarrassing to find the organization in a position where it cannot pay bills or meet its payroll, especially when the board has approved a balanced budget. One alternative is to borrow money but this is usually expensive unless the organization can draw on the largess of a wealthy friend or board member who will make an interest-free loan. On the other hand, with an adequate reserve fund, the organization can borrow from itself. That is, it can take money from the reserve fund early in the year and replenish it later when the projected income is finally received. It is important to remember, though, that even this procedure has a real cost. By taking money out of a reserve fund, the organization is foregoing certain income by forfeiting interest. It is important to keep this in mind so that the staff does not become cavalier about drawing on the reserves. It is always better to maximize a good cash flow position by doing adequate cash flow planning several months before the beginning of the fiscal year (see "Cash Flow," later in this chapter).

Reserve Funds Functioning as Endowment
Some nonprofit administrators and board members are concerned that too large a reserve fund can be a disincentive for funders inasmuch as it looks like the organization may not need money. The fear is that a foundation, corporation, or government agency will look at financial reports that show

a healthy reserve and conclude that such funds could be used to support the activities that the organization is seeking support for. This is particularly true in cases where organizations, through prudent fiscal management, allow their reserve funds to grow very large.

One way to address this issue is for the board to designate a portion of the reserves as "funds functioning as endowment." An endowment is a reserve fund with special rules and restrictions as to its use. Generally, endowments consist of invested funds (principal) that must be left intact (only income from the investment can be utilized by the organization). Funders understand the rules governing endowments and so when they see endowment funds listed in an organization's financial statements they do not expect that the organization will be able to invade principal to pay for current expenses.

Thus if the board of an organization designates a portion of the organization's cash reserves as endowment, it looks as though there is much less cash available to draw on. In truth, the board can undesignate the endowment conditions and restore these funds to unrestricted cash reserves at any time. Nevertheless, from the point of view of the presentation of the finances to outsiders, the organization does not look as flush with available cash when reserve funds are designated in this way.

THE BUDGETING PROCESS

If budgeting is a form of financial planning, then it is important to know what specific procedures are involved in doing it effectively. There are two important considerations:

☐ Budgeting should always be related to the overall planning process of the organization. No one is in a position to plan for the future without a clear sense of what the available resources are. Conversely, sensible budgets, or financial plans, cannot be put together without knowing where the organization is going. Simply allocating money is not enough. Using it strategically is what the budgeting process ideally should be about.

☐ The board of directors should be involved in both the budgeting and general planning process. Because board members must set long-range goals for the organization, decide on program priorities, and ultimately assume fiscal accountability, it is important that they be involved in the budgeting process both in the forecasting stages and later when the budget is monitored.

Beyond these general considerations, there are eight steps that an organization should take to complete a successful budgeting cycle.

Step 1: Make a Wish List

The first step in budgeting has nothing to do with numbers or dollars. It concerns an annual review of what the board and senior staff want the organization to accomplish in the year to come. At the beginning of the budget cycle, they should consider a number of questions about the upcoming year:

☐ What should the organization be doing in the next year?
☐ What core activities are essential?
☐ What additional activities might be undertaken if cost were not an object?
☐ What staff needs are associated with these activities?
☐ Are there special one-time expenditures that might be considered for things such as equipment, the improvement of physical facilities, special consultancies in evaluation, or marketing?

This step is essential because it forces the board of directors to think systematically about the organization's activities, its mission, and its programs. It provides an opportunity to review the purposes for which the organization was formed, its long-range goals and plans, and its short-term objectives. Making a wish list is fun because it does not require a close monitoring of costs. It is the last time in the budgeting process that such an opportunity presents itself.

Step 2: Cost Out the List

How much will it cost to carry out the activities listed in Step 1? Obviously, there are some basic costs that have to be covered just to keep the organization going. There is the office, core staff salaries, and expenses related to the basic programs that were done last year and that will continue. Each of these must be carefully "costed." In addition, the expenses associated with new activities will also have to be evaluated.

Determining how much things will cost is not an easy process. There are two approaches commonly used:

☐ The first approach, called the *incremental budgeting* method, leans heavily on information contained in previous years' actual expenses and income. If an organization is carrying out an activity that it has done for several years, then the easiest way to prepare a budget for the coming year is to add a percentage increment for inflation and other factors to the figures contained in the previous year's financial statement (referred to as actuals) or the current year's budget.
☐ The second approach, called *zero-based budgeting,* requires that each line item of a budget be calculated anew. Staff members are told that any

item in the budget will be zero unless they can provide a full justification for some other figure.

Obviously, some combination of these two approaches is desirable in the budgeting process. The previous year's expenses together with projected expenses for the current year will be immensely helpful in estimating not only the next year's expenses but also income for the period. On the other hand, each item in the budget should also be examined carefully without reference to another year's figures. An assessment should be made, item by item, of whether the expenditure is required and if so, how large it should be. In addition, new projects and activities require estimates for which the previous year's actuals and budget are not very helpful.

In costing out the wish list developed in Step 1, two things are important to remember:

☐ Costs should always be estimated on the high side. Add at least 10 percent to all expense figures. Those people who budget expenses at a level they think will be correct (with no percentage added) are almost always underbudgeted.

☐ As you consider the costs of *new* programs and activities, remember that they will add to your central administrative costs. It is not enough simply to estimate how much you will actually spend on a new program. The simple addition of the program puts an added burden on the core staff, space, office equipment, and so on.

COMPTON HOSPITAL'S INVISIBLE EXPENSES

As an example of how a new activity almost invisibly seems to increase central administrative costs, consider the case of Compton Hospital, which decided to undertake a prenatal education program. Staff members costed out all anticipated expenditures connected with the new program. However, they forgot that the hospital published the *Information Bulletin,* in which each hospital class was given a one-page description. By adding the prenatal class, the hospital was required to add a page to a publication that was paid for out of its central administrative budget. It is crucial, as the costing process goes forward, that realistic overhead increases such as this are built into the budgets of new initiatives.

If project budgeting (see earlier discussion) is being used by an organization, projected expenses should be allocated to proper categories (figure 6.4).

FIGURE 6.4. Compton Museum Project Budgeting

EXPENSE PROJECTIONS

	Education Program	Permanent Collection	Traveling Exhibition	Membership	Fund Raising	Administration	Total
Salaries	$22,500	$18,000	$ 9,000	$10,000	$25,000	$20,000	$104,500
Benefits	3,375	2,700	1,350	1,500	3,750	3,000	15,675
Fees	16,000	2,000	0	0	5,000	4,000	27,000
Supplies	2,700	500	500	1,100	800	3,000	8,600
Telephone	300	600	600	500	200	2,000	4,200
Travel	0	50	700	100	2,000	2,000	4,850
Printing	2,000	2,000	2,000	2,000	2,000	2,000	12,000
Equipment	1,000	1,500	500	500	500	2,000	6,000
Shipping	0	500	2,000	0	0	0	2,500
Utilities	600	1,500	300	300	300	600	3,600
Insurance	800	11,000	5,000	200	200	1,000	18,200
Total	$49,275	$40,350	$21,950	$16,200	$39,750	$39,600	$207,125

Source: Compiled by the author.

Step 3: Allocate Income

Using the same list of activities developed in Step 1 and costed out in Step 2, it is now time to consider how much income can be expected from each activity. Again, last year's actuals and the current year's updated budget projections can be helpful. However, this step has some built-in complications because it is likely that there are certain funds specifically earmarked for particular activities and other income that has no such restrictions and can be put anywhere.

Here it is important to differentiate between unrestricted and restricted funds. Unrestricted funds are monies received with no particular instructions or limitations as to how they are to be used. Admission, memberships, earned income from publications or a shop, and general donations are all examples of unrestricted funds. Restricted funds, on the other hand, are those received with special conditions placed on their use. The conditions can apply to the time period during which they are to be used, the purpose of their use, or both. A grant for a new piece of equipment or a contribution to a scholarship fund can only be used for the purpose that the donor specified. Similarly, a grant for the fiscal year beginning July 1, 1991, cannot be used before that date or after June 30, 1992. An organization can always request that the person or organization that imposed a restriction lift or change it. However, until such permission is given, restricted funds must not be used for any other purpose.[1]

Once restricted funds and unrestricted funds have been separated, the process of allocating income is as follows (see figure 6.5):

1. Put all restricted income into the proper program activity or category. That is, any income clearly attributable to a specific project should be put into that category and marked. Later on, if the budgeting team begins cutting back programs or reallocating income, it is important to remember that these funds cannot be transferred from one program category to another.
2. Cover all of the most basic administrative costs with unrestricted income.
3. Allocate the balance of unrestricted income across all the programs and activities listed. You may want to allocate it on a percentage basis as was discussed in connection with expenses in the section on project budgeting. Or you may want to use a simpler method and divide the money up on a roughly equal basis among programs. The first method, although more work, does help you assess the relative cost-effectiveness of programs.

FIGURE 6.5.   Compton Museum Income Projections with Restricted and Unrestricted Funds Separated

	Program Education	Permanent Collection	Traveling Exhibitions	Membership	Fund Raising	Administration	Total
Membership	$ 0	$ 5,350	$ 0	$16,200	$ 7,500	$ 7,500	$ 36,550
Admissions	10,000	0	0	0	15,000	15,000	40,000
Rental fees	0	0	14,000*	0	0	0	14,000
Tuition	28,500*	0	0	0	0	0	28,500
Museum shop	0	0	0	0	7,500	7,500	15,000
Individual donations	0	30,000	0	0	9,750	9,600	49,350
Government grants	0	5,000	2,500	0	0	0	7,500
Corporate grants	2,500†	0	0	0	0	0	2,500
Foundation grants	2,000†	0	0	0	0	0	2,000
Endowment income	4,000†	0	1,000	0	0	0	5,000
Total	$47,000	$40,350	$17,500	$16,200	$39,750	$39,600	$200,400

Source: Compiled by the author.

Note: Only unrestricted funds can be switched from one column to another. If there is a decision to eliminate the education program, for example, only the $10,000 of unrestricted income from admissions can be switched. The funds with a dagger in that column will be lost as income unless restrictions are lifted by donors. The asterisked funds in that column ($28,500 in tuition fees) will be lost revenue and therefore cannot be reallocated.

*Income generated by program.
†Restricted gift.

4. Understate all income estimates by at least 10 percent. Just as you left some margin for error on expenses, so must you be equally conservative on income forecasting.

Step 4: Compare

This is often called the read-it-and-weep step. It should be clear by this time that some activities must be given up if the budget is going to balance. There is simply too much expense and not enough income. In fact, if the board discovers that income is adequate to cover expenditures at this point in the budgeting process, there should be great concern that the organization is not reaching far enough or being ambitious enough. Put another way, if the board can pay for all of its wishes *at this point in the budgeting process,* it is not wishing hard enough. Its reach should exceed its grasp so that it can continue to grow in its ability to provide services and programs to the public. However, the board is not acting responsibly when it ultimately undertakes more than it can pay for. Many projects should be considered even though only some will be undertaken immediately. The examination of a potential activity one year is valuable in planning for that activity another year.

In evaluating one program activity against another, the board should be careful about using the criterion of cost-effectiveness. There are certainly appropriate questions that can be asked in this area. Which activities come closest to paying for themselves? Which have the highest cost relative to the income that they bring in? But these are the kinds of questions that are more compelling in profit-making companies. While they are certainly of more than passing interest to any nonprofit organization, it is important to remember that nonprofit organizations are not in business primarily to make money. Their missions may dictate that they *should* carry on certain activities that are not cost-effective. How would we feel, for example, if the only activities engaged in by a certain church were its profitable rummage sales and bingo games? We (and, most likely, the IRS) would be concerned that a more fundamental mission of the church was not being fulfilled. Thus cost-effectiveness, while one criterion, is only one. The primary criterion should relate to the mission of the organization, its purposes, goals, and objectives.

Step 5: Set Priorities

Any board member or staff person who has sat through a budget balancing session knows how traumatic it can be. Everyone seems to have a pet project. Every expenditure appears to have its defender. Yet at the same time everyone knows that the organization must be more fiscally restrained. In the end, a priority-setting session must relate not solely to dollars and cents but to a fundamental assessment of the organization's reason for being. It is too easy in the heat of the moment to argue for or against a proposed expenditure on its own merits or on cost-effectiveness. But it is important to ask questions such as the following ones:

☐ Is this activity really central to what the organization is about?
☐ Does it help the organization get where it should be in a year, in two years, in five years?
☐ Might it be more important to build a reserve to protect the organization over the long term than engage in a new activity area?

These are difficult questions, but in asking them the board is fulfilling a fundamental role in deciding what course is best for the organization and most clearly in the public interest.

Step 6: Adjust and Balance

Once activities have been put in some semblance of priority order, a little negotiation is still possible as the budget is adjusted and put into balance. If the Compton Museum's Traveling Exhibition program is a high priority but there is simply not quite enough income to cover it, perhaps some money can come out of the Acquisitions budget. If the program is dropped instead, monies that were allocated to it can be moved to other areas if those monies are unrestricted. One must be careful, obviously, not to move monies that can only be used for the traveling exhibition program itself. For example, if there is a grant for that program or if there was income projected from exhibition rentals, that income is now lost to the organization.

There is one other danger at this point in the budgeting process and that is going back and exaggerating income in order to avoid making the hard budget cuts. Consider the following case:

THE BUDGET SESSION OF THE COMPTON YMCA

The finance committee of the Compton YMCA had spent three evenings trying to balance the budget for the coming year before presenting it to the full board. The group had arrived at an impasse. They could find no more cuts and expenses still exceeded revenues by about $70,000 on a budget of $1.3 million. The contingency line of the budget had already been cut from $65,000 to $30,000, which was the precise amount of income projected from two questionable grants that were written into the budget. As the third evening's meeting was coming to an end, the head of the committee said, "Let's just increase the line of the budget for Individual Giving by

$70,000. It will mean everyone will have to work a little harder this year."
In order to balance the budget, the fatigued group agreed to increase the
line for Individual Giving to a figure that was 50 percent higher than that
recommended by the development committee.

Was this a responsible step for the budget committee to take? Probably
not. While the budget numbers were now in balance, they were based on
unrealistic income projections. The development committee had made its
best estimate of contributed income and the finance committee had exceeded it by a large margin. Such action simply increases the risk of a
deficit at the end of the year.

The budgeting process, as discussed so far, has guaranteed that figures
will be skewed conservatively. Income has been understated, expenses
overstated, and roughly 5 percent of total income has been put in the
contingency/reserve category. Even though the budget is balanced on
paper, it would appear that there is far more money coming in than going
out. Careful budgeting, however, requires this approach. It is almost always the case that certain expenses have been forgotten, and certain anticipated income will come in short. In the event that the actual financial
picture results in income far exceeding expenses, the board has the enviable
task of deciding what to do with the additional money.

Step 7: Approve

Now that the budget has been worked out, it is necessary for the full board
of directors to discuss and approve it. This is more than a mere formality.
In voting through a budget, the board exercises its fiduciary responsibility
in setting financial limits and boundaries for the staff. The board is also
implicitly agreeing to meet the projected revenues through a commitment
to fund raising. A board of directors should never approve a budget based
on a wish and a prayer that projects unrealistic fund-raising goals. If such
a budget is approved, and the funds are not raised, it is the trustees who
must take responsibility. Thus a good question to ask during the approval
process is, "Do we really know how every projected revenue dollar will be
earned or raised, who will be responsible, and whether the targets are
realistic?"

On the expense side, a responsible board member should ask how estimates were determined. For example, if the line item for Postage is $2,500
and the board member is told by staff that the number was arrived at by
taking last year's figure, a good question might be, "Is that a realistic figure
given the fact that postal rates have increased by 20 percent and we have
added 3,000 people to our mailing list?"

Indeed, because the previous year's budget is so often the primary document on which so many estimates are made, it is easy for the budget preparers to forget to take obvious changes into consideration. Trustees should challenge the budget document, not because they doubt the ability of the staff or finance committee, but because it is they who are ultimately responsible for the fiscal health of the organization.

Step 8: Monitor and Amend

One common mistake in the budget process is to assume it has come to an end once the board approves the final document. Indeed, the very word final is a misnomer when talking about a budget. Few budgets can hold up over time unless they are amended and modified to accommodate new information and new conditions as the year wears on. For this reason, board and staff must set up a process by which the budget can be reviewed when necessary and changed.

Two extremes should be avoided. The board should not insist that the document they have approved "is it" and force the staff to stick to it without modification throughout the fiscal year. On the other hand, the board should not be willing to say that the budget document is only a rough approximation and give staff instructions to "come as close as possible." Rather, board-approved policies and procedures should be set up to allow staff some flexibility but give the board the final say on any significant changes in the budget figures.

For example, in a $100,000 budget, the board may tell the executive director the following (which would be documented in the minutes of the board meeting at which it was approved): "So long as you feel you can balance the budget, you may shift up to 15 percent or $2,000 (whichever is less) out of, or into, any account. However, if more significant changes are to be made, you must present a revised budget to the board for approval."

By way of example, let us say that the line item Equipment has a budgeted amount of $20,000. Using the guidelines previously listed, the director may, at his or her discretion and without board approval, move up to $2,000 to some other expenditure category or may choose to spend $2,000 more in that category. The director should not do the extra spending, however, unless he or she is relatively confident that the budget can still be balanced with additional income or by shifting the $2,000 from some other category where it is not needed. If the director anticipates that an additional $4,000 is necessary for equipment, then the full board must be consulted and an amended budget must be submitted and approved.

A budget can serve as a valuable measuring stick against which the growth of an organization (or project) can be evaluated. Although it is important to revise a budget to reflect special circumstances or opportunities, the original budget for a particular year can be a valuable tool when making projections for the future. Changes made during the year should be reviewed by the staff and finance committee members when making new projections so that errors made (such as underestimation of costs or overestimation of income) can be avoided when a new budget is prepared.

FRAMEWORK BUDGETS

Limiting the budgeting process to one-year projections the way many nonprofit organizations do can cause problems for medium- and large-size organizations. This is because many of these organizations have to make plans several years in advance. Frequently staff members must make commitments for major expenses months or even years before the budgeting cycle begins, as is the case for a museum planning exhibitions with a lead time of three years or a school developing a new department. The danger is that by the time the board and senior staff review and are ready to approve the coming year's annual budget, large sums of money will have already been committed. This may significantly limit the ability of board members to react to a changing financial climate.

How can this problem be overcome? One way is through a process called *framework budget planning,* a strategy designed to provide timely long-range budget forecasts. As discussed earlier, budget planning is an integral part of any organizational planning process. The framework budget planning component furnishes a plan, particularly a long-range plan, with a crucial—and often overlooked—component: the necessary structure for board and staff to develop multiyear estimated budgets based on the specific program plans for the future.

The first stage in developing a framework budget is not unlike the beginning stage of the normal annual budgeting cycle. The staff compiles one year of historical budget figures and provides estimates of the current year's projected figures. Also included is the coming year's proposed budget once it is completed. These three sets of figures are projected in columns in such a way that all the budget categories are comparable from one year to another (see figure 6.6). Once this information has been gathered, it can be used to analyze trends and make projections for the future. Ideally, this framework is input into a computer spreadsheet to facilitate calculations in the subsequent analyses.

Once the historical figures have been established, two separate income and expense projections for the next three or four years—called the optimistic and conservative scenarios—are developed in consultation with board members and staff. The optimistic version tends to project higher levels of earned and contributed income while the conservative version

FIGURE 6.6. Framework Budget for Anyplace Community Center

CONSERVATIVE VERSION

	Actuals	Projected Current	Approved Budget		Estimated Budgets	
	1989	1990	1991	1992	1993	1994
Income						
Tuition/workshops	$ 10,223	$ 11,100	$ 13,800	417,000	$ 21,000	$ 25,000
Corporate membership	3,250	3,350	3,750	4,300	5,100	6,100
Other contributions	2,780	2,750	2,800	3,100	3,500	4,200
Government grants	0	5,000	6,500	7,000	7,000	7,000
Total Income	$ 16,253	$ 22,200	$ 26,850	$ 31,400	$ 36,600	$ 42,300
Expenses						
Staff salary	$ 5,500	$ 7,500	$ 8,500	$ 9,750	$ 10,500	$ 13,000
Professional fees	8,750	9,950	10,775	12,000	14,400	16,000
Art instruction material	1,100	1,545	1,750	2,500	3,370	4,100
Classroom rental	3,000	3,500	4,000	4,750	5,500	6,000
Contingency/reserve	0	0	1,340	1,570	1,830	2,115
Total Expenses	$ 18,350	$ 22,495	$ 26,365	$ 30,570	$ 35,600	$ 41,215
Excess (or deficit) of revenues	($ 2,097)	($ 295)	$ 485	$ 830	$ 1,000	$ 1,085

OPTIMISTIC VERSION

	Actuals	Projected Current	Approved Budget		Estimated Budgets	
	1989	1990	1991	1992	1993	1994
Income						
Tuition/workshops	$ 10,223	$ 11,100	$ 13,800	$ 18,000	$ 23,000	$ 28,000
Corporate membership	3,250	3,350	3,750	5,000	6,200	8,100
Other contributions	2,780	2,750	2,800	3,500	4,000	4,800
Government grants	0	5,000	6,500	7,500	9,000	10,000
Total Income	$ 16,253	$ 22,200	$ 26,850	$ 34,000	$ 42,200	$ 50,900
Expenses						
Staff salary	$ 5,500	$ 7,500	$ 8,500	$ 11,000	$ 13,500	$ 17,000
Professional fees	8,750	9,950	10,775	13,000	16,500	19,000
Art instruction material	1,100	1,545	1,750	2,600	3,500	4,400
Classroom rental	3,000	3,500	4,000	4,800	5,500	6,100
Contingency/reserve	0	0	1,340	1,700	2,110	2,545
Total Expenses	$ 18,350	$ 22,495	$ 26,365	$ 33,100	$ 41,110	$ 49,045
Excess (or deficit) of revenues	($ 2,097)	($ 295)	$ 485	$ 900	$ 1,090	$ 1,855

Source: Compiled by the author.

shows easily achievable revenue targets. The expenses in each scenario may also be adjusted based on these alternative assumptions about income or they may be kept the same in both versions, in which case the bottom line of the two scenarios will vary by the amount of the differing income assumptions.

The advantage of framework budgeting is that it allows board members to understand what the future may have in store given different assumptions about the future and it allows them to make plans accordingly. Sometimes, by seeing what the conservative projections look like, the board may defer certain activities. In other cases, they may adjust fund-raising goals. In either case, they will be making decisions based on better and more complete information.

By developing budgets for several years, framework budget planning provides a longer budget cycle that more accurately reflects the planning needs of many institutions. Equally important, by offering at least two alternative versions of the multiyear budgets, framework budget planning can forge a link between the budgeting and planning functions and ensure that planning decisions are based on sound analysis of the future.

Like any good planning process, framework budgeting should not be seen as a one-time procedure, but as an ongoing management tool. Each year, the board should not only review and approve a proposed budget for the coming fiscal year but it should also review two versions of proposed budgets for three subsequent years. In this way board members can see an overall five-year financial and program plan on an annual basis.

CASH FLOW

We prepared a conservative budget and thought we were in good shape. Three months into the fiscal year we found ourselves out of money. Bills were coming in faster than we received cash. The state agencies that provided tuition money for certain kids were often three to six months behind in their payments and the federal government wouldn't allow us to keep any of their funds on hand (we could only request what we had spent). We had never heard the term cash flow before but we sure learned the hard way what a cash flow problem is.

These words came from the director of a daycare center. Her experience is not unusual. Like so many people who devise a sensible budget, she thought she would have no financial problems. She never thought about the fact that an annual budget only tells an organization how things should end up at the end of the year. It does not tell how much cash to have on hand at various points during the year. It is important to figure this out

so that the staff knows whether it will need to make some special arrangements in order to pay the bills.

Cash flow projections are most commonly prepared on a monthly basis
for the upcoming fiscal year. In the analysis, an organization's income and
expenses are projected for each month. The budget is laid out on a wide
sheet of paper (or preferably a computer spreadsheet) with separate columns for each month (the first column lists the total yearly budget). Each
horizontal line (or row, if using a computer spreadsheet) lists budget items.
Listed next to each item is the annual budget total (in the first column)
followed by monthly breakdown of anticipated receipts or expenditures in
the subsequent columns. For example, if salaries for the year are $120,000,
and if they do not change from month to month, the line item Salaries
would appear with its annual total of $120,000 followed by the various
monthly totals of $10,000 next to it. The first three months would look like
this:

	Total	January	February	March
Salaries	$120,000	$10,000	$10,000	$10,000

On the other hand, if all of the income from a fund-raising event is anticipated in March, the line item Fund-raising event would look like this:

	Total	January	February	March
Fund-raising event	$5,000	0	0	$5,000

In preparing a cash flow projection, if you are not sure when a particular
expenditure is going to be due, it is best to be conservative, plan for the
worst, and figure that it is going to be due on the early side; to practice
the same prudence with income, you should err on the late side in predicting when cash is going to come in.

Once you have listed your estimated monthly income and expenses, you
can compute your monthly net income (or loss). A monthly net income
(loss) is simply the difference between total income and total expenses
during that month. If after preparing your monthly budget chart, you
anticipate that your organization will take in $6,812 in July and spend
$6,467, you will have a net income for July of $345. If for August you show
income of $5,673 and expenses of $6,529, you will have a net loss for
August of $856 (see figure 6.7).

All of this is useful to know, but it becomes even more valuable when
you are able to analyze your changes in cash flow position from month to
month. What you really want to see is how the ups and downs of your
monthly cash balances affect a cumulative flow of cash. The way this is

FIGURE 6.7.   Hippy Dippy Day Care Cash Flow

	July	August
Expected income		
Parent Fees	$2,500	$1,810
Title XX	2,211	2,106
School lunch program	926	882
United Way	875	875
Fund raising	300	0
Other income	0	0
Total income	$6,812	$5,673
Expected expenditures		
Staff salaries	$3,468	$3,468
Substitutes	280	350
Fringe	544	556
Legal and audit fees	100	100
Program development/training	50	0
Rent/mortgage	425	425
Utilities	50	40
Food	950	890
Equipment, supplies, services	200	550
Insurance	250	0
Loan repayment	150	150
Total expenditures	$6,467	$6,529
Monthly net income (or loss)*	$ 345	($856)
Cash flow summary		
Opening cash balance†	$ 200	$ 545
Monthly net income (or loss)	345	(856)
Ending (cumulative) cash balance	$ 545	($311)

Source: This example is adapted from Roger Neugebauer, "Money Management Tools—Cash Flow Analysis," Child Care Information Exchange 19 (May 1981): 10.

*Equals total monthly income less total monthly expenses.

†Equals amount of money in the bank at the beginning of the month (the same as the ending cumulative cash balance of the previous month).

done is shown in the cash flow summary at the bottom of figure 6.7. To begin with, you show how much cash you will have on hand in the bank at the beginning of the month (opening cash balance). To this amount you add (or subtract) your net monthly income (or loss)—the difference between income and expense for that month. The sum of these two numbers is your ending, or cumulative, cash balance for the month. This bottom line tells you where you stand at one month's end and tells you how much you will have to start the next month with. Thus the ending cash balance for July becomes the opening cash balance for August and so on.

If you do cash flow projections early enough (four to six months before the start of the fiscal year), you are usually in a much better position to solve a potential cash shortage problem. For example, you might make a special plea to a funder to put you first on the payment list, you might decide to do your fund-raising event earlier in the year, or you might negotiate with your printer to spread your payments over two months rather than just one. People are generally much more flexible about these requests if you give them plenty of warning. By way of contrast, if the day of reckoning comes and you have not attempted to make prior arrangements with creditors to help alleviate your cash flow problems, they will become very impatient and they will tend to remember your bad planning the next time you attempt to do business with them.

If all else fails and you will have a cash shortfall during the year, you have several alternatives. One is to take money from your reserve fund if you have one. For this reason, many organizations leave a substantial portion of their reserve in some liquid savings instrument so they can get at the cash quickly when they need it. If you do not have a reserve fund, you may be forced to borrow money for a short period of time. Ideally, a trustee (or several) might loan you the cash interest-free. Otherwise, you will have to borrow from a bank, which can be extremely expensive. If cash must be borrowed and interest must be paid on the loan, be sure to build the interest payment into the expenses of your budget.

This chapter began with a quote from a board member who has never taken an interest in the financial affairs of the nonprofit organization that he serves. It is hoped that he and others like him will realize that there are aspects of the financial affairs of the corporation that are, quite properly, part of their responsibilities as trustees. Although these trustees will not be expected to prepare the budget, they must at least familiarize themselves with it so they can make responsible decisions based on the information it contains. They should also understand something about cash flow and other financial matters. Leaving things completely to others is simply too risky a course.

CHECKLIST QUESTIONS FOR CHAPTER 6

1. Does the timing of your organization's fiscal year allow for meaningful financial comparisons to be made between one year's activities and the next?
2. Does your organization's chart of accounts provide sufficient detail to allow for necessary financial analysis of performance?
3. Does your organization's budgeting system allow board and staff to analyze the comparative cost of various programs and activities?
4. Has your organization developed a cash reserve fund?
5. Does the budgeting process allow for the input of board members? Is the process sufficiently conservative to prevent the incurring of unintended deficits at the end of the year?
6. Does your organization do multiyear budgeting for long-range planning purposes?
7. Does your organization do regular cash flow analyses?

7
Financial Statements and Fiscal Procedures

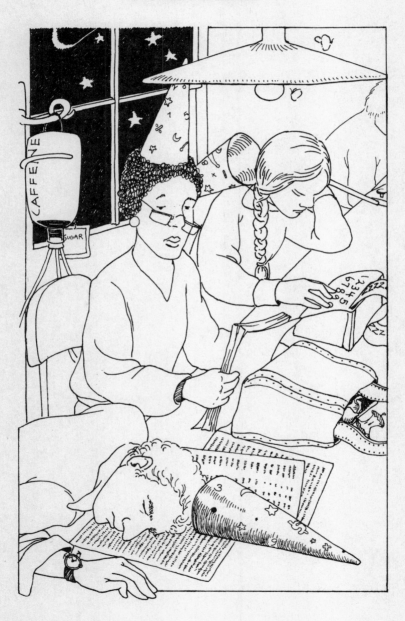

Samuel Snyder is the director of finance for the Creighton Home, a residential treatment center for drug addicts. His wife claims not to understand how this could be the case. "Sam's boss told me last month that he is the most meticulous person she had ever seen. He rides herd on finances—monitoring expenses and income, doing complicated final reports on grant budgets, and working with the accountants at the end of the fiscal year on the audit. But he is so casual about finances at home that I am the one who keeps our personal checkbook in balance. Last year, Sam overdrew our account three times because he forgot to enter checks. And, as far as our taxes go, forget it. If I didn't do them, they wouldn't get done. Sam is the modern version of Dr. Jekyll and Mr. Hyde. By day, he stabilizes the financial ship at the Creighton Home. But when he leaves work, he doesn't bring his financial head home with him."

Samuel Snyder knows a very important fact. Nonprofit organizations do not enjoy the luxury afforded to individuals who can conduct their financial affairs in a relatively casual and lax manner and get away with it. Individuals can forget to enter a check that they have written, or assume the bank is correct when monthly bank statements arrive and simply skip doing a reconciliation. Nonprofits must maintain records carefully and should have these records reviewed periodically by an independent outside examiner who can certify that the organization is operating legally and according to *generally accepted accounting procedures.* Because nonprofit organizations enjoy numerous financially lucrative privileges and benefits (as we saw in chapter 1), they must be able to demonstrate that their fiscal houses are in order. Board members are ultimately fiscally responsible for these organizations and must be able to read financial statements and be aware of reporting requirements and fiscal systems. It generally falls to staff people such as Sam Snyder to implement these systems.

In this chapter, we continue our discussion of finances beginning with an explanation of accounting systems, then focusing on financial statements, and ending with a description of financial controls and reporting requirements. Again, an effort will be made to explain financial terminology and to outline those areas that are critical to fulfilling the fiscal responsibilities that accrue to board members and staff.

ACCOUNTING

Accounting is the term used for financial record keeping. There are two common accounting methods. The first, *cash basis accounting,* has the advantage of being simple and straightforward; the second, *accrual-based accounting,* is more complex but gives a more complete view of the organization's fiscal health.

Cash basis accounting. Most people are familiar with cash basis accounting because they do it when they maintain financial records for their checking and savings accounts. Financial transactions are recorded *only when cash changes hands.* When a person receives money and deposits it in the bank, the deposit is recorded as income and is added to the bank account balance. When cash is withdrawn from the bank (or when a check is written which is the equivalent of a withdrawal), the transaction is recorded as an expense and the amount is subtracted from the bank account balance. The cash basis accounting system is quite straightforward if all a person needs to know is how much money is in the account. However, what it does not reveal is the financial health of the person maintaining the account, because it tells nothing about what that individual owes and how much is owed to him or her.

Accrual-based accounting. For many individuals, credit cards have forced a kind of informal accrual-based accounting into their personal systems of financial record keeping. This system takes into account not only their actual payments and deposits but also what they owe and what is owed to them. Although few of us do formal accrual-based accounting, a lot of us do something very much like it when we estimate whether or not we will have enough cash to pay the mortgage or rent during the next month. If we see a nice article of clothing and try to figure out whether we can afford it by thinking about our outstanding bills and yet-to-be-received paychecks, we are engaged in informal accrual-based accounting.

Accrual-based accounting recognizes expenses not only when money changes hands but also when expenses are incurred and income is committed. If the Compton Community Center purchases office supplies for $125, an accrual-based system recognizes the $125 as a financial obligation from the moment the purchase order is written and the amount is deducted from the organization's net worth at that time. Similarly, if the Compton Community Center receives an official notification from a funding agency of a $5,000 grant, the $5,000 is added to the net worth figure for the organization as soon as the letter is received. In the case of the $125 owed for supplies, the amount is reflected in the financial statements as a *payable* until the check is actually written. In the case of the $5,000 grant, the amount is entered on the books as a *receivable* until a check is actually deposited.

In the case just cited, if the Compton Community Center has $3,000 in the bank on the day that it charges $125 worth of office supplies and receives the grant letter for $5,000, a cash basis accounting system ignores these transactions and only indicates the organization's bank balance of $3,000. An accrual-based accounting system, on the other hand, adds the $5,000 grant receivable and subtracts the $125 payable showing a net figure of $7,875, which is a truer picture of the organization's net worth (see figure 7.1).

It should be obvious that knowing the financial condition of an organization is more revealing than knowing its bank balance, if the organization's financial health is the main consideration. For example, an organization with no money in the bank could borrow $30,000 to pay $20,000 of outstanding bills and then deposit the remaining $10,000 in its bank account. On a cash basis, a financial accounting would only reveal a positive cash balance of $10,000. On an accrual basis, the outstanding loan of $30,000 would be taken into account and the organization would show a net worth of −$20,000. From the point of view of a prospective trustee, a funder, or anyone else attempting to assess the organization's fiscal health, the second figure would give a more accurate picture.

Choosing Methods

Cash basis accounting is much simpler than the accrual method and provides many people in the organization with enough financial information most of the time. It keeps accurate track of income and outflow, and it tells people whether there is sufficient cash in the bank to pay the bills. Occasionally, however, the information from an accrual-based system is also necessary. For that reason, many organizations, even those with budgets in excess of a million dollars, use what is called a *modified cash basis accounting* system. According to this system, the books are kept on a cash basis except for a few accounts that are kept on accrual and that are usually updated only at the end of the month or at financial reporting time. Generally, these accounts include those in which regular or important outstanding obligations need to be monitored. These accounts usually

FIGURE 7.1. Cash Versus Accrual

	Cash	Accrual
Beginning cash in bank	$3,000	$ 3,000
Purchased supplies (payable)	0	− 125
Grant commitment (receivable)	0	+5,000
Ending cash in bank	$3,000	
Net worth		$ 7,875

Source: Compiled by the author.

include federal taxes payable and state taxes payable—the accounts that show how much money has been withheld from employees' salaries and how much needs to be paid to federal and state taxing authorities. Accounts kept on the accrual basis may also include what are called plant fund accounts, particularly when an organization is purchasing equipment, land, or buildings over a period of years. In such cases, it is advantageous to show the amount of the annual budget committed to (or due) the plant fund for these long-term purchases. When accounts are maintained in this way, the obligated monies are factored into the accounting system so that the organization does not spend the cash on other things just because it happens to be sitting in the bank.

In either a modified cash basis system or a strictly cash basis system, it is necessary, at least once a year, to convert *all* of the accounts to accrual. At the end of the fiscal year, as part of the annual audit, an accountant will take all the payables and receivables and factor them into the financial statements, thus allowing the organization to show its entire financial operation on an accrual system. It should be pointed out that this practice—presenting year-end financial statements on an accrual basis—is one of the "generally accepted accounting procedures" approved by the accounting profession. Only very small organizations with budgets of $75,000 or less, should try to get by with closing statements that are not presented in this way. For organizations whose boards of trustees (or funders, or regulatory agencies) may require more frequent complete accrual-based statements, the books can be converted to full accrual more often.

FUND ACCOUNTING

A small organization may have a simple budget for its entire operation—a kind of composite statement of the predicted expense and income for the entire organization. The *single fund budget* shown in figure 6.1: is a good example of such a budget. As organizations grow more complex, however, they may need to develop several subdivisions of this type of budget in order to gain an accurate analysis of the operation. One such method was described in the last chapter under "Project Budgeting" and an example was shown in figure 6.3.

Fund accounting is a method that allows organizations to track their financial resources according to various categories or "funds." Each fund becomes its own accounting entity, with its own categories of revenue and expense, its own assets, and its own liabilities. Some funds that are commonly established include:

☐ *Unrestricted current fund.* Any monies received, expended, held or owed by the organization without conditions as to their use.

☐ *Restricted current fund.* Any monies received, expended, held or owed by the organization with conditions placed either on when they may be used or for what purpose they may be used.

☐ *Plant fund.* Any monies received, expended, held, or owed by the organization in conjunction with land, buildings, and major equipment as well as the value of such items held by the organization.

☐ *Endowment fund.* Any monies received, expended, held, or owed by the organization in conjunction with an endowment.

The total of activity in all funds becomes the total activity of the organization.

Figure 7.2 shows a financial statement using fund accounting. The first column summarizes the income and expenses associated with general activities. The second column summarizes income and expenses associated with two contributions restricted for use in connection with a program for gifted and talented children. The third column summarizes income and expense associated with improvements to the school building and the fourth column represents the sum of the first three.

FIGURE 7.2. Multiple Funds of the Compton School

	Unrestricted Current	Restricted Current	Plant Fund	Total
Income				
Tuition	$41,222			$ 41,222
Book store sales	10,173			10,173
Foundation grant	5,496	$50,000		55,496
Business scholarship	5,000			5,000
Individuals	15,621	1,000	$ 8,000	24,621
Total	$77,512	$51,000	$ 8,000	$136,512
Expenses				
Salaries	$47,500	$24,500		$ 72,000
Benefits	7,122	3,621		10,743
Honoraria	2,500	16,586		19,086
Supplies and materials	5,287			5,287
Equipment rental	3,401			3,401
Promotion	6,526			6,526
Utilities/heating	3,212			3,212
Repairs/maintenance			9,997	9,997
Contingency/reserve	711		2,900	3,611
Total	$76,259	$44,707	$12,897	$133,863

Source: Compiled by the author.

FINANCIAL STATEMENTS

Just as accounting systems are standardized, so are financial statements. When trustees and others want to assess the organization's financial health, they will look at two financial statements, the balance sheet and the income statement. A health metaphor is appropriate here because the two statements are used as a diagnostic tool in much the same way medical reports are used. Consider, for example, a doctor wishing to diagnose a sick patient. The first thing a doctor checks is the patient's vital signs chart, which reports such things as temperature, pulse, and blood pressure *at a particular moment in time.* The second thing the doctor checks is the patient's medical history, a record of the patient's health *over the course of time.* Neither record by itself is adequate. Two patients with the exact same vital signs may be in very different states of health—the one recovering from a serious illness, the other on a decline from previously good health. Unless the doctor can assess progress over time, a vital signs chart is inadequate. Yet, the medical history is not adequate by itself either. It may be fine to know how a patient has been treated for various ailments over a period of five to ten years, but without an up-to-date reading of the patient's vital signs, there is no way to assess the current state of health.

The balance sheet and the income statement serve the same function in the financial area as the vital signs chart and the medical history do in the health area. The balance sheet, like the vital signs chart, is similar to a freeze frame, a snapshot of the organization's financial condition as of a particular date (often the last day of the month of the fiscal year). It summarizes the organization's vital financial signs—the value of what it owns, what it owes, what is owed to it, and how much is left over. The income statement, by way of contrast, is like the medical history. It summarizes financial activity over a period of time (often a month or a year). Unlike the balance sheet, which tells only where the organization's finances stand as of a particular moment in time, the income statement helps the financial diagnostician determine whether the manner in which the organization arrived at that state was "healthy." Armed with the income statement, more formally referred to as the statement of revenue and expenditures, it is possible to determine whether the organization had a surplus, a deficit, made any unusually large expenditures, or had any revenue windfalls.

THE BALANCE SHEET

The balance sheet (see figure 7.3) is so called because each half adds up to the same total number. One half of the balance sheet (shown at the top of the statement) lists all of the organization's assets (that is, everything that the organization owns). The other half (shown on the bottom of the state-

FIGURE 7.3. Balance Sheet as of June 30

Assets	
Cash	$ 1,101
Accounts receivable	211
Prepaid expenses	1,016
Land and buildings	50,000
Total assets	$52,328
Liabilities and fund balance	
Liabilities	
Accounts payable	$ 532
Notes payable	11,012
Mortgage	25,221
Total liabilities	$36,765
Fund balance	
Excess (or deficit) of revenues	$ 1,611
Starting fund balance	13,952
Total fund balance	$15,563
Total liabilities and fund balance	$52,328

Source: Compiled by the author.

ment) lists both the organization's liabilities (everything that it owes) and its fund balance. Thus the *balance* in a balance sheet is between assets on the one hand and liabilities and fund balance on the other. Put in mathematical form:

Assets equals Liabilities plus Fund Balance: $A = L + FB$

Understanding this formula, we can easily see how the fund balance itself is calculated. If we know how much we own and how much we owe, the fund balance is simply the difference between the two numbers:

Fund Balance equals Assets minus Liabilities: $FB = A - L$

In a profit-making corporation, the fund balance is referred to as *profit* or *owner's equity.* In a nonprofit organization where there are no owners and no profits, the fund balance shows the organization's financial net worth when all of its financial obligations are subtracted from all of its cash and noncash assets. The fund balance provides a link to the income statement, because the organization's financial net worth is obviously affected by the net income (or loss), the so-called bottom line from the income statement.[1]

Let us look more closely at a balance sheet to find out what it is really telling us. First, look at the Assets section of the statement in figure 7.3. Assets are what the organization owns: cash in the bank, land, buildings, a collection of paintings, and equipment (such as typewriters and copiers). In addition, because balance sheets are commonly prepared on an accrual basis, all the money owed to the organization is counted as an asset. These are called the receivables and might include things like grants on which the letter of commitment but not the check has been received or items sold and invoiced but for which the organization has not received payment.

Prepaid expenses are another category counted as assets. An example of a prepaid expense is a rental security deposit. Technically, the amount paid to the landlord is a prepayment for the final month or two of rent or for damage that may occur to the space. Because neither of these events has occurred at the time the balance sheet is prepared, the actual obligation to the landlord has not been incurred at that time. For this reason, the payment should technically not be subtracted from the organization's net worth. In order to compensate for this, and to give a more realistic picture of the organization's financial health, the prepaid expenses are added back to the Assets total.

Moving to the other half of the balance sheet, there is a listing of all of the organization's liabilities (what it owes). On the first line under Liabilities are all of the unpaid bills (the accounts payable). Next are the longer term obligations such as outstanding loans (the notes payable). Finally, the principal balance of the mortgage is shown.[2] All of these liability categories are then totaled and the sum is subtracted from total assets. The resulting difference produces the fund balance.

What does all of this information tell us? Beginning with the fund balance, we know the organization's net worth. In the case of the organization whose balance sheet is shown in figure 7.3, the net worth is $15,563. Often a large fund balance connotes a healthy organization. But not always, and this is precisely the reason why the other numbers on the balance sheet are so important. In figure 7.3 for example, the organization shows a fairly sizable fund balance. But on closer examination we see that the reason for this is because it owns land and buildings. Its cash position is poor. It has only $1,101 in the bank and owes $11,544 (exclusive of the mortgage). In one sense, the organization could be called healthy. If it sold its land and buildings it could pay its debts and have plenty of money left over. On the other hand, if it hangs on to the property, it will have to raise a good deal of cash to pay its debts. Generally speaking, an organization that has to sell assets to pay debts is not considered financially healthy.

The balance sheet is an excellent tool for prospective trustees, funders, regulators, and others to decide whether the organization is a good financial risk. Prospective trustees will want to check whether the organization is saddled with debt because this will provide a clue about whether they will spend a lot of time on the board scrambling for funds; potential funders will want to see whether an organization has large accumulated deficits because this often means that it will be so preoccupied with debt that it will be unable to focus on its programs and other activities; for the regulator, debt-ridden organizations are often tempted to draw on restricted funds to cover operating needs. Indeed, it is not uncommon for government auditors to check on whether restricted public funds have been properly used in financially troubled organizations.

The balance sheet can be most important to trustees and employees of an organization as a diagnostic tool if there is an understanding of how to use it. Unfortunately, many people are mystified by all the numbers. They are content to study the income statement, which is more familiar to them and easier to understand. The assumption is that it contains all the information they really need to know, especially if it is a statement that includes changes to fund balance. But this is not the case, as we have just seen. An organization may have a surplus on the income statement (and/or a large fund balance) and be in serious financial trouble. Only the balance sheet will reveal this. Consider the following case.

THE CONSERVATION TRUST

Before joining the board of a conservation organization, a prospective trustee asked what the net worth of the institution was and was told that the figure was $2 million. Content that he was joining a financially healthy organization, he agreed to serve on the board. Later, when he was shown the balance sheet he was shocked. The museum owed over $1 million. However, its land and buildings were valued at over $3 million, hence the high net worth figure. Because the organization could not sell most of its real estate given the terms by which it had been donated, the value of the holdings had little meaning as equity against debt. The trustee spent the next three years as a full-time fund-raiser, something he had hoped he would not have to do when he joined the board.

Had this trustee studied the balance sheet *before* joining the board, he would have had a more complete picture of the organization's financial situation.

THE INCOME STATEMENT

If the balance sheet tells us what we need to know about an organization's financial health at a particular moment in time, why is another financial statement necessary? The reason is simply that we not only need to know what the organization's health is today but must view the progress of that health over time. Two organizations may have identical balance sheets but one may be improving its financial condition and the other's financial health may be rapidly deteriorating. The income statement (figure 7.4) shows these financial trends over time and gives the historical perspective, which the balance sheet ignores.

Historical perspective is not the only value of an income statement. It also gives an idea of an organization's income sources and its expenditures. Revenues and expenditures are subdivided into categories that reveal such things as how much of the organization's income is earned, how dependent the organization is on certain kinds of grants, how much is spent on personnel, or how much it costs to maintain the physical plant.

Unlike a balance sheet, in which a large number of the line item categories are predictable and similar from one organization to another and from one industry to another, the various revenue and expenditure categories on the income statement vary greatly (they usually closely parallel an organization's budgetary chart of accounts). The bottom line (Excess of revenues over expenditures) shows whether the organization had a surplus or deficit for the year (or whatever time period is reported on); it is calculated by subtracting total expenditures from total revenues and is carried over to the balance sheet (figure 7.3).

Sometimes the income statement may include the fund balance at the

FIGURE 7.4.   Income Statement (Statement of Revenues and Expenditures from July 1 to December 30)

Revenues	
Membership	$ 14,225
Tuition	26,234
Government grants	12,000
Corporate gifts	15,750
Individual donations	12,655
Other	11,222
Total revenue	$92,086
Expenditures	
Salaries and benefits	$32,213
Professional fees/contractual	21,123
Office supplies/telephone	2,987
Travel and subsistence	5,531
Printing and promotion	7,298
Educational materials	4,091
Utilities and insurance	2,755
Mortgage interest	6,643
Grounds maintenance	4,000
Other	3,834
Total expenditures	$90,475
Excess (or deficit) of revenues	$ 1,611

Source: Compiled by the author.

bottom part of the report. (This is most frequently the case on year-end audited statements.) In this case, a line for the starting fund balance is added to the net income to produce a new ending fund balance as is done on the balance sheet. If these lines are included (as is shown in figure 7.5), the bottom of the income statement looks much like the bottom of the balance sheet and the report becomes known as the statement of revenue, expenditures, and changes in fund balance.

The income statement, like the balance sheet, is an important tool in analyzing the financial health of an organization. Knowing how to read the two statements and knowing what the various categories mean are extremely useful.

FIGURE 7.5.   Bottom Lines Included on the
Statement of Revenue, Expenditures, and
Changes in Fund Balance

Excess (or deficit) of revenues	$ 1,611
Starting fund balance	13,952
Total fund balance	$ 15,563

Source: Compiled by the author.

READING MORE COMPLICATED FINANCIAL STATEMENTS

The balance sheet and income statements presented above are very simple financial reports and may bear little resemblance to those from an organization that has been in operation for several years or that has a sizable budget. Accordingly, figures 7.6 and 7.7 show statements that are more complicated and more typical of a larger organization.

What can be said about the Morse School by looking at the balance sheet in figure 7.6? And how does one approach a financial statement like this without feeling intimidated? The challenge is actually similar to that of a detective searching for clues to solve a mystery—the information is there, it is simply a question of how to track it down. And the method to do so is the same as the one described above for reading a simpler statement.

One thing that may look familiar on this statement are the columns, which are similar to those discussed earlier under "Fund Accounting." From these columns, a reader can determine three things. First, the Morse School has a physical facility. Further examination shows that in fact the school owns the facility (note Real estate line valued at $431,203 under Plant Fund column) and it has performed some substantial renovations (Building renovations line valued at $45,903). Second, the Morse School has an endowment of over $2 million (Investments at market line valued at $2,165,748 under Endowment Fund column). Finally, the Morse School provides loans to its students (Loan Fund column).

As discussed earlier, the fund balance line on the balance sheet can be

FIGURE 7.6. Morse School Balance Sheet from June 30, 1989

	Operating Fund	Loan Fund	Plant Fund	Endowment Fund	All Funds Combined	
					June 30, 1989	June 30, 1988
Assets						
Cash and cash equivalents	$29,064			$ 6,695	$ 35,759	$ 32,175
Investments at market		$15,786		2,165,748	2,181,534	1,458,663
Accounts receivable—students	13,001				13,001	12,756
Other receivables	6,339	1,485		30,540	38,364	43,550
Inventory, at cost	6,227				6,227	6,104
Real estate			$431,203		431,203	431,203
Building renovations			45,903		45,903	29,394
Equipment			68,241		68,241	78,277
Art objects			14,250		14,250	14,250
Prepaid expenses	21,904				21,904	3,137
Loans receivable		27,800			27,800	21,300
Total assets	$76,535	$45,071	$559,597	$2,202,983	$2,884,186	$2,130,809
Liabilities and fund balances						
Accounts payable	$26,321				$ 26,321	$ 9,542
Mortgage			$ 80,551		80,551	91,627
Other liabilities	11,162				11,162	24,599
Deferred income—tuition	25,750				25,750	13,500
Unexpended balance of restricted grants	8,402				8,402	343
Advanced endowment income	4,900		0	($4,900)	0	0
Total liabilities	$76,535	0	$ 80,551	($4,900)	$ 152,186	$ 139,611
Fund balance	0	$45,071	$479,046	$2,207,883	$2,732,000	$1,991,198
Total liabilities and fund balances	$76,535	$45,071	$559,597	$2,202,983	$2,884,186	$2,130,809

Source: Compiled by the author.

very revealing inasmuch as it indicates the net worth of an organization. To begin with, one can look at the fund balance under the All Funds Combined column as of the close of the 1989 fiscal year (the second to last number at the bottom of the fifth column). The Morse School appears to have a healthy fund balance at this point in time ($2,732,000). It is also clear from comparison with the previous year (sixth column) that the net worth of the school is increasing, another good sign. If the breakdown of the fund balance between the various columns is examined, it is clear that most of the school's net worth is reflected in the endowment, which shows a fund balance of $2,207,883. This dependency on the endowment in the net worth of the school may or may not be a problem (having an endowment is not the answer to every need as endowment funds are frequently severely restricted), depending on the needs of the school and the restrictions placed on the endowment. It is also clear when comparing the two All Funds Combined columns of the Investments at market line that the increase in fund balance is almost entirely attributable to the increase in the value of the endowment, which could simply be the result of market fluctuations (although it might also be due to additional funds donated to the endowment). It is also apparent however, that the income from the endowment, or at least a portion of it, can be used to support the operations of the school (note the Advanced endowment income line, which shows that $4,900 of income has been advanced to the operating fund).

Another key indicator of health is the cash position, as was discussed in connection with the simpler statement. Operating fund cash is $29,064 (Cash and cash equivalents line), with total liabilities of $37,483 (combining Accounts payable with Other liabilities in the Operating Fund column). This indicates that the school is cash poor and may be forced to increase tuition or expand fund-raising efforts to cover expenses, depending on the restrictions on the endowment.

Part of the fund balance comes from the Loan Fund column, which has a fund balance of $45,071. This student loan fund has nearly $28,000 in currently outstanding loans plus another $15,786 in unutilized funds. This may be of particular interest to a trustee concerned about the accessibility of the school to those unable to afford the tuition. It also indicates a potential source of income for the school in the form of interest payments on loans; however, because the principal amount outstanding is not large, the income will not be substantial.

A picture of the Morse School is beginning to be formed based on the information garnered from our detective work with the balance sheet. Can anything further be learned about this school by examining the income statement in figure 7.7?

In looking at the income statement in figure 7.7,[3] an obvious place to

FIGURE 7.7. Morse School Income Statement and Changes in Fund Balance for Years Ended June 30, 1989, and June 30, 1988

	Operating Fund	Loan Fund	Plant Fund	Endowment Fund	All Funds Combined	
					June 30, 1989	June 30, 1988
Income						
Earned income						
Tuition and fees	$ 864,905				$ 864,905	$ 863,804
Financial aid	(127,090)				(127,090)	(144,805)
Tuition (net)	$ 737,815				$ 737,815	$ 718,999
Investment income	7,543	$ 1,704		$ 163,347	172,594	163,804
Proceeds from events	1,854				1,854	831
Other	5,487				5,487	5,768
Total earned	$ 752,699	$ 1,704		$ 163,347	$ 917,750	$ 889,402
Contributed income						
Unrestricted						
Individual	$ 135,271				$ 135,271	$ 151,653
Foundation	2,500				2,500	2,500
Restricted						
Individual	7,360			30,000	37,360	35,951
Foundation		8,000	11,800		19,800	20,700
Total contributed	$ 145,131	$ 8,000	$ 11,800	$ 30,000	$ 194,931	$ 210,804
Total income	$ 897,830	$ 9,704	$ 11,800	$ 193,347	$1,112,681	$1,100,206

	Operating Fund	Loan Fund	Plant Fund	Endowment Fund	All Funds Combined	
					June 30, 1989	June 30, 1988
Expenses						
Instruction	$ 604,818				$ 604,818	$ 607,143
Kitchen	65,191				65,191	62,032
Plant operation and maintenance	108,081		$ 23,661		131,742	122,582
General and administrative	177,206			$ 100	177,306	185,299
Student supplies and services	41,674				41,674	39,655
Headmaster discretionary	13,110				13,110	14,914
Special program	4,330				4,330	4,475
Total expenses	$1,014,410		$ 23,661	$ 100	$1,038,171	$1,036,100
Net income (or loss)	($116,580)	$ 9,704	($11,861)	$ 193,247	$ 74,510	$ 64,106
Endowment income transferred	$ 116,580		0	($116,580)	0	0
Final net income (or loss)	0	$ 9,704	($11,861)	$ 76,667	$ 74,510	$ 64,106
Fund balance, beginning	0	$35,367	$ 490,907	$1,507,589	$2,033,863	$1,619,671
Change in market value of investments	0		0	$ 623,627	$ 623,627	$ 307,421
Fund balance, ending	0	$45,071	$ 479,046	$2,207,883	$2,732,000	$1,991,198

Source: Compiled by the author.

start is the Final net income (or loss) line. Morse School ended the year with a surplus of $74,510 (fifth column). The school shows approximately $10,000 additional in surplus in 1989 than for the previous year ($64,106 for 1988). It is interesting to note that this surplus results from the income earned on the endowment—see the Net income (or loss) line in the Endowment column, which shows $193,247. Without the endowment, the school would show an operating loss of $116,580 as is shown in the Net income (or loss) line of the first column. However, the income from the endowment covers this deficit in the Operating Fund (note the Endowment income transferred line).

Some additional information about the school is apparent from this statement. Contributed income for the school ($194,931 for all funds) is 18 percent of all income. This is not a particularly high percentage, and indicates that should enrollment drop or faculty salaries be increased, there may be some room for expanded fund-raising efforts to increase the income of the school. Comparison of this figure with that of the previous year ($210,804) indicates an 8 percent drop in contributed income, which may be of concern. On the expense side, instruction costs ($604,818) are nearly 60 percent of total costs for the school. Increases in faculty compensation rates could thus have a major impact on the expenses of the school, because this figure is such a large portion of total expenses.

The bottom four lines indicate changes in fund balances and are simply a summary of changes in the net worth of the school. Net income (or loss) for each fund is added to the fund balance (or net worth) from the previous year to give an ending fund balance figure, which is carried over to the balance sheet's Fund balance line (in figure 7.6). There is one additional adjustment to the fund balance, which is the change in market value of investments for the endowment. This entry is necessary as the securities are carried at market value on the balance sheet. As we guessed from examining the balance sheet, the increase in market value of investments is a major part of the increase in net worth for the school.

Clearly there is much information to be gained from examining the financial statements of an organization. The intimidating columns of figures can actually be quite revealing if the reader has a sense of where the most important information lies. Responsible board members will take the time to familiarize themselves with at least the highlights of each statement in an effort to be as informed as possible about the organization they are overseeing.

CONTROLS

One of the major responsibilities of board members is to establish fiscal policies that protect the organization from either intentional or unintentional misuse of funds. They must decide how money will be handled internally to ensure that it will be safely received, recorded, deposited, and expended in a manner that seems appropriate. The policies that board members set in this area are called *controls* and there are guidelines that they can follow. Any responsible accountant can advise them on what are generally accepted and appropriate procedures. For example, many fiscal controls are based on the notion that two people are far less likely to make a mistake, either intentionally or unintentionally, than one. So one kind of financial control is to be sure that two people are involved in transactions involving the receipt of cash, the preparation of financial statements, the expenditure of funds, and other financial matters. Other controls are discussed below.

Budget Monitoring and Amending Procedures

Budget monitoring and amending procedures were discussed in the previous chapter where it was suggested that trustees should be consulted on any significant change in the budget. However, a suggestion that trustees be consulted is not deemed sufficient control. It does not assure the trustees that such consultation will take place. Nor does it assure a funder that the board is in a position to monitor carefully the staff's spending of its dollars. To establish a reliable procedure, the board generally requires that two people should be involved in processing all payments. One person who is familiar with the budget, the organization's operation, and the appropriateness of specific expenditures, should be responsible for approving payments. That person is often the director of the organization. Another person should actually write the checks and monitor the expenditures for the trustees. If the director stays within the limits established by the budget, or the limits beyond the budget set by the board, a check can be written. If the director requests payments that exceed these limits, the matter must be referred to the treasurer, the finance committee, or the full board for approval or for an amended budget.

There is a simple method for documenting the processing of payments. The organization should invest in a rubber stamp with the following designations:

> Date Received:
> Date Paid:
> Account:
> Check Number:
> Approved:

Every invoice, before it is paid, gets stamped. When no invoice exists for a particular item, a dummy invoice is prepared by the staff and stamped.

The executive director, or the person responsible for approving invoices, fills out the first, third, and bottom lines. The first line indicates the date the invoice was received, the third indicates the account or line item that the expense gets charged to, and the final line allows the director to indicate his or her approval of the payment with a signature. The person responsible for writing the checks fills out the second and fourth lines after making sure that there is enough money remaining in the budget account to pay the bill. After the completion of the transaction, the invoice is placed in a file so that an auditor can review the paper trail backing up the particular payment. For organizations with a fairly heavy volume of transactions, it is recommended that there be a separate file for each account or for each month.

Other Controls on Check Writing
It is generally not recommended that the person who writes checks have the power to issue a check to himself or herself without at least a countersignature on the check. While banks probably will not monitor this, the policy can be recorded in the minutes of a board meeting and a person can be held in violation of a fiscal policy if the rule is not followed. One control that banks may be willing to monitor is that of requiring two signatures on all checks over a certain amount ($5,000, for example). To further monitor expenditures, use of checks made out to "cash" should be forbidden or severely restricted.

It is a great deal easier to monitor check writing and other financial activity if organizations do not maintain a large number of bank accounts. Ideally an organization should have only two cash accounts: checking and savings (money market). To the extent that it is feasible, all checks and deposits should be to one account (the checking account), with the second account serving solely to hold cash reserves or unexpended restricted funds. Some may argue that more than one account is necessary to be sure that restricted funds are not used for other than their intended purpose. But proper accounting methods can ensure that this does not happen. Furthermore, maintaining separate bank accounts can be time-consuming and wasteful if smaller amounts of cash that could earn interest if held in aggregate are held in several noninterest-earning accounts or if service charges are accruing on several accounts. From the point of view of controls, more accounts require more monitoring by an accountant when the books are audited.

Controls on Incoming Monies
Again, in this area, the assumption is that two people are less likely to err than one. Where incoming monies are involved, the person who opens the

mail should record all incoming checks and cash and keep a list. Checks and cash should then be forwarded to the fiscal officer who prepares the deposit slip and keeps a record. Periodically, someone other than these two people (the board treasurer or the executive director) should check to see that the two sets of records agree. In addition, all incoming money, whether cash or check, should be deposited promptly in the organization's bank account before it is used to pay a bill.

Bonding
Bonding is a form of insurance that protects an organization from financial losses stemming from either intentional or unintentional irregularities in the handling of money. Generally, those people who handle money and sign checks are listed in the bonding document. Like any form of insurance, a limit is placed on the amount an organization can collect in the case of a loss. The greater the limit, the greater the annual premium. As a general rule of thumb, an organization should not use total annual expenses as the bonding limit figure even though at first glance this would seem to be prudent. The total budgeted dollars are rarely available to spend at any one time, and so it is unlikely that any loss would be so great. The organization should determine the maximum amount of money it anticipates having in the bank at any one time, increase the figure by 20 percent, and use that number as the bonding limit. Some funding sources require evidence of bonding before they will contribute dollars to a nonprofit organization. Whether or not they do, it should be a comfort both to funders and trustees to know that such insurance against loss is in place.

Physical Controls and Security Measures
Physical controls such as fireproof filing cabinets or safes and off-site storage of computer back-up disks or tapes provide additional protection for a responsible fiscal system. If appropriate (in the case of gift shops and other retail outlets), the use of electrical or mechanical equipment such as cash registers in the recording and execution of transactions can reduce the likelihood of errors or irregularities.

REPORTING REQUIREMENTS
Nonprofit corporations may not have to file income tax forms, but there are other forms that must be filed each year for an organization to maintain its nonprofit status. Although generally the forms are prepared by staff or by the independent auditor who reviews the books each year, it is important for board members to be aware of the reports that must be filed in order to ascertain that it is done in a timely manner. Because requirements vary from state to state, board members should check their own state

regulations to determine what specific state forms should be filed. The following is a general overview of federal forms required:

☐ *Annual return.* Most nonprofit organizations must file an annual information return with the IRS called Form 990. This form provides information on the ongoing activities of the organization in support of its tax-exempt status and includes statements regarding all income and expenditures for the year. The returns are due on the fifteenth day of the fifth month following the fiscal year end. Failure to file can result in civil and criminal penalties.

☐ *Unrelated business income tax.* In recent years, nonprofit organizations have come under increasing scrutiny as more inventive and atypical methods of raising money have been implemented. Tax must be paid on "unrelated" business income, which is income produced by regular activities that are not substantially related to the exempt purpose of the organization (excluding income from passive investments such as money market interest, stock dividends, etc.). This income (if it exceeds $1,000) must be reported on Form 990-T, which is due with Form 990. As it is sometimes complicated to determine whether or not income is considered unrelated, it is best to consult with the independent outside examiner who prepares the Form 990 or conducts the annual audit as to whether or not this form is required.

☐ *Employment taxes.* All organizations with employees are required to withhold income taxes and social security (FICA) from salaries and to pay and report amounts withheld to the IRS. Nonprofit organizations other than 501(c)(3) organizations must also pay federal unemployment taxes (FUTA) on salaries paid. Income taxes and social security are reported on Form 941, which is due one month after the end of each calendar quarter. FUTA is reported on Form 940, which is due by January 31 of each year. In addition, all employers must prepare form W-2, which is the annual wage and tax statement for each employee. This form must be mailed to the employee by January 31 of each year and copies must be filed with the IRS by February 28 of each year with form W-3. Details on payment of withholding and FUTA are available from the IRS through the publication *Circular E—Employer's Tax Guide.*

☐ *Other information returns.* Form 1099-MISC must be used to report on an annual basis any nonemployee compensation paid in amounts exceeding $600. This form is due by February 28 of each year, and should be filed with Form 1096 with the IRS. Form 8282, Donee Information Report, must be filed with the IRS if a donee organization sells, exchanges, or otherwise disposes of gifts of property other than money or publicly traded securities within two years of the gift. This form is not required if the gift was valued at less than $500.

COMPUTERS

With the rapidly decreasing costs of microcomputers and the availability of affordable prepackaged software to handle accounting needs, organizations are increasingly choosing to computerize their financial records to ease burdens on staff. Even relatively small organizations with single fund statements kept on a cash basis can benefit from using standard off-the-shelf accounting packages to maintain ledgers and create financial reports. There are also customized accounting packages for nonprofit organizations that provide some specific adaptations of standard accounting procedures, terminology, report design and links to membership and fund-raising packages. Computer spreadsheets are invaluable tools for budgeting and cash flow analyses, simplifying projections and recalculations and reducing the possibility of errors. (For a detailed discussion on use of computers, see chapter 10.)

Use of a computer for financial record keeping requires additional control procedures to ensure a responsible fiscal system. These may include control of access to records and data entry through use of passwords, regular review of output and reconciliation to assets on hand (especially cash) by a second staff person, specific requirements on systems back-up, and clear documentation of data entry and report generation procedures.

In addition to in-house computer systems, many organizations hand all of their payroll record keeping over to a specialized computer payroll accounting service. This service may include the preparation of paychecks, the maintenance of tax and benefit information, the issuing of W-2 and 1099 forms, and other payroll-related tasks. For organizations with frequently changing payrolls (hourly staff) and numerous contracted services, these services are often less expensive and more accurate than having comparable tasks done by staff because they are fully computerized and are performed by those specializing in payroll services.

This chapter has explained accounting procedures, financial statements, and financial controls and has reviewed reporting requirements that nonprofits need to meet to maintain their special tax status. Too many nonprofit organizations have failed because of lack of attention to these areas. Staff members may have been lax in the maintenance of financial records or trustees may not have bothered to analyze the financial statements or put controls in place. Although the plethora of procedures and reports described in this chapter may seem overwhelming, no nonprofit organization can afford to be casual about its financial affairs, if it wants to protect its nonprofit status and ensure its continued survival. No board member can afford to be casual about these matters either if he or she is to meet the responsibilities of public trust, which are part of the conditions of trusteeship.

CHECKLIST QUESTIONS FOR CHAPTER 7

1. Has your organization determined which method of accounting is most appropriate for its needs (i.e., cash basis, modified cash basis, or accrual)?
2. Does your organization have a properly prepared balance sheet and income statement that together accurately report the organization's net worth and fiscal year's financial activity?
3. Has your board developed a regular procedure for monitoring income and expenditures and amending the annual budget?
4. Are there proper controls over check writing, dealing with incoming money, and handling cash in your organization? Is the organization properly protected through bonding against financial loss?
5. Does your organization file required financial forms in a timely manner (including IRS Form 990, Form 990-T, Form 940, Form 941, Form W-3, Form 1099-MISC, and Form 1096)? Does your organization provide the necessary forms to employees and independent contractors in a timely manner (including IRS Form W-2 and Form 1099)?

8
Fund Raising

Josephine Tierney is a seventy-two-year-old widow who is still an active volunteer in Compton. Over the years she has supported many causes. She has donated time and money to more organizations than she can count. She is greatly beloved by her community. She is also a fund-raising target for a large number of nonprofit organizations.

Josephine Tierney is opening her mail a week before Christmas. Of the seventy-two pieces of mail before her, there are twenty-two Christmas cards and the same number of requests for money. This is not an unusual day for her. In fact, during the month of December alone, she will be receiving more than 500 letters asking her to support some charity or other. Many of these requests will go straight into the wastebasket unopened, but others will receive at least a cursory review. Mrs. Tierney will take the time to open some of the envelopes, scanning the contents of the packet. Of this material, most will also be thrown away. But some of the packets she does save. If a letter is from one of her particularly favorite charities—an organization that she is planning to contribute to anyway—she will put the letter and enclosed material on what she calls the yes pile on her desk. With the remaining letters, if her eye happens to pick up something that makes her hesitate, she will put the letter on another pile, her maybe pile. Everything else will be thrown into the wastebasket.

What keeps letters out of the wastebasket? To quote Mrs. Tierney, "I certainly do have favorite charities and their requests are always attended to. But with the others, I take the letter in my hand and as my arm is moving toward the wastebasket, I am scanning the material, checking to see whether there is any personalized message. Has someone handwritten a personal P.S. or is the letter typed to me personally? If not, and now my hand is very close to the wastebasket, I check to see if I recognize any of the names of people on the board—this list is usually printed on the letterhead, or should be. Finally, I may be struck by the kind of activity the organization is engaged in—the big organizations for cancer or world hunger can't personalize their messages but I support them anyway. In the case of the others, it is the personal aspect of the request that keeps the letter out of the wastebasket. If someone has taken the time to write something, or if one of my friends is on the board, I know I need to be a little more careful. Mind you, this doesn't mean I am going to make a contribution. It just means I will consider it."

Mrs. Tierney's daughter, Roberta Sims, is a corporate contributions officer. This month her company will receive more than 1,400 requests for money. The requests will come from colleges and universities, from hospitals, from social service agencies, from cultural organizations, and from other kinds of nonprofit organizations. Roberta Sims knows very little about any of these fields. Her background is in corporate finance and she was assigned to her position with no special training or expertise in philanthropy. She has a staff of two people working for her. Her assistant organizes her paperwork and calendar and tries to protect her as much as possible from people who call on the phone. The secretary attempts to stay on top of the incoming mail, answer the phone, and type her correspondence. Both have little time to spare.

Twice a year Roberta Sims is expected to make recommendations to the contributions committee, keeping track as she does so of the various members' favorite charities. Her strategy, as she has often admits to herself, is to make order out of chaos. She identifies for the company the obvious blue-chip organizations that it should be supporting—for example, the United Way, the university teaching hospital, and the orchestra—and for the balance of the giving program she tries to put together a package that is consistent with the goals of the company's contributions program. She wants to get the most for the company's charitable dollar, and she wants the company to look good to its customers, its employees, and the community. Just as important, she wants to avoid all contributions that have any potential of becoming an embarrassment for the company.

Roberta Sims smiles as she divides the proposals she receives into three piles. It is just as her mother says. One pile is for those organizations she knows the company will fund no matter what. A second pile—the analogue to her mother's wastebasket—is for those proposals that are clearly not fundable. The organizations are too small or badly managed, the projects will not serve her company in any visible way, or the projects involve too much risk. Then there is a third pile, which Roberta Sims intends to check out more carefully, her maybe pile.

Roberta Sims's brother, Charles Tierney, is a research psychologist with a teaching appointment at the local university. Periodically he is invited to serve as an outside reviewer for a federal funding agency. Although his regular teaching job and his research are very demanding and represent more than a full-time commitment, he always responds enthusiastically when called on to lend his expertise to the review of grant applications. Twice a year, the federal agency expects him to read proposals and then go to Washington to discuss the material and make recommendations about funding. Three weeks before the Washington meeting, he receives a large cardboard box in the mail. He opens the box to find three black notebooks full of proposal summaries (there is a total of 312 proposal summaries in the notebooks). He is instructed to read through these summaries. In addition, he finds another package that contains fifteen complete proposals together with back-up material; he is told to review these in depth and to rate them according to scoring criteria that are included in the package. He will be responsible for reporting on these fifteen proposals at the Washington meeting.

Says Charles Tierney, "The first time I received the box I wondered whether the federal agency was really aware that I had another job; I spent every night for three weeks reviewing the material. Conservatively, I would say I spent twenty hours and still did not finish to my satisfaction. When I arrived in Washington, I found most of my fellow panel members much less prepared than I. My hunch is that some looked at the material the night before or on the airplane on their way to Washington. It was very revealing and quite shocking. To say our review of the proposals was superficial is an understatement. As a result, the predictable occurred. It was another version of what my mother and sister do—sorting requests into three piles. The key organizations in our field received most of the funding, organizations that didn't have their act together weren't even considered, and we spent the bulk of our time fighting like cats and dogs about who would get what the established organizations hadn't walked away with. What the experience taught me is that a great fund-raiser is not someone who can raise money for an established organization—any fool can do that. It is someone who can raise money for an organization on the next rung of the funding ladder where the competition is really fierce."

These three family members—all of whom are involved in different branches of philanthropy—share certain dilemmas. They know that the great majority of requests that they must review will not be funded. They all have a limited amount of time to look over the material that is sent to them. They are all aware of the constraints—both social and political— that make it difficult to say no to certain established organizations. There is also something else that these people have in common. They are strong-minded individuals who have their own definite ideas about what should and should not be funded. Like most people who have been in the philanthropic field for some time, they have developed a technique for very quickly dividing requests into three categories: Those that should be funded no matter what, those that should not be funded no matter what, and all the rest. In fund raising, this is what some people call the three-pile phenomenon. There is a yes pile, a no pile, and a maybe pile.

Many nonprofit organizations that are responsibly managed and provide a service to their communities are placed in this third category—the maybe pile—much of the time when they request funds. Those that are successful manage to accomplish two difficult tasks. First, they beat out the competition on a fairly regular basis among the other maybe's. Second, they manage to get themselves placed in more and more funders' yes piles. The techniques for accomplishing both of these feats is the subject of this chapter. It is essential to keep in mind that even those who have accomplished them are accustomed to failure much of the time. The successful fund-raiser, like a talented major league baseball batter, will be unsuccessful more often than successful. In baseball, a 30 percent success rate in hitting (or a .300 batting average) is considered very good. In fund raising the odds are even tougher. Good fund-raisers do not expect to be successful all the time. Good fund-raisers learn that the secret of success is in improving their average every year.

THE ROLE OF THE BOARD IN FUND RAISING

Chapter 2 dealt with the need for board members to contribute cash to an organization and to assist in the general fund-raising effort. Many funders will be interested in answers to three questions:

1. What percentage of trustees are contributing to an organization (the answer should be 100 percent)?
2. How much, in total, does the organization receive in board contributions (the answer should be a substantial proportion of the total individual contributions—perhaps 20 to 30 percent)?
3. How active is the board in soliciting funds (the answer should be very active)?

As one contributor put it, "Trustees are the bellwether. They provide the leadership. If they are not giving generously themselves, if they are not out there asking for money, the organization is going to have some problems."

Mrs. Tierney, whose funding approach was described at the outset of the chapter, is always interested in who is on a board and how much they are giving. "It helps me to know whether to give and how to scale my gift," she says. Similarly, Roberta Sims claims that her corporation does not contribute to organizations unless there is strong board involvement—not only in giving money but in raising it. "We talk around here about the three 'Gs' for trustees—Give, Get, or Get off. While not all trustees will feel comfortable asking for money, they still can involve themselves in the general fund-raising effort. For those not comfortable with direct solicitation there are other activities. These include working on a fund-raising event, updating mailing lists, analyzing donor records, scripting telethons, writing or typing personalized fund-raising letters, researching funding sources (like corporate and foundation donors), hosting fund-raising lunches or breakfasts. There are plenty of jobs for everyone."

The most important reason why trustees have to be active in fund raising is because people give to people, but most especially peers give to peers. To the extent that the trustees are active in the community, are givers themselves, and are not afraid to ask for money, the organization will be more successful in the fund-raising effort. Furthermore, the fiscal health of the organization depends on the extent to which the trustees feel that the income gap (the difference between what is earned and what is expended) is their responsibility. Board members can be extremely helpful in direct solicitation and in arranging fund-raising calls for the staff. Their involvement is one way that the funding community takes the measure of the organization's vitality and health.

UNRESTRICTED GIFTS AND INDIVIDUAL CONTRIBUTORS

All money raised by nonprofit organizations is not of equal value to its operation. Certain gifts are most useful because they can be used for any purpose that is consistent with the organization's mission, including basic administrative costs. These gifts are called unrestricted because the donor has not attached any strings to them. The other category of gifts, the so-called restricted ones, can only be used for a specific purpose, or at a specific time or both. Organizations that rely entirely on restricted gifts often find it difficult to cover basic operating expenses. Furthermore, restricted gifts can occasionally get an organization into serious trouble because a single gift may partially fund an expensive new project that requires substantial additional money. Instead of getting the organization ahead financially, the gift forces it to set even higher fund-raising goals.

Clearly, the most valuable money is that which is unrestricted, because it can be directed in so many ways. It can be used to pay for staff salaries, occupancy costs, utility bills, telephone, and other office costs. For many nonprofit organizations, finding adequate unrestricted income is a constant worry. Funders always seem to want to pay for projects and programs but are less enthusiastic about making a general gift. For that reason, fund-raising planning must concern itself with identifying first and foremost the sources of ongoing unrestricted support.

By far the greatest source of unrestricted income comes from individuals. Healthy nonprofit organizations generally work hard to build a relationship with individual donors that continues year after year. Indeed, the underpinning of most sound fund-raising programs rests on a base of *many, small, ongoing, individual, unrestricted gifts.* While each individual donation may seem small and hardly worth the effort, the total take can be very large. If a single individual gives $100 each year for ten years, and if the funds are unrestricted, this person represents an important asset to the organization. For this reason, many fund-raisers tend to work on building loyalty among their individual contributors and raise more from them each year. This involves two efforts:

- Increasing the number of donors giving unrestricted funds on an annual basis
- Upgrading the amounts that these individual donors give from year to year

It is desirable to identify several donors who will contribute substantial sums—board members should figure prominently in this category—but it should be kept in mind that as individuals make larger and larger contributions, their willingness to keep these gifts unrestricted diminishes.

Individuals can be solicited in a number of ways—in person, by mail, by phone, through fund-raising events, even through the media. Whatever technique is used, *the more personalized the approach, the greater likelihood of success.* Some organizations have fund-raising committees, volunteers, or paid callers that undertake in-person solicitations and this is generally a very effective approach. Whether it is part of a program of carefully orchestrated face-to-face meetings or simply part of a door-to-door community campaign, the success rate for person-to-person solicitation is far greater than that for any other kind of fund raising. However, because this approach can be time-consuming, the telephone offers an alternative for targeted personalized fund raising from individuals. Schools and colleges have found great success with "telethons" in which alumni, parents, and students solicit funds from individuals who have had some kind of connection with the institution and are likely prospects for support. The least personal approach is direct mail, but it has the advantage of reaching the largest number of prospects for the least amount of money.

Direct Mail

Direct mail allows great efficiency in time spent and people reached, but unless it is carefully tailored to give the impression of a personal approach, it is often unsuccessful. The "Dear Friend" fund-raising letter, printed by the thousand and sent out bulk rate in envelopes with mailing labels affixed to them, often ends up unopened in wastebaskets. Large nonprofit organizations that mail hundreds of thousands of pieces of mail must resort to these impersonal approaches, but these organizations usually have the advantage of universal name recognition, broad appeal, and media coverage, which helps spread their message. For smaller local groups, which are less well known and which appeal to a more specialized group, a personal approach in direct mail is an absolute must.

How can direct mail be personalized? Individual letters can be written to known supporters or constituents by board members and other volunteers. Preprinted letters can also be personalized either by the addition of a handwritten P.S. or by the addition of short individual notes written on personal stationery. But other aspects of the direct mail packet itself can be made to appear more personal. For example, a good direct mail packet will consist of the following pieces.

The External Envelope. The purpose of the external envelope is to get the packet opened. Toward this end, a hand addressed envelope is quite effective (a personally typed envelope—or one produced on a letter-quality printer—is also good). Envelopes with mailing labels affixed, or those produced by dot-matrix printers are least effective because they look the most impersonal (or as many donors claim, like junk mail). Envelopes with stamps—perferably large colorful ones—are more effective than those with preprinted or metered postage. First-class stamps are preferred, but even those organizations mailing at a bulk rate can get stamps from the post office for these mailings.

The Letter. Most letters will not be read in detail. They should be short, which means for most organizations only one page. If detailed information needs to be conveyed, it can be included in a separate flyer. The easiest way to compose a good fund-raising letter is to ask board members and volunteers to save good examples of such letters from other organizations. They provide a wealth of good ideas about style, flow, content, even choice of words, and it is often easy to compose an entirely original letter by combining ideas from several other organizations' letters.

Perhaps the most important thing to remember about a general appeal letter for unrestricted funds is that the wording must *not* specify that the funds will be used for a particular project. For example, if the letter asks for funds to support the scholarship fund, it becomes a request for restricted funds and the money that comes in can only be used for the scholarship fund. Some organizations that wish to be more specific in their appeals for general support use a device where they list several areas where the funds may be applied (e.g., the scholarship program, the seniors program, the inner-city program) and end the list with the short phrase, "and other activities." This allows the contributions, when they come in, to be considered unrestricted.

One organization that has a remarkably high rate of return on its fund-raising letter campaign makes sure that every letter that goes out has some personal message handwritten at the bottom of the letter (the organization sends out 3,000 pieces). One week each year, trustees and volunteers gather in the evening and each is handed a stack of letters and a list of people to whom a personal message must be written. Some people on the list they may know. Others they do not know. Beside each name is an indication of whether the prospect has given in the past two years and the size of the gift. Trustees are then told to write such messages as: "Your $50 meant so much to us last year. With our programs increasing, we hope you might consider a larger gift this year." Or, "As a volunteer, I have become convinced of the good work of this organization. We hope you will become part of our loyal network of supporters." The message itself is less important than the fact that someone took the time to personalize what would otherwise have been an impersonal request.

The Return Device. The return device, generally printed on a card, should include at the very least the categories (or amounts) of donations as well as lines where the donor can indicate name and address. Occasionally, the return device also includes a space where the donor can write a message (e.g., information for the alumni bulletin in the case of a school or college or indications of program preferences in the case of a musical organization). A typical return device is shown in figure 8.1:

FIGURE 8.1. Sample Return Device

Yes! I wish to contribute as follows (check one):
_____Benefactor ($1,000)   _____Patron ($500)   _____Sponsor ($250)
_____Contributor ($100)   _____Donor ($50)   _____Friend $_____
Please indicate your name as your wish it to appear in our annual report
Name _____
Address _____
City _____ State _____ Zip _____
Check here if you do not wish to be listed _____

There are several features of the card shown in figure 8.1 that are important. First the categories of giving are listed with the highest categories first. This makes it less simple for the donor simply to check off the lowest category. Second, the smallest *listed* amount ($50) is larger than the smallest anticipated gifts (which may be $15 or less). This encourages smaller donors who are uncertain precisely how much to give to gravitate to a higher level of giving. Third, donors are asked to show how they want their names listed—and it is very important that their instructions are honored. Finally, there is an opportunity for donors to keep their gifts anonymous.

The Return Envelope. The return envelope has the organization's name and address preprinted on it for the convenience of the donor. There is some debate about whether or not it should also have prepaid postage; research on this question is inconclusive. Some organizations include preprinted return postage that they only have to pay if the envelope is used; others forego this expense and simply include a printed note in the upper right hand corner that says, "Your stamp helps our efforts. Thanks."

However, there is one group of donors where it is useful not only to include prepaid postage on the return envelope but to include an actual stamp. These are the organization's lapsed donors, the so-called LY-BUNTS, donors who gave *L*ast *Y*ear *B*ut *N*ot *T*his. There is an extremely strong likelihood that an organization will get a contribution from these individuals if it keeps at the effort, and because these donors tend to be the kind of people who put a first request aside and forget about it, sending a second packet with an actual postage stamp on a return envelope commands a bit more attention and often elicits a quicker response.

Informational Flyer (optional). Some organizations like to include another piece in the direct mail packet that gives facts and figures about the organization. Where complex information has to be conveyed, or where detailed financial information is important, such a flyer or brochure can be included, although it does add considerably to the cost of producing the direct mail package and, occasionally, to the cost of mailing.

Once funds are received from individuals, the organization must acknowledge the gifts immediately. A short personal note of thanks should be sent to every contributor together with a receipt for tax purposes: "The XYZ organization thanks John R. Moneybags for his generous gift of $100 received on July 4, 1990." Some organizations have thank-you parties and receptions for donors who contribute over a certain sum. Others recognize their contributors in printed material such as annual reports, program booklets, and even newspaper articles. It is important to think carefully about how to say thank you. Done properly, it can create a positive feeling on the part of the donor that will make next year's request for funds even easier.

Unrestricted Income Through Events

Another way to generate unrestricted income is through fund-raising events. There are several advantages of fund-raising events:

- Fund-raising events widen an organization's donor pool by attracting people whose interest may be in the event rather than the organization

- Fund-raising events can generate good public relations and exposure for an organization
- Fund-raising events allow an organization to raise additional money from people who are already making contributions; if someone buys a ticket to a dinner dance, purchases items at a silent auction, or pays to attend a benefit concert, that person may still make a general gift
- Fund-raising events provide a vehicle by which board and volunteers without any particular fund-raising experience can assist in bringing in contributed money

The disadvantage of events is that they often involve a great deal of planning and work and can overtax the organization's volunteer pool. For organizations with a seemingly inexhaustible supply of volunteers (schools with a great number of parents, for example, and colleges with a large number of alumni), numerous events may turn out to be practical. But when organizations do not have such a large supply of volunteers and have to rely either on their paid staffs or on their already overworked volunteers, even one event a year may be a stretch.

In planning events, there are certain rules that are important to follow:

☐ Set a dollar goal early in the planning process and stick to it. Many events planners get off course by confusing public relations functions with fund raising. The logic seems to be that if the organization does not make a lot of money, at least everyone who comes will have a good time and there will be good coverage in the local paper. A dollar goal reminds volunteers that the primary purpose of the event is to make money and it gives them a criterion by which success can be judged.

☐ Remember, the secret of success is *net* income not gross income. What counts is how much the organization has left over after all the expenses for the event have been paid. Budgeting for an event must be done carefully and realistically, always with an eye toward the bottom line.

☐ Plan an event that people will enjoy. It is easier to get people to participate if the event itself is a drawing card as well as the organization sponsoring it. Avoid events that are esoteric and will not have wide appeal.

☐ Establish a committee to work on the event. There should be a chairperson (or two or more cochairs). Keep in mind that those who serve on the committee may themselves represent part of the draw for others to attend. For that reason, it is always good to include several very prominent people on the committee as honorary officers (e.g., elected officials, their spouses, corporate leaders, or media personalities).

☐ Exaggerate the number of volunteers and dollars you will need in order to make the event a success. Like budgeting, planning for a fund-raising event usually requires overstating needs at the beginning of the planning process.

☐ Allow plenty of planning time. Things always seem to take longer than expected and there should be plenty of margin for error in a timeline for a fund-raising event.

☐ Build in plenty of ancillary ways to pick up money in conjunction with the event. An auction can include a preauction cocktail party (with income-producing cash bar), a potluck dinner (for which people have to buy tickets), a raffle for some high-priced items, a souvenir table, a game room for youngsters, and so on.

☐ Involve local merchants. While local businesspeople may be reluctant to make a cash contribution to a nonprofit organization, many are more than willing to donate goods and services for an event. Keep in mind that when merchants are willing to give an organization things "at cost", the recipient may be saving 40 percent to 60 percent off the retail price. When the gift is made outright, it is a lot less expensive for the merchants than if they gave cash. It is also a way for them to get a little free advertising for their wares.

☐ Attempt to find a type of event that works for the organization and stick to it for several years. As knowledge of the event spreads, people will begin to plan for it, building it into their calendars and their budgets. It is always best if the event can happen at a predictable time each year (like the first Saturday of a particular month) so that people do not have to wait for an announcement to save the date.

The variety of fund-raising events is almost endless. Dances, special dinners, fairs, auctions, theater or concert benefits, art shows and sales, raffles (except where prohibited by law), garden and house tours, wine tastings, and trips to exotic or interesting places represent only a beginning list. Other ideas include showcase houses (where decorators and contractors each participate in the renovation of a house that is then toured by participants), food festivals (in which local restaurateurs and caterers compete for prizes), and fund-raising "nonevents" (in which participants pay for the privilege of not attending a fund-raising event). The creativity surrounding the event theme and the image that this projects will often determine the event's draw for participants.

Using the Phone
One of the most popular fund-raising tools today is the telephone. Although many donors complain that telephone solicitation invades their

privacy, research shows that it is one of the most effective devices for bringing in substantial sums of money.

Some organizations will do telephone solicitation to find new donors. This is particularly true of the larger ones whose image is already well established. Smaller organizations may prefer to limit their calling to individuals with a known history of interest in the organization. In particular, those people with a history of giving are the best prospects and the telephone is an ideal way to get them to upgrade their gifts.

Paid employees or trained telephone solicitors can be used but donors will feel far more comfortable with volunteers, particularly those who identify themselves as such on the phone. What they may lack in polish and experience, they gain in credibility. If volunteers are used, they must be trained and they must be scripted. Training can be done by combining a meeting explaining the process with an actual series of phone calls in a group session. First-time volunteers can be paired with those who have more experience during their first evening of a telethon. This helps overcome the initial fear of the process.

Scripting the Volunteers. It is essential that the volunteers are provided with a script from which they can work. In the beginning, the script may be followed verbatim; later, as the volunteers acquire more confidence, they may vary what they say and improvise conversation. However, even the most seasoned caller will sound more knowledgeable and be more secure with a script.

In addition to a script, organizations should also provide a prospect information card for each individual who is to be called. The cards give the caller the necessary background information to customize and personalize the script. In addition to giving a prospect's name and address, the card might tell what the prospect has donated over the last few years as well as other pertinent information (e.g., for a college, the card might typically give the year of graduation, the departmental major of the prospect, and whether he or she played on any athletic teams). If the caller is asking the prospect for an increased gift, the amount sought will usually be listed.

In the following example, a parent/volunteer for Abbott Academy, the small private school described in chapter 5, was given the prospect card shown in figure 8.2 for a telethon that took place in 1990:

FIGURE 8.2. Prospect Card

PROSPECT: Benjamin Smith
SALUTATION: Ben
ADDRESS: 112 Holden Street, Compton, Massachusetts 02138

PHONE: 617–294–4111
YEAR OF GRADUATION: 1978
COLLEGE: Swarthmore College (B.A.)
          Harvard Graduate School of Education (Ed.M., Ed.D.)
OCCUPATION: college professor of music
WIFE: Denise (not Abbott Academy graduate)
CHILDREN: Sally (age 5), Joshua (age 2)
1989 GIFT: $25
1988 GIFT: $25
OTHER INFORMATION:
1. Smith is a musician; while at the school he played flute in the orchestra, sang in the choir,
    and won the music prize in his senior year; be sure to tell him about this year's choir trip
    to Europe
2. Smith has given every year since graduation; be sure to thank for this
3. Be sure to address Smith as "Dr." not "Mr."; use "Ben" if you feel comfortable in doing
    so

The conversation that resulted from the prospect card (together with the
script and outline provided by the school) offers a glimpse of a well-
executed call. The parent/volunteer who made the call was Sam Evans
whose son was a senior at the school. Evans himself did not attend Abbott
Academy so he could not rely on the "fellow alumnus, remember our great
years at the old alma mater" approach. Nevertheless, by taking the basic
script and then improvising, he created a special approach to the prospect.

Phone rings.

SMITH: Hello.

EVANS: Is this Dr. Smith?

SMITH: Yes.

EVANS: This is Sam Evans, a parent/volunteer calling on behalf of Ab-
        bott Academy. Do you have a few minutes?

SMITH: Yes.

EVANS: I am calling for the alumni fund drive and though I am not an
        alumnus myself, I think the reason I was selected to call you, Dr.
        Smith, is that my son is also a flutist and his ambition is to win
        the music prize as you did when you were a senior. I gather you
        have continued with your music since then.

SMITH: Well, yes, actually I have. I continue to play a few concerts now
        and then though my teaching keeps me quite busy. I have always
        been grateful to Abbott Academy for giving me so much encour-
        agement.

EVANS: Yes, that is one of the reasons my wife and I are so enthusiastic
        about the school. The choir is going to Europe to perform this
        coming summer and our son will get to go on the trip.

SMITH: That's wonderful. He is a lucky kid just as I was.

EVANS: Well, we're lucky to have graduates like you, Dr. Smith, and actually that is one of the purposes of this call. On behalf of the school, I want to thank you. You are among that special group of alumni that has given every year since you graduated. That is terrific and we all appreciate it.

SMITH: It's the least I could have done. I often feel greater loyalty to my high school than I do to the college and university I attended afterward.

EVANS: Well, I know the school is grateful. But we are also concerned about the future. There are so many new plans and we really need special help from alumni like you who understand what we are doing and who can make a difference. This call is important because we want you to consider a substantially increased gift this year to the alumni fund.

SMITH: I see.

EVANS: Yes, we wonder if you would consider a gift of $200.
Pause.

SMITH: That's an awfully large increase.

EVANS: Would $150 be more comfortable?

SMITH: Yes, it would.

EVANS: Well, I know the school will appreciate a gift of $150. In fact, I personally want to thank you. This kind of gift will make it possible for the school to move ahead and continue to do the things that both you and I feel are so important. May I send you a pledge card tomorrow for the $150 amount.

SMITH: Okay.

EVANS: Now let me confirm the information. *(Evans checks Smith's name, address, and amount of gift.)* Many, many thanks for your support. I know the committee will be thrilled with your generosity.

SMITH: You're welcome.

EVANS: Good night.

After the phone call, Evans sent Smith the pledge card with a personal note of thanks. After Smith sent in his contribution, another personal letter came from the headmaster of the school thanking him for his increased gift.

As it turned out, this call not only resulted in a gift that represented an increase of $125 over the previous contribution, but the following year the donor, without a special call, decided to give at the $100 level (representing $75 more than the base year gift). Thus by using a personal approach to request the initial upgrade and by making the donor feel good about himself and his gift, a permanently higher level of giving was achieved.

Local Business Giving

Properly cultivated, local businesses can provide another source of ongoing unrestricted income. Any particular business's contribution—often coming in the form of a membership—will probably be small, but if there are enough of them they can provide an important source of revenue. In some cases, the contributions are in forms other than cash. The local supermarket may contribute food toward a fund-raising event, a law office may contribute free legal help, or the bank may contribute its advertising space in the newspaper to help promote an event. All of these contributions should be encouraged no matter what form they come in. The idea is to be as inclusive as possible in soliciting from local businesses—and the more contributors an organization has, the easier it is to get more.

In soliciting from local business, there are certain rules to follow:

☐ Always have a suggested dollar range for unrestricted contributions from local business. The minimum should never be less than $50 and the maximum should not be too high (perhaps between $500 and $1,000). Remember, the idea is to get ongoing gifts from the same sources year after year and this is only possible if the amounts requested are modest.

☐ If a new building or special project is planned, fund raising for this can be done separately and larger amounts can be requested. Such one-time requests for special items should not interfere with the regular annual campaign.

☐ Make it more convenient for existing donors to give again than to drop out of the annual-giving program. You might send a letter at the beginning of your campaign asking them to let you know if they do not wish to be listed as a donor again in your program booklet. Once the booklet is printed, send them a copy, underscore the firm's name, and suggest that this would be a good time to send the check.

☐ Figure out a way to thank businesses publicly. They are contributing to the organization in order to be good community citizens and they want everyone to know that they have done their part. In addition to printed acknowledgments in publicity and press materials, a thank-you party or other gesture of gratitude is important.

☐ First-time solicitation of businesses for the campaign should be done by peers. It is desirable to have a special committee, chaired by a local businessperson, who is responsible for this campaign. This person should find others in the business community to assist with solicitation. If there are not enough businesspeople available, board members and volunteers who are good customers of particular business concerns can also be used.

☐ Use service clubs such as the chamber of commerce or the Rotary Club to let the business community know of the organization's activities. No one wants to contribute to an organization that is not well-known in the community.

☐ Do not confuse program advertisements from local businesses with contributions. An advertisement may be an important first step in winning the support of a business firm, but the ultimate goal should be to get that same business to make a contribution as well.

In general, local business support is important both for the revenue it brings in and for what it tells other funders—especially large corporate donors, foundations, public agencies, and even some wealthy individuals—about community support. Similarly, while funders are generally quite understanding of a nonprofit organization with little support from large corporations, they look askance if there is no support from the local business community. It tells them something about the kind of profile the organization enjoys at home.

PREPARING TO RAISE LARGER GIFTS

Asking for a larger gift will almost always produce restricted funds—that is, it will almost always involve a particular project, activity, or capital need. For that reason, much work needs to be done before a particular request is made for such a gift. Potential donors (individuals, corporations, foundations, and government agencies) need to be identified, researched, and rated (a rating determines a potential dollar range for a potential gift). Matches have to be established between specific programs and projects of the organization and donors' own philanthropic interests. Promotional literature must be assembled. Prospect cards must be prepared (these are similar in format to the Prospect card shown in figure 8.2, but they contain additional information such as how much will be asked for, what the money will be used for, etc.).

The Case for Support

In preparing to solicit larger gifts, an organization must develop a convincing case for support. The case for support is a series of statements that can be used in oral presentations in meetings with prospective donors and can also be incorporated into written proposals and grant applications as will be discussed later in this chapter.

For nonprofit organizations, there are three steps to developing a credible case for support:

1. Identify the important problems or needs that the organization intends to address with the help of the larger contributions
2. Demonstrate the organization's capability to address these needs
3. Match the proposed areas of organizational activity with the funder's own philanthropic interests

Problem (or Needs) Statements. Nonprofit organizations are established for the purpose of solving societal problems and addressing the needs of particular constituencies. Fund-raisers who wish to solicit larger gifts must develop short, tightly written problem (or needs) statements that clarify precisely what these needs are and what constituencies they serve. To the extent possible, these statements should be expressed in quantitative terms. For example, an organization offering financial aid to college-bound students in Compton might state, "In the town of Compton, two out of three graduating seniors cannot afford to attend college without some form of financial assistance." A social service organization might state, "In the past three years, requests for free meals at the Compton facility have increased by 37 percent." An organization that can prepare a varied list of these statements is developing a "menu" of giving opportunities that can suit a number of potential donors with different philanthropic agendas.

Capability Statements. In developing the case for support, an organization must also be prepared to answer an implied series of questions from the funder, "Why you? What makes your organization so special? Why shouldn't I give my money to some other organization?" The way the questions are answered is through so-called capability statements. The big four capability statements that every organization must be able to express clearly are as follows:

- The program and activities of the organization are of high quality
- The organization provides service to a broad constituency
- The organization is well managed and has fiscal accountability
- The organization provides service cost-effectively

In arguing that the programs and activities of the organization are of high quality, it is desirable to use either outsider opinions or specific quantitative indexes. Favorable press statements about an organization's service to the community or documented statistics on client usage will always be more effective than flowery self-assessments.

Funders are concerned that nonprofit organizations serve a broad public because "level of service to the public" is one criterion that many use to determine whether or not an organization is deserving of funding. If an organization serves a multicultural clientele, low-income people, the handicapped, senior citizens, students, or other special constituencies, that fact should be documented and stressed. Organizations should be able to point to the number of people they are serving and show a broad mix of constituent types.

Finally, capability can be argued on the basis of organizational efficiency, prudent financial management, and cost-effectiveness. Other organizations may be able to solve the same problems and may be able to show the same program quality and service to the public. But can they provide the same level of service with the same assurance of financial stability, quality board, and experienced staff? Can they provide the same level of service at the same price? If not, they are at a strategic disadvantage in fund raising. Funders, like the rest of us, like to get more quality for less money.

Strategic Fit. Unfortunately, it is not enough to prove that an organization is serving a societal need and is deserving of money. The needs of the organization must be matched with the funder's own philanthropic interests. No funder can afford to be interested in everything and so people or organizations that give away money have their own special interests, their particular reasons for giving, and their unique philanthropic predilections. Organizations that are successful in garnering funds are those that take the time to learn all about donor preferences and idiosyncracies.

How is this information collected? In the case of public agencies, there are usually published guidelines that make clear what the agency will support, and there is almost always a staff person to clarify any ambiguities in these guidelines. Some corporations and foundations also have printed guidelines; others will have annual reports that show the patterns of past grants. In addition, there are many resource libraries—including the national network of cooperating collections of the Foundation Center in New York—that provide large data bases of information about foundation and corporate donors. Learning how to use these research facilities effectively may significantly improve an organization's success with these funders.

With individual donors, determining strategic fit may be a less predictable process. Some organizations have large development committees that assemble information on potential donors through what one skilled fundraiser calls "systematic gossip." Other organizations collect annual reports and other published donor information from several nonprofits in town, cross-referencing donor lists and trying to establish the capability and interests of particular individual donors. Finally, an organization's own donor history records is a good way to review the giving pattern of individual contributors over time.

It is important to add a cautionary note here. There is sometimes a temptation to respond to a donor's enthusiasms by developing a special program to meet his or her interests. Although this can sometimes produce more cash in the short run, it can also produce financial problems in the long run. What happens if the donor does not fully fund the new program? What happens when he or she loses interest and stops funding it after a year or two? In either case, the contribution can force an organization into having to increase its fund-raising goals while diverting staff time to a program that is not critical to the organization's mission or long-range plans.

A good example of this problem was described by the director of a touring opera company several years ago. "We undertook a tour of the opera 'Carmen' against our better judgment, because a large national foundation was willing to contribute several hundred thousand dollars, but only for that project. In retrospect, that grant almost bankrupted us. We had never toured such a large production. We ended the tour with a near million dollar shortfall. I learned that a contribution can often get you further behind financially than you were before you started."

CORPORATE SUPPORT

One source of larger contributions is corporations.[1] In trying to understand what will motivate a corporation to give money, it is important to remember that the business of a profit-making company is to make money, not to give it away, and its decision to act in a philanthropic way is usually related to some business interest. Generally, one of three factors motivates a corporation to give:

- The gift will influence public opinion about the corporation
- The gift will benefit employees
- The gift will assist in marketing efforts

Influencing public opinion. There are many companies that have generous philanthropic programs because they wish to impress the public that they care about their community, the environment, the needy, or some special cause. Oil companies, major utilities, and companies that manufacture war machinery are just three kinds of corporation that have used corporate giving as a means to counteract a specific public image problem. Other companies maintain an edge over their competitors by projecting an image of strength, generosity, and power through charity.

Employee benefits. Some companies use philanthropy as a way to enhance loyalty and positive feelings among employees. Sometimes the benefits for employees can be very direct such as company-supported daycare centers or cash-matching programs for employee giving. Sometimes they are indirect—such as gifts to major nonprofit organizations in cities and towns where their employees live.

Marketing. When a company comes out with a new product, it is sometimes advantageous to give away free samples as a marketing device. When the recipients of these freebies happen to be nonprofit organizations, the company gets credit for a charitable contribution as well. Another kind of marketing uses philanthropy more subtly to get customers to participate jointly in a philanthropic effort by buying a company's product. Typically, in this form of *cause-related marketing,* the company agrees to contribute a share of the profit from each product sold to a particular nonprofit organization.

Given these sorts of motivating factors, it is extremely important to find out precisely what is behind a corporation's contributions policy before a proposal is submitted. What kinds of contributions has it made? Which kinds of organizations have benefited? Where have they been located? How much, on average have they received?

There are several ways to find out this information and there is a logical sequence of steps to follow:

1. Do some basic research about the corporation. There are several initial things to determine. Is philanthropy handled by a corporate giving department (or some variant such as community relations) or is it handled by an independent corporate foundation? In the case of the former, the level of money to be given away will be closely related to company profits in the previous year; in the case of the second, giving levels will be more predictable from year to year because the corporate foundation's assets are less tied to annual profit figures. It is also important to find out who might be a key person to talk to in the corporation. Sometimes there are several departments involved with nonprofits such as employee relations, marketing, and contributions—a nonprofit group might eventually want to talk to representatives from each of them. Get whatever material you can (such as the company's annual report) and see whether you can get any clues about what kinds of activities were supported in the past.

2. Spend a considerable amount of time seeing whether you can find someone from the company who will get involved with your organization as a volunteer or who will come visit. Later, that person can help you get an appointment with a decision maker in the company.

Alternatively, see if you can find someone outside the company (e.g., another corporate funder or a friend of an officer) who can introduce you either by phone or letter to the funder. At the very least, find someone who agrees to allow you to use his or her name as an introduction.

3. If your contact has called or written on your behalf, requesting that the company representative talk to you for a few minutes, call and ask to speak to that person telling the secretary that your contact told you to call.

4. If you are introducing yourself, you can either send a letter ten days ahead saying that you will call in about a week or you can attempt to get through using your contact's name without a letter.

5. Be polite but firm with the secretary. Do not explain why you are calling or why you wish to speak to the company representative. Simply reiterate that your contact told you it was important to speak to the company representative directly.

6. If and when you finally get through (it may take several calls), explain to the person at the other end of the line that your contact said that he or she could be helpful to you as you plan your fund-raising efforts and that you would like to take fifteen or twenty minutes to discuss your plans. If the person appears negative about your getting money from the company, explain that you really want general advice on your strategy, on other contacts, and on your program and that a short conversation would be very valuable in any case.

7. When you get your interview, keep several things in mind:

☐ The most important purpose of your visit is to find out as much as you can about the company's approach to contributions (the best way to find this out is to get the company representative to feel comfortable and to talk freely; start the conversation with something informal such as asking about the family photograph on the desk).

☐ The second most important purpose is to get the names of other business representatives you should be talking to (ideally, you would like this person to make other introductions for you by phone, more often than not, however, the best you can hope for is being able to use his or her name when you make the calls—but this is a good deal); try to get five names before you leave.

☐ You do want to say something about your organization (remember, though, the person you are talking to is not an expert in your field and will be bored by details); keep your description of your

organization short and practice at home making a cogent six-
minute presentation that emphasizes how your organization's
projects can be helpful to the corporation.

☐ Be sure to ask when is the best time to submit a proposal, what
the range of actual grant amounts have been in the past year, and,
if possible, what kind of project your organization might undertake that would most likely be funded; do not beat around the
bush, you are there to get this information and the person you are
talking to expects to be asked these questions.

☐ *Know when to leave;* plan on staying no longer than twenty-five
minutes and watch carefully to be sure the person you are talking
to is not getting bored (don't mistake politeness for enthusiasm;
if you are unsure about whether you should continue, test the
waters with a comment such as, "I know you must be awfully
busy and I do not want to take too much of your time," this gives
the person a chance to move you out comfortably or to keep you
around a little longer).

☐ Send a thank-you note within a day of the visit summarizing the
advice you were given; this will provide good background material when your proposal actually comes into the corporation (if
you do not send a proposal within three months, keep in contact
with regular letters informing the person of your activities; you
have broken the ice and you must keep the contact alive).

An important piece of information that should be garnered from the
interview is the proper form for a written proposal. Some corporations just
want a one-page letter with a budget. Others want a more formal proposal.
Unless specifically told to do so, nonprofit groups should not submit anything longer than four pages double spaced. Ideally, it should have a
one-page introduction that summarizes the project and financial need
(preferably this page should be in large-size type), a two-page detailed
description, and a budget page. Additional supporting material, such as the
organization's tax determination letter, financial statements from the last
completed fiscal year (preferably audited), and promotional material may
also be requested.

In most cases, support from a corporation will be for a restricted purpose
and it will be only for a short period of time. Organizations that receive
substantial unrestricted gifts from corporations on an ongoing basis are
rare. This is why nonprofit organizations must assess very carefully
whether it is worth spending the time and effort in approaching corporations. They must ask themselves whether they have a program that will
give the company the kind of exposure or benefits it seeks, whether they

have the staff resources to research and cultivate corporate relationships, and whether they want to invest so much time and effort raising money for specific short-term projects.

WRITING PROPOSALS FOR FOUNDATIONS AND PUBLIC AGENCIES

Foundations and government agencies are other important sources of larger restricted grants. In general, research identifying which prospects might be potential funders is quite different for foundations on the one hand and government agencies on the other. In the case of foundations, the best place for a nonprofit organization to begin is at one of the Foundation Center's regional collections. These reference centers—located throughout the United States—vary in the amount of material they contain but most have extensive libraries of books and periodicals, and many include foundation annual reports, newsletters, and, in some cases, foundation tax returns. Some offer user services and the beginning grant seeker may need this kind of help in learning to use such sources as the Foundation Grants Index, the Foundation Directory, sourcebook profiles, state and regional directories, the *National Data Book,* IRS Form 990s, and other materials.

In the case of government funding, the search for funders is more challenging. It is true that the *Catalogue of Federal Domestic Assistance* contains information on every federal funding program with program objectives, types of assistance, uses, and restrictions. But the sheer volume of material in the catalog reduces its effectiveness in locating potential sources of grants. Furthermore, it provides no information on grants that may be available from city, county, and state sources. A more effective way to proceed might be to talk to representatives from other nonprofits in the field to find out where they traditionally apply for money. If the field has a national service organization, this too is an excellent source of information. Finally, public officials and civil servants will often be helpful not only in providing information on where dollars may be available, but may also help in securing the funds. Elected officials especially like to see money coming to the areas they represent and they like to help voters who might help to elect them in the future. They should not be overlooked in seeking government support.

Some foundation and government funders will have detailed forms to fill out, which make the application process easier because the expectations of the funders are clear. In every case, it is important to read the accompanying instructions carefully and give *exactly* the information that is asked for. Whenever possible, the person filling out the forms for the applicant organization should have a conversation with a representative of the foundation or the agency to clarify precisely what is wanted and how the forms are to be filled out. In certain cases, it may even be possible to find out the kinds of emphases the funder might wish to see in the responses to particular questions.

Where forms are not provided, foundations and government agencies will often simply request a proposal, without specifying in detail what it should consist of. Again, it is best to seek as much clarification as possible before writing a proposal and to customize each proposal to the specific funder who will receive it. One may want a very short proposal with an emphasis on the personnel who will be carrying out the activities. Another may wish to know a great deal about how the activities will be evaluated. In every case, it is important find out how many pages, on average, successful proposals have run and to make sure the proposal that is produced conforms closely to this model. Sometimes a foundation or agency staff person may be willing to send a sample successful proposal (always ask to see one), and at other times staff may be willing to review and comment on a proposal before it is submitted.

While proposals vary in length and content, there are certain standard formats that funders expect to see. A typical proposal outline might have the following sections.

☐ *Introduction/abstract.* Typically the proposal begins with an introduction that contains all the pertinent and critical information. It might start with the following words:

> The [name of applicant] seeks [amount requested] from [name of funder] for [purpose of grant]. Funds are sought for the fiscal period beginning on [begin date] and ending on [end date]. The total cost of the project is [amount] and matching funds will be provided by [give either the names of specific funders if you know them or give anticipated categories of matching support such as earned income, individual contributions, government grants, etc.]. This project follows the successful completion of [a board planning retreat, a feasibility study, a pilot program, six years of successful programming, or something else that makes it appear logical in the organization's development].

☐ *Problem/needs statement.* Some description of the problems and needs that the applicant organization will be addressing and the constituencies being served needs to be in the proposal. It is often appropriate to follow the introduction with this section.

☐ *Goals and objectives.* The proposal should go on to describe what is to be accomplished in general terms as well as the specific quantitative objectives and targets to be achieved by the proposed project. For example:

> The goal of the project is drug prevention and it will be accomplished through educational programs for junior-high schoolers. Specifically, in the course of one year, five certified drug counselors will meet with thirty-two junior-high classrooms in the greater Compton area for at least four forty-five-minute sessions.

In drafting the specific time-bound quantitative objectives, it is important to remember that evaluation of the project (assuming the proposal is funded and the project goes forward) will involve assessing whether these targets were met.

☐ *Program description.* This section of the proposal addresses the basic logistical questions of how the program will be carried out and by whom. Timelines and program details are appropriate for this section as well as a description of the qualifications and backgrounds of the individuals who will have primary responsibility for the project. (In some cases, the résumé of the project head may be included as an appendix to the proposal.)

☐ *Capability statement.* Capability statements were discussed earlier in this chapter. They provide a rationale for why the applicant deserves to be funded. Some proposal writers like to put capability statements near the beginning of a proposal (after the abstract); others like to place it later after the project description. Either format is acceptable.

☐ *Evaluation strategy.* Accountability is extremely important to funders and they want to know that the applicant organization intends to evaluate the success of the activity in which they are being asked to invest. At the very least, the proposal should specify how the applicant organization intends to measure whether the objectives and targets were met and how the funder will be informed. On larger scale projects, outside professional program evaluation may also be appropriate.

☐ *Budget.* The budget should show that project expenses will be met by income from all sources (including the requested amount from the funder). On the income side, it is understood that not all contributions and grants will have been firmed up and anticipated amounts can be used. On the expense side, most funders do not like to see high overhead figures; program-related expenses, which may include the salaries of program personnel, should not fall below 80 percent of the total. Some grant seekers like to build in-kind contributions into their budgets. The preferred method of presenting a budget is to include only cash income and expense in the budget itself and to list the value of in-kind contributions separately.

DEFERRED GIVING

In most organizations, individuals provide a substantial number of the large gifts and in many instances, innovative ways are found to extend the advantages of giving to this very important segment of donors. Deferred giving offers many contribution vehicles that provide substantial benefits to a number of different kinds of donors.

Deferred gifts involve arrangements by which a donor makes a commitment of funds but defers the actual transfer of cash, securities, or tangible assets for a period of time. On the surface, it would appear that deferred gifts would be discouraged by nonprofit organizations, especially those that have a need for immediate cash. However, deferred gifts can be so advantageous for donors that these individuals may make much more substantial contributions under such arrangements. Ultimately, nonprofit organizations can benefit handsomely and many build endowments almost entirely through gifts of this type.

What are some situations in which a deferred gift might be appropriate?

☐ An individual would like to make substantial contribution to a nonprofit organization but feels that he cannot give up the security of the income that these funds would provide him and his wife during their lifetimes.

☐ Another donor would like to establish a scholarship fund in honor of her husband but feels that she must hold on to her assets while her aged parents are still living in case they incur large medical bills.

☐ A businessperson who has just sold his company wishes to receive a large charitable income tax deduction in a particular year but does not have enough cash to make a gift that would be sizable enough to realize such a large deduction.

☐ A fifty-year-old woman has just been named president of a company and wants to defer income during her peak earning years; she wants to enjoy this income later when she is in a lower tax bracket.

☐ A forty-year-old man wants to set up an endowment to honor his father but does not have enough cash for an outright gift; he wants to find some way to make annual payments toward the endowment but he wants the fund guaranteed should he die before all the money has been provided.

☐ A woman has inherited stock that has appreciated tremendously in value but that pays no dividend; she does not want to incur substantial capital gains taxes by selling the stock but she would like to figure out some way she could derive income from it.

For each of these individuals—and for many others—there are a variety of deferred giving instruments that allow them to accomplish their goals and help a nonprofit organization at the same time. A few of the most important are discussed below.

Bequests

A bequest is a gift that is made through a donor's will. The advantages to the donor are as follows:

☐ By deferring the gift until after a donor's death, the individual has the use of the assets during his or her lifetime.

☐ A bequest usually provides a tax savings because the gift is deductible from the adjusted gross estate.

☐ A bequest can be changed during the donor's lifetime; it is not an irrevocable gift until the donor dies.

From the nonprofit organization's point of view, a bequest can be welcome but its revocable nature is problematic. Whereas a donor may feel positively toward an organization today, he or she may feel less so at a later date and may change the will. A second disadvantage of a bequest is that there is no guarantee that there will be adequate money in an estate to provide the specified funds. Indeed in some cases, such as a residuary bequest (in which a nonprofit is named to receive the *remainder* of an estate after specific legacies have been fulfilled), the assets of the estate may be inadequate to provide any funds. Nevertheless, bequests have provided the major portion of endowment funds held by nonprofit organizations and their importance in fund raising from individuals should not be underestimated.

Gifts of Life Insurance

Gifts of whole life insurance policies, those that buy protection for a lifetime rather than for a limited time period (as is the case with term insurance), are another important type of deferred gift. Commonly an individual will purchase a policy with a certain face value (the amount the company will pay when the individual dies) and a schedule of premium payments. The individual who wishes to make a gift of life insurance must assign ownership of the policy to a nonprofit organization making it the beneficiary of the policy as well. In order to secure a tax deduction, the individual will make a contribution of the premium payments to the nonprofit organization which in turn pays to the insurance company.

A gift of life insurance offers the following advantages to donors:

☐ As soon as the policy is purchased, the gift is secured; thus even if the individual dies immediately after making the first premium payment, the organization is assured of the gift in full.

☐ The donor enjoys the pleasure of planning the uses of the gift during his or her lifetime.

☐ In the case of younger donors (those under forty-five years of age), a sizable fund can be created with a rather modest investment (for example, a nonsmoking forty-year-old man created a $225,000 gift by purchasing a policy that required contributions of $4,000 a year for seven years).

Life insurance gifts also offer benefits to the nonprofit organization. The *cash value* of the life insurance policy can be listed as an asset on the organization's balance sheet even during the donor's lifetime and this can be used as equity against loans. A life insurance gift can be an excellent way to develop an ongoing relationship and other cultivation opportunities with a donor. The most substantial disadvantage is that the donor can choose to stop paying premiums before the policy is paid up. Under these circumstances, the nonprofit organization itself can choose to pay the premiums or it can cash in the policy for whatever its cash value is at the time.

Charitable Trusts

Charitable Remainder Trust. There are several types of charitable trust that are used as deferred gifts. The most important is the *charitable remainder trust,* which allows a donor to make a substantial gift but to receive income based on the value of that gift for a period of time—either a fixed number of years or the balance of a lifetime (or lifetimes). The donor creates a formal trust and provides a certain sum (usually a minimum of $100,000 which is often given in the form of securities although it can be cash or even real estate). The asset is transferred to the trustee who is responsible for managing the funds during the specified time period of the trust. When the specified period is over, the asset passes to the nonprofit organization. Depending on the type of vehicle, the trust can:

☐ Pay a fixed percentage of the fair market value of the original investment to the beneficiaries (the donor, a spouse, or anyone else named in the trust agreement) for the time period specified in the trust; such is the arrangement with a *charitable remainder unitrust.*

☐ Pay the actual amount of income earned by the trust to the beneficiaries, as is the case with an *income only unitrust.*

☐ Pay a specified fixed amount annually to the beneficiaries, as is the case with a *charitable remainder annuity trust.*

It should be noted that a variety of other special pay-out arrangements can be arranged to meet the needs of specific donors.

There are several advantages to donors:

☐ The most obvious advantage is that the donors need not give up potential income by making a large gift; an income stream can be directed to designated beneficiaries for a specified amount of time thus reducing the risks involved in giving up capital.

☐ Donors get an immediate tax deduction based on what the U.S. Treasury estimates will be the remainder of the original asset after all income has been paid out (for example, a fifty-five-year-old female sets up a trust with a $100,000 contribution that is to pay her $6,000 annually during her lifetime; her tax deduction in the year of the gift is approximately $50,000).

☐ In the case of gifts of securities that have appreciated in value while held by the donor, the trust can sell and reinvest these securities without any capital gains taxes (this is particularly helpful in cases where the original securities were paying no dividends and the donor wishes to get income from them).

☐ Donors are relieved of the responsibility of managing an investment portfolio.

☐ Donors derive the considerable satisfaction of making a major gift during their lifetimes.

The advantage to the nonprofit organization is also considerable:

☐ The gift is irrevocable, which means that even if the donor becomes disenchanted with the organization, it will still receive the funds at the end of the income pay-out period.

☐ Often the donor will make a larger gift because he or she is not giving up income that would be lost if the gift were made outright.

☐ Because the organization has not had to wait for the donor's death to get a significant commitment, there is time for further cultivation for additional gifts.

Charitable Lead Trust. It should be pointed out in passing that there is one other type of charitable trust that allows donors to retain not the income derived from the gift made to the nonprofit but the principal. In a so-called charitable lead trust, the donor transfers income-producing assets to a trust for a period of time. During that period, the income from the trust is paid to one or more nonprofit organizations. At the end of the period the asset—securities, real estate, or cash—returns to the donor.

One of the main advantages of certain types of charitable lead trusts to donors is that their tax deductions on the gift can be accelerated into the first year of the gift (as is the case with trusts established for periods of less than ten years). Thus for someone who wants to offset a particularly high income year with a substantial tax deduction, a charitable lead trust may be an answer. However, because the donor is the owner of the trust, all income earned by the trust will be taxable (this is one reason why such trusts are often created with tax-exempt securities).

For nonprofit organizations, charitable lead trusts produce predictable flows of funds—this is one reason why they are often used to pay off multiyear pledges for capital campaigns (short-term fund-raising drives for new buildings, endowment, or other uses). However, because the asset portion of the trust passes back to the donor, they are often considered a lower priority in the nonprofit organization's fund-raising portfolio.

Pooled-Income Funds

One of the more recent deferred giving vehicles, which dates from the tax reform act of 1969, is the so-called pooled-income fund. A pooled-income fund operates much like a mutual fund. It is set up by a nonprofit organization to attract donors. A donor makes a gift by buying shares (or units) in the pooled-income fund. These are invested by the fund's manager (either the nonprofit organization itself or a designated trustee) in a large diversified portfolio. The donor receives income based on the proportionate value of his or her investment. On the death of a specified beneficiary or beneficiaries (e.g., the donor, a spouse, a friend), the original investment passes out of the pooled-income fund as a direct contribution to the non-profit organization.

Many of the advantages to the donor of a pooled-income fund are similar to those offered by charitable remainder trusts:

☐ The donor need not give up income associated with contributed funds.
☐ The donor can get higher yields on capital appreciated stock in his or her portfolio (the pooled-income fund manager simply sells these and reinvests the proceeds without any negative capital gains tax consequences for the donor).
☐ Donors are relieved of the responsibility of managing an investment portfolio.

In addition, there are some other benefits offered by pooled-income funds:

☐ Unlike charitable remainder trusts, individuals can participate for a relatively small investment—some nonprofit organizations price a unit (or minimum gift) as low as $2,500.

☐ Unlike a charitable remainder trust, a pooled-income fund allows donors to add to their initial contribution as often as they wish.

For nonprofit organizations, pooled-income funds offer the same advantages as charitable remainder trusts in that the gifts made to them are irrevocable and they often encourage larger and more frequent gifts from major contributors. However there are some disadvantages. Perhaps the most serious one is the requirement that the organization must either manage the pooled-income fund or find a trustee to do so. Unless a pooled-income fund is sizable and will end up paying a large return to the institution, it may not be worth the effort and responsibility associated with its management.

THE TEN COMMANDMENTS OF FUND RAISING
Volumes and volumes have been written on the subject of fund raising, with far more advice than can fit into this chapter. Nevertheless, a few more tips follow. These tips, the so-called ten commandments, represent a distillation and condensation of many ideas that, together with good old common sense, make ordinary people into skilled fund-raisers.

Commandment 1: Remember, Only Prospectors Find Gold
A good fund-raising team spends far more time assembling lists of prospects and researching funding sources, than it does actually asking for money. Knowing who to ask is more important than knowing how to ask.

Commandment 2: Be Sure that Courtship Precedes the Proposal
You would never dream of asking someone to marry you before you had a chance to get acquainted and find out whether you were compatible. In the same way, it is far preferable to ask for money after you have had a chance to get to know someone and to find out areas of compatibility between your organization's activities and his or her approach to philanthropy.

Commandment 3: Personalize the Pitch
Every request for money should be tailored, to the extent possible, to the predilections of the giver. Obviously, it is not always practical to customize every request. Nevertheless, every different type of small giver deserves a special approach and every prospective large donor deserves a specially tailored request that takes into consideration everything you know about his or her likes and dislikes. Blanket fund raising is rarely as successful as targeted requests.

Commandment 4: If You Want Bread, You Need Dough

What is true for the baker is equally true for the fund-raiser. Money rarely materializes without something to prime the pump. People who give money are conservative and they are more likely to contribute to an operation that already has a long list of donors associated with it. Public agencies will require matching funds; corporations may wish to see substantial earned income. But in almost all cases, donors will want to see that you have other sources of cash before they join in.

Commandment 5: When Asking for Money, Assume Consent

Do you remember the last time someone tried to sell you life insurance? He or she never used the words "*if* you buy this policy," but rather "*when* you buy this policy." He or she avoided being tentative and did not give you many opportunities to say no without actually being rude. A good fund-raiser should use the same approach, always assuming in all communication that the prospective donor will ultimately be making a contribution.

Commandment 6: In Written Requests, If You Can't Scan It, Can It

Most fund-raising letters and proposals are not read carefully, they are scanned. All other things being equal, those that receive the most thorough review are the ones that are most legible and easy to read at a glance. Fund-raising letters should be short with ample margins; proposals should have plenty of headings, bulleted lists, underlinings, and other scanning devices. Also, of course, brevity is the greatest of all virtues. As one funder says, "The success of proposals being funded is in inverse relation to their length and weight."

Commandment 7: In Designing Budgets, Use the Old Math

For those lucky souls trained in what was once called the new math, they have a sophisticated understanding of mathematical concepts even though they may be a bit rusty on their multiplication tables. When asking for money, however, these individuals better get hold of a calculator and make sure their figures add up correctly. Nothing makes a poorer impression than a budget that is incorrect. It gives funders little faith in the organization's ability to handle money if the numbers do not even look right on paper.

Commandment 8: When in Doubt, Communicate in English

Why is it that fund-raisers think that jargon impresses? There is nothing as nice as a clear, short sentence, composed of words of one syllable or less. (Obviously, there is no such thing as a word of less than one syllable, but funders wish there was.) Nouns and verbs, especially when they are very specific, are the meat and potatoes of a good proposal or letter. A large number of adjectives and adverbs is usually the mark of a weak request. When you claim that your organization is wonderful, the funder is unimpressed—after all, what else are you going to say? If you want to include such value judgments, at least have the good taste to quote someone else.

Commandment 9: Don't Take a No Personally

Fund raising is hard on people who are sensitive and do not like rejection, because even good fund-raisers hear the word *no* more often than they hear the word *yes.* But after a time, the experienced fund-raiser looks on a no answer to a request as a challenge—it may be no this year, but it will be yes the next time around. The good fund-raiser should insert an internal translator in his or her brain that converts the word *no* to the words *come back.* Persistence, after all, usually pays, especially in fund raising.

Commandment 10: No Matter How Many Times You Said Thank You, Say It Again

The secret of fund raising is not in getting the donor's first contribution, it is in getting the second and third. Developing an ongoing group of loyal supporters is essential and can only be done if just as much attention is paid to donors after they give as before. For those contributors who give large amounts of money, there should be regular correspondence updating them on the progress of the organization's activities. For smaller donors, an occasional newsletter may be much appreciated. Mention of contributors in press materials or a special thank-you party is another way of showing your gratitude. Never take your contributors for granted and never miss an opportunity to say thanks.

CHECKLIST QUESTIONS FOR CHAPTER 8

1. Has your organization developed strategies to increase the number and amount of ongoing, individual, unrestricted gifts?
2. Does your organization evaluate its direct mail solicitations before sending them out? Are letters personalized? Are there follow-up mailings to those who do not respond?
3. Does your organization do at least one fund-raising event annually? Are volunteers utilized effectively? Does income from events increase each year as it should?
4. Does your organization fund raise by phone? Are callers properly trained and scripted? Is adequate research done on each prospect and his or her giving history before a call is made?
5. Does your organization fund raise from a wide variety of local businesses? Is solicitation done by peers (other local businesspeople) and/or customers? Is there a convenient way for businesses to renew their gifts each year without responding to a special request for funds?
6. Has your organization developed appropriate problem/needs statements for inclusion in proposals? Has it developed capability statements?
7. Does your organization do extensive research on corporate prospects and visit them before submitting proposals? Do proposals to foundations and public agencies reflect the guidelines and priorities of the funder?
8. Has your organization explored bequests, gifts of life insurance, charitable trusts, and pooled-income funds? Does the organization educate donors about the advantages of these and other deferred giving vehicles?

9
Planning

In the 1950s, in an imaginary part of the United States, two mousetrap companies enjoyed halcyon days. Business was good—sales were strong, profit margins were large, employees were happy. While the two companies vied for the title of number one in the mousetrap manufacturing business, demand for the product was so strong that the competition was friendly. The two companies manufactured quality mousetraps that were hardly distinguishable from one another except for the company labels: the traps had a wooden base and the spring action mechanism connected to it was of high grade copper wire. Indeed, the very names of the two companies— Better Mousetraps, Inc. and The Superior Trap Company—gave an accurate indication to consumers that the products being manufactured were top of the line.

Although the products manufactured by these companies were similar, their respective styles of management were very different. Better Mousetraps Inc. (BMI) was a fourth-generation family business. Its president prided himself on running the company the way his father, grandfather, and great-grandfather had. "We make the same product the same way we always have," he used to boast, "and I have no doubt that four generations of our customers have used our product with complete satisfaction." The president of The Superior Trap Company (STC), a relative newcomer to the industry, was a business-school graduate who was constantly involved in product and market research as well as in strategic planning. While BMI's president took larger and larger profits out of his company, STC's president used some of his company's earnings to fund a planning division that experimented with alternative materials in the manufacture of traps, considered other uses for its products, and assessed possible changes in consumer demand.

In the 1970s, both companies experienced some serious reversals brought on by greatly increased costs for materials and a decreased demand for mousetraps. The price of copper doubled in a period of less than eighteen months and there was a mysterious, gradual, and unexpected drop in consumer demand. Mousetraps simply were not selling as well as they had in the 1950s in spite of the increase in the general population. This seemingly unexplainable shift in demand turned out to be the result of the

231

oil crisis of the early 1970s. Because the price of oil had shot up so rapidly and gasoline was in short supply, many people were traveling less and staying home more. The increased hours at home were so lonely that a large number of these people decided to keep pets. The majority of the pets were cats, and because cats perform the same services in the mouse-elimination business as traps do, the need for mousetraps decreased.

For BMI, the double reversal of increased cost and decreased demand spelled disaster. The president, who had done everything the way three generations of his family had done it, was convinced that bad times would pass and that persistence, hard work, and tradition would pay off. He was wrong. In 1981, BMI declared bankruptcy. For STC, the situation was quite different. When the price of copper increased, the company sub-stituted a scented shiny steel wire, claiming, as it did so, that ten years of product research had proven that this new, less expensive trap was 22 percent more effective than the old models. For the next five years, STC captured a larger and larger share of the trap market, thereby further exacerbating BMI's problems. But STC's president knew that this was only a temporary solution and that, indeed, the trap business was doomed by changes in consumer habits and living patterns.

In 1977, STC created a wholly owned subsidiary, SuTraComp. The high-tech–sounding name stood for Superior Trap/Computer, which was appropriate given the product the company became best known for. That product was a high-quality computer printout clip—a clip that looked remarkably like the mousetrap the parent company was manufacturing except that its wooden base was decorated not with the head of a mouse, but with a pictorial rendition of a computer terminal and printer spewing forth reams of paper that were gathered up in a compclip (as the product was called). STC spent the next three years marketing the compclip. Ten years of research and planning had indicated that the compclip would be a tremendous seller and, thanks to the company's patent, would be without serious competition.

In the same year that BMI declared bankruptcy, STC discontinued its manufacture of mousetraps. Or, perhaps it would be more accurate to say that STC discontinued calling its product a mousetrap. The compclip was now selling so well that STC's president bought up the remnants of the BMI business and hired the former employees to manufacture the "deluxe compclip," as the copper wire mousetrap was now called. That same year, STC went public and gained a listing on the American Stock Exchange; its president turned down the top job at ailing General Motors. That was also the year that he managed to pay back all of his outstanding loans to business school.

The preceding apocryphal story illustrates the importance of planning.

Two companies, both with identical products and markets, ended up at very different points principally because one was willing to allocate resources to long-range planning and the other was not. The successful company (STC) was willing to forego some of its profits in order to underwrite the cost of a planning team; the less successful company (BMI) was not. STC's planners evaluated the company's current operations, charted long-range trends in the marketplace, and considered the ramifications of a variety of alternative scenarios; BMI did none of these things. Although BMI appeared to be more profitable than STC in the 1950s, the failure to allocate some of its resources to planning proved very costly in the end. The company's president learned too late that planning is not a luxury, it is a necessity.

PLANNING FOR NONPROFIT ORGANIZATIONS

In the environment of the profit sector, planning is fairly straightforward. This is because the mission of profit-making companies is clear: They are supposed to make money. In the nonprofit world, where the missions of organizations revolve around the more nebulous concept of public service, planning is less straightforward. Whereas profit is an easy thing to measure, public service is not. In a profit-making company, a planner can devise and evaluate a number of strategies for making more money and can measure the relative effectiveness of each through quantitative tests. But when the same planner looks to the future in a nonprofit organization, he or she may discover that the governing group does not even agree on the central mission of the organization. While all may agree that the organization is supposed to serve the public, the form of this service is a bit different in each person's mind. For example, a hospital may define its central mission as providing quality healthcare to the public, but each member of the board and staff may interpret that mission a little differently. One person may believe that the emphasis should be on quality care (top-flight doctors, up-to-date equipment, and a university affiliation), while another may believe that service to the public mandates healthcare for a very broad group of clients, including the indigent and others who cannot or will not pay.

If the lack of agreement over mission is one problem in planning for nonprofit organizations, disagreements about strategies to accomplish the mission is another. Supposing that the board and staff can reach a consensus about an organization's mission, they must then debate the best strategy for carrying out that mission. Should a senior citizen service organization emphasize information and referrals to its clients or should it run programs such as Meals on Wheels or recreational activities? Should a multiracial, multiethnic daycare center support itself through government contracts or by a sliding scale tuition? Should a food co-op fulfill its mandate of political activism by developing position papers for political candidates or by boycotting the purchase of lettuce and grapes harvested by nonunion workers? Because the missions of the respective nonprofit organizations are general at best and ambiguous at worst, the strategies for accomplishing them are not clear-cut.

Finally, as if the problems over missions and strategies were not enough, there is an additional problem in determining success criteria and evaluation strategies in nonprofit organizations. How does a nonprofit know whether it is doing a good job in carrying out its mission and accomplishing its goals? For the profit-making company, the measurement of success is relatively simple. It is accomplished through an examination of the financial balance sheet. A series of numbers shows whether the company is succeeding and compares its current performance with performance in other years. Unfortunately, in the nonprofit world, success is not only more difficult to measure but it is even difficult to define. One trustee of a community theater might argue that the cost-effectiveness of the organization's inner-city program is an appropriate measure of its success, another may feel that the proper criterion is the number of clients served, and still another may argue that success should be judged by the critical response to the program by the media.

With so much disagreement over mission, strategies, and success criteria, it is no wonder that many nonprofit organizations resist planning. The reasons for not planning are varied. Typically, nonprofit organizations will argue that:

- Planning takes too much time and effort—staff and board are already overworked (a variant of this argument is that this is simply not the right time for planning because there is too much work or too many crises to deal with)
- Planning is too expensive—there is no extra money in the budget for consultants, the costs of meetings, and other expenses
- Planning saps organizational initiative—a long-range plan does not allow an organization to remain open and responsive to constituents

Not one of these arguments is justified. To argue that staff and board do not have enough time to do planning is a bit like arguing that the fiscal officer does not have time to prepare a budget and the treasurer does not have time to review it. Because these tasks are a part of their job responsibilities, they must make time. To argue that there is no money in the budget to pay for planning is like saying that there is nothing in the budget for rent and utilities. If the money is not there, it should be put there. To argue that an organization should be responsive to its constituency is an argument *for* planning, not against it, because planning involves an analysis of the needs of the constituency both in the present and in the future.

There is only one justifiable argument against planning. When planning is done badly, it is not only a waste of time but it also saps the energies and the spirit of an organization's board, staff, and sometimes even its constituency. Long, laborious, expensive planning processes that result in voluminous documents that no one reads are an argument against planning. Yet, planning is so important, and its absence leaves an organization so vulnerable, that it is worthwhile to attempt to find a planning process that can work, which is the subject of the balance of this chapter.

WHAT IS A PLANNING PROCESS?
Planning is an ongoing process involving several steps that are listed below.

Step 1: Set parameters and boundaries
Step 2: Identify limiting conditions
Step 3: Change limiting conditions where possible
Step 4: Design a plan of action
Step 5: Carry out the action plan
Step 6: Evaluate what you have done
Step 7: Repeat what you have done

Planning a Garden
In order to gain a better understanding of what each step involves, imagine that you are a gardener and that you have been given the task of taking a plot of land, turning it into a garden, and maintaining that garden year after year. If you went through the seven steps, you would do the following things.

Set Parameters and Boundaries. First, you would determine the boundaries of your garden, taking into account your property lines, the general contour of the land, how much you wanted to produce in the garden, and how hard you were willing to work. You would make your decisions with care, thinking about the long-term future of this garden. After all, once you decided on the boundaries, prepared the ground, built fences, and put in the surrounding trees and lawn, you would be reluctant to go through the time, expense, and stress that would be required to make a change.

Identify Limiting Conditions. Second, you would identify conditions that determined what you could plant in your garden. Climate would be the first limiting factor: When does the ground freeze and thaw? How much rainfall is there and how long are the dry periods? How many hours of daylight and how much direct sun will different parts of the garden receive? A second factor would be soil conditions: Is the soil acidic or alkaline? Sandy or clay? Does it have adequate organic nutrients? A third constraint would involve your budget: How much money are you willing to spend on the garden? How much help are you likely to get (both in manpower and dollars) to stretch the resources that you have?

Change Limiting Conditions Where Possible. Third, you would now see if there were ways to change some of the limiting conditions you had identified in the previous step. For example, if you had determined that the ground stayed frozen until late March, yet you knew you wanted to start some of your vegetables well before that time, you might consider investing in a greenhouse or a cold frame, or you might decide to buy seedlings instead of seeds. If you discovered that an oak tree shaded half of the garden for three hours in the afternoon, you might decide to cut it down or at least remove some of its limbs. If you found out that your soil was poor, you would seriously consider adding fertilizer. But how much money would you be willing to spend in preparing the soil and making some of these other changes? Remember, your limited budget has to cover these modifications plus the cost of the garden itself. Or does it? Is your budget really inelastic or is this another limitation that you may be able to modify?

Design a Plan of Action. Fourth, you are now ready to plan the specific actions you will take. In essence, you are ready to lay out the garden. You will decide how to prepare the ground, what seeds and plants to buy, whether to do some preplanting in a greenhouse or cold frame, when you need outside help, when to harvest the produce, what you must do to winterize the garden and protect certain plants from harsh weather after the first growing season, and on and on. Unfortunately, there are many gardeners (even experienced ones) who initiate the planning process at this point, without completing the essential preparatory steps. While they may have excellent gardens, the gardens themselves tend to look the same year after year. The boundaries have been established years before and there has never been any thought about changing them. The gardeners have learned, often by trial and error, what grows and what does not, so they tend to plant the same thing in the same place year in and year out. But despite the fact that their gardens look nice, these gardeners are creatures of habit. This can be a problem if changes occur over which they have little or no control (a sudden shrinking of budget, acid rain, a need to expand the boundaries of the garden). These gardeners have few strategies for respond-ing to such change.

Carry Out the Action Plan. Fifth, you are now ready to carry out the plan for the garden. If you have done all the preceding steps correctly, your garden should end up growing well. There will be some surprises and some disappointments, but for the most part, your garden should look quite acceptable. If it does not, chances are you skimped on your planning because you were so excited about actually starting right in on planting. This, unfortunately, is the plight of most inexperienced gardeners. They actually begin by planting their gardens and the results are often unfortu-nate. Because they have done virtually no planning, they do not know what grows best or what they can do to improve the conditions for growth. They go to a nursery and buy lovely healthy plants only to see these plants wither in the ground two weeks later. They complain that they do not have the proverbial green thumb, not realizing that green thumbs are not inherited but are earned by good planning and hard work.

Evaluate What You Have Done. Sixth, if your garden is growing well, you are probably more worried about weeds, rodents, and insects than you are about next year's garden. But as you plant, cultivate, and weed, and as you pick your flowers and harvest your vegetables, you must carefully observe your successes and your failures with an eye toward next year's garden. Evaluation is an essential component of good planning because it allows you, the gardener, to test your hypotheses and adjust them in the future based on actual events.

Repeat What You Have Done. Seventh, it is time to repeat the process for next year. Actually, the process is a bit different the second time around. As you were planning your first garden, you spent a great deal of time on Step 1 determining the shape, contours, and boundaries of the garden. During the second year, it is unlikely that you will spend nearly as much time thinking about this. However, you will find it important periodically to review Step 1. As your resources increase, you may become more ambitious and want to add a rock garden where you originally thought gardening was out of the question; as you grow older, you may want to shrink the boundaries of your garden so that you can still manage things without too much strain. Whatever you decide, you want to do it with adequate thought and deliberation, not just on impulse.

There is one other observation to make about your garden planning. Although a sequence of steps has been given, it is quite possible that a skilled gardener may be working on several steps at the same time and may be planning for several different years at once. For example, a gardener may be thinking now about changing the boundaries of his garden five years hence. At the same time, he or she may be planning the ramifications this will have on budget, soil preparation, and cold frame construction over the next three years while planning the specific layout of this year's garden. A skilled planner knows that planning is an ongoing process in which many things interact simultaneously.

Planning in a Nonprofit Organization
In a nonprofit organization, each of the steps just described must take place in a planning process.

Set Parameters and Boundaries. When the organization is first set up, the broad parameters of its activities must be established. They are generally documented in a mission statement. Periodically, this mission statement should be reviewed so that trustees can make sure the organization is still operating within the established boundaries. If it is appropriate, the mission statement should be amended to set new boundaries for organizational activities. Indeed, an organizational planning process should always involve a careful review (and, if necessary, a reworking) of the mission statement.

Identify Limiting Conditions. Planners for a nonprofit organization must also look at those factors that constrain its activities—budgetary considerations, government regulations, the wishes of its constituency and membership, societal trends, increased competition, and a negative public image—to understand what limitations must be taken into account in planning.

Change Limiting Conditions Where Possible. The planners must then decide which of those constraints can be modified or changed and which are worth changing. For example, additional fund raising might eliminate some budget constraints, a public relations or education campaign might reverse a negative public image, and political activism might lead to changes in certain government regulations.

Design a Plan of Action. After changing what limiting conditions they can, the nonprofit organization's planners must map out a specific action plan for the immediate future. The plan should include goals, objectives, activities, and a budget (which makes priorities clear).

Carry Out the Action Plan. The specific activities described in the action plan must then be implemented.

Evaluate What You Have Done. The activities must be evaluated to help future planning.

Repeat What You Have Done.

LEVELS OF PLANNING

One way to think about planning is to view it sequentially as a series of steps as we have just done. This can be somewhat misleading because a group of planners will probably not wait for one step to be completed before beginning on another. In fact, several planning steps may be taking place at the same time. For that reason, it is probably more useful to talk about levels of planning as follows:

- The level of purpose or mission
- The level of goals
- The level of objectives and targets
- The level of strategies (timeline, action plan, budget)
- The level of actions
- The level of evaluation

Planning levels relate closely (but not precisely) to the planning steps described in the previous section. Let us look at this more carefully. A planning process is a road map to help an organization make a journey from one place (here and now) to another (some point in the future):

- Level one, *purpose or mission,* reveals why the organization is making the journey
- Level two, *goals,* provides the general direction it is heading
- Level three, *objectives and targets,* reveals the destination
- Level four, *strategies,* tells specifically how the organization will get there
- Level five, *actions,* is the trip itself
- Level six, *evaluation,* determines whether you arrived

How can these levels be translated into a planning process for a nonprofit organization? The question can be answered by looking at planning within a specific nonprofit organization.

THE COMPTON MEMORIAL HOSPITAL

The *purpose* or *mission* of the hospital was set out at its inception, is reviewed periodically, and occasionally, is even amended. A mission statement tells the world why the organization exists and the general categories of activities within its purview. The mission of the Compton Memorial Hospital is "to provide quality healthcare to the residents of Compton." At first glance, it would appear that such a mission statement would never have to be revised. After all, providing quality healthcare is what a hospital is all about. Yet, it is quite possible that in fifty years hence a new, more modern hospital may be established in Compton. At that point, Compton Memorial must decide whether it wants to compete (with its outdated plant and equipment), wants to go out of business, or wants to change its mission (it might become an out-patient facility). At that point, its governing group must examine the mission statement and determine the nature and scope of changes that need to be made.

At the second planning level, the level of *goals,* a more specific series of statements must be developed setting the direction of the organization's activities for the shorter term. Thus while the Compton Memorial Hospital's mission is "to provide quality healthcare to the residents of Compton," its specific goals for the next five years might be:

- To establish an out-patient unit
- To improve administrative practices, particularly in the areas of record keeping and billing
- To pursue collaborative planning of healthcare delivery with surrounding hospitals
- To establish greater financial stability through increased fund raising

Although goal statements are more specific than a mission statement in setting a direction for the organization, they do not state exactly what the organization is going to do, how it is going to do it, and what the criteria will be to determine success. What goal statements do provide is the framework for deciding these more specific questions.

It is at the third planning level, the level of *objectives and targets,* that the goals are interpreted, made more specific, and quantified. An objective is a destination statement. It describes very specifically where an organization wishes to go. Every objective carries with it either a stated or implied target, a measurable benchmark that determines whether the organization achieved the objective. Thus goals give a general indication of direction, objectives indicate the destination, and targets offer criteria for judging whether the destination was reached.

For example, one of the hospital's goals is "to improve administrative practices, particularly in the area of record keeping and billing." The problem with that statement by itself is that it is too general. No one knows specifically what things need to be achieved in order to carry out the goal successfully. Therefore, an objective and a target must be developed such as computerizing the entire billing system within two years. Another goal of the hospital is to establish greater financial stability through increased fund raising. A related objective and target might be to increase private donations by 10 percent a year for three years.

At this point in the planning process, great care must be taken to set realistic targets because the targets will determine the success criteria by which performance will be evaluated. In the case of the computerized billing system, staff members should not agree to an unrealistic timetable; in the case of the increased fund-raising target, board members should be confident that they have the time and are willing to make the commitment that such an optimistic target suggests. In the end, success is judged not by the optimism of the original objective but by whether the target was achieved.

The fourth level of planning involves *strategies* for carrying out the objectives and reaching the targets. Strategies are also called action plans. If objectives tell us where we want to get, strategies and action plans tell us how we are going to get there and how much it will cost. (A complete action plan includes a detailed budget.) Because action plans assign specific costs to particular objectives, they are generally worked up by staff and fully discussed by the board before a set of objectives and targets is approved. For example, the board of the Compton Memorial Hospital did not agree to increase private donations by 10 percent a year for three years until the staff had come up with an action plan to show how this could be accomplished and how much it would cost. The action plan budgeted for a fund-raising consultant during the first year of the campaign, called for additional volunteers (to be recruited by a board committee) to work on an annual telethon, mandated another board committee to organize an annual auction beginning in the second year, and suggested the need for a senior-level staff person (with clerical assistance) to coordinate the campaign. These strategies represented only a small part of the staff's total action plan for this objective.

The fifth level of planning is the implementation of the action plan itself *(actions)*. Very little actual planning goes on at this level as this is more of a doing phase. However, careful monitoring must take place to be sure that the implementation is proceeding on schedule. For example, the Compton Memorial Hospital assigned two board members to develop a volunteer list for the telethon. After two months, nothing had been done

(one board member had had a death in the family and the other was simply overwhelmed by the task). For that reason, modifications were made in the action plan—four board members were asked to find volunteers and a staff person was assigned to assist this group on a half-day-a-week basis.

The sixth and final level of planning is *evaluation.* Evaluation asks the questions: Did we achieve our targets? Why or why not? How can we do better next time? Evaluation is an extremely important planning tool because it provides concrete information on the organization's performance potential based on past experience. As a result, it makes future planning easier and more realistic. For example, when the board of the Compton Memorial Hospital examined the performance of its fund-raising drive after three years, it found that private donations had not increased significantly for the first eighteen months of the campaign but thereafter increased 25 percent in a twelve-month period. The evaluator's conclusion was that it takes several months to set up a good fund-raising campaign and that the board should not have expected concrete results immediately. This fact was extremely useful to the board as it planned its fund-raising target for the next three years. The target called for a 30 percent increase over a three-year period with the increases phased annually at 5 percent, 10 percent, and 15 percent.

Planning Level Responsibilities

One of the advantages of looking at planning in terms of levels is that it can be a more useful framework for determining who is responsible for what in the planning process itself. For example:

- The board of directors, with the assistance of the chief executive, bears primary responsibility for the mission statement
- The board, with the assistance of senior staff, is responsible for setting goals
- Board and staff are jointly responsible for setting objectives and targets
- Staff, with some assistance from the board, is responsible for determining strategies
- Staff is responsible for implementing the action plan
- Board and staff are responsible for approving an evaluation plan; ideally some evaluation should be done by an objective outsider

Although planning level responsibilities are allocated between board and staff, it is important to keep in mind that others may also participate in the process. These include:

- Constituents, funders, and other important community representatives whose opinions might be sought in the process of planning
- Organizational volunteers, who can be used strategically in gathering information and participating in planning discussions
- A community resource person (or several), unconnected with the organization, who might be invited to become part of the core planning group to provide an objective view of issues
- A paid consultant who might assist with setting up a planning process and schedule, might lead discussions, do research, write reports, and assist the staff with logistics

PLANNING MODELS

There are numerous approaches to planning in nonprofit organizations. It is probably not very important for administrators and board members of nonprofit organizations to become familiar with each and every one of them. What is important is to understand the two underlying approaches to planning—linear planning and integrated planning—which ultimately dictate what planning approach is chosen. Each of these approaches has its own particular advantages and disadvantages. Once these are fully understood, the governing group of a nonprofit organization, together with its senior staff, can develop a specific model of planning that seems appropriate both for the organization and the particular planning situation.

Linear Planning

Most of the planning that has been described in the chapter to this point has been based on fairly classic planning models. For the most part, these models are based on a linear approach that begins with a general discussion by the governing group concerning organizational purpose or mission and ends, much later, with the issuing of a formal document detailing long-range goals, objectives, strategies, and so on. This approach assumes that planning is initiated periodically at particular periods in an organization's history and that such a planning "intervention" will have a beginning point and an end point. The linear model is usually quite comprehensive and can be undertaken for several reasons:

- Plans of this type can be carried out in order to create new organizations
- Organizations can produce such plans on a periodic basis (e.g., every five years) so that mission, goals, objectives, and action plans for the interval have been self-consciously developed and approved by the governing group

- Organizations may be required to do such plans by a funder as a condition of receiving grant support
- Organizations taking on major new programs, building a building, undertaking a capital campaign, or considering a change in direction can find this approach useful in developing a clear vision of the future
- The linear approach is often used when an organization needs to demonstrate wide involvement of the general public in the planning process or has to draft a plan that will become a public document open to review and comment by friends and foes alike

Linear planning proceeds by a process of condensation and distillation following the steps outlined earlier in the chapter. It considers a whole range of options at each level of planning (mission, goals, objectives, and strategies) and in each case eliminates all but the very few that appear most reasonable and sensible. The linear planning model is best described visually by a triangle as shown in figure 9.1. The triangle, a visual metaphor for linear planning over time, reveals two special characteristics of this approach to planning. First, it shows how linear planning always proceeds from a process of broad mission and goal formulation to the more narrow

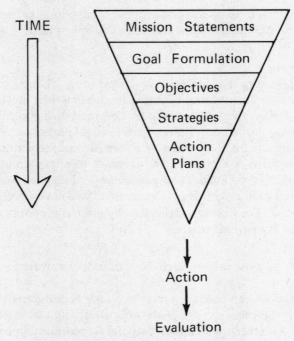

Figure 9.1. Linear Planning

and specific process of writing action plans and, second, it shows how linear planning tends to slough off many options and narrow down to a very few.

Linear planning has advantages and disadvantages. The principal advantage is its comprehensiveness. When a nonprofit organization wants to look at itself in a systematic way, evaluating and speculating about its future in a wide variety of areas, the linear approach works well. Similarly, when the organization undertakes a controversial, risky, or expensive new project, or significantly changes its mission, it can prove to the world at large that the new direction has not been undertaken lightly, that many people have been consulted, and that many options have been considered. Another advantage is that a linear planning process often generates a formal public document that provides the framework for actions and protects the organization from pressures to consider other approaches.

Unfortunately, the very comprehensiveness of linear planning is one of its major disadvantages. It is often a slow and frustrating process. Many organizations spend months drafting mission statements, begin to tackle goals, and simply give up in exhaustion without a plan and without a willingness to continue planning in the future. Inflexibility is a second disadvantage. Once a plan has been drafted and approved, it can be very difficult to change. Should conditions change, if opportunities arise, if the plan itself does not seem to be on track, the plan is not easy to modify. Additionally, such a lengthy process often places an organization in a holding pattern that restricts the implementation of new initiatives. A good way to see how a linear planning process might work is to review how one organization managed the task.

THE CRAFT SOCIETY

The Craft Society is a thirty-year-old nonprofit whose activities have included the exhibition and sale of contemporary crafts, the establishment of a permanent craft collection, and an educational program. The group decided to undertake a planning process after a major funder stated that a five-year plan would be required if the organization wished to apply for a major challenge grant to develop an endowment.

The first step in the process was to lay out a schedule and budget for the planning process itself. This was done by a planning committee of the board, which included the executive director as a member. The schedule and budget for the planning process were reviewed by both the staff and the full board. After making some changes based on suggestions from these two groups, the board approved the schedule for planning. A budget range was also approved and an effort was made by some of the trustees to secure outside funding. In the end, a $10,000 grant was secured toward a $22,000 planning budget. Funds were to be used for consultant assistance ($15,000), temporary assistance to ensure sufficient staff release time ($4,000), and miscellaneous travel and office expenses ($3,000).

The next step was to identify potential consultants who could assist with the planning process. Through phone calls to similar organizations around the country, six consultants were identified. Five expressed interest and sent material about themselves and their firms, but one of these was far too expensive to be considered by the society and two did not seem to have the right mix of experience. The remaining two were interviewed by the executive director and members of the planning committee. A consultant was ultimately selected whose expertise, approach, and personality seemed best suited to the Craft Society's needs.

The kickoff for the planning process itself was a two-day retreat planned and led by the consultant. The retreat was designed to give the board and the staff an opportunity to *review the mission statement* and then to evaluate each of the society's major areas of program activity (exhibition, collection, education, and sales) and organizational areas (governance, staffing, fund raising, and general administration). Participants were also asked to develop a list of the most important activities the society should engage in over the next decade, put them in priority order, and then identify the organizational changes that would be required to accomplish these things.

After the retreat, the planning process continued. Committees were appointed by the president of the board to focus on the various programs, activities, and functions of the society identified and discussed at the retreat. These committees were composed of board members, staff, and some community people not formally associated with the organization (it was felt that this latter group could contribute a great deal to the discussion). For the next six months, the committees met to flesh out the priorities for the areas assigned to them. To accomplish this task, additional research was needed in certain cases. Staff members and the consultant were used to investigate the feasibility of certain activities, conduct market research, and interview key committee leaders, funders, and media representatives.

At the end of the six months, each committee had a short written document representing the group's consensus. It began with a statement that outlined the importance of the area in the overall functioning of the society. It also included:

- A *list of the goals* to be accomplished by the program during the time period covered by the plan (including *specific and measurable objectives* for each goal)
- A preliminary description of budget and staff implications of the goals
- An outline of the necessary fund-raising, marketing, and other activities needed to accomplish the goals

The material from each committee was collated and summarized by a staff person and sent to all participants. A second board retreat was organized to review all of the material presented, to set priorities, and to begin to assemble and approve the goals and objectives of the long-range plan. Senior staff was invited to participate in this retreat and to provide a reality check on whether the directions, targets, and activities being considered by the board were reasonable and achievable.

The next step involved completing the action plan for a five-year time period. The consultant wrote a report consisting of:

- A summary of the goals and objectives already approved by the board
- A five-year timeline, broken down into six-month units, showing when particular activities would occur
- A narrative description of what would be taking place in each of the activity areas
- A discussion of staffing issues including staff additions and reorganization
- Two versions of a five-year budget—one based on conservative assumptions about revenues (and activity levels and expenses), the other based on more optimistic assumptions (this product was similar to the framework budgets described in chapter 6)
- A five-year fund-raising plan
- An evaluation plan

The planning document was circulated to the full board a month before the final planning meeting. This allowed adequate time for board members to read the report carefully. At the meeting, which was led by the consultant, the board asked questions, raised concerns, made modifications, and ultimately approved a somewhat revised version of the plan. The consultant then made the revisions in the planning document.

In designing this process, the society ran into some problems that required special solutions:

☐ *The make-up of the working committees.* Ideally, the committees were to be composed of board members and other individuals, including senior staff and community resource people. However, in some cases, there were limitations both on the time board members were willing to commit to the process and the availability of others outside the organization. Thus the society used two other approaches to prepare the initial planning papers. First, the board itself served as a planning group for some areas, making sure that efforts were made to gather ideas and opinions from a larger body of interested individuals. Second, a consultant was used to research other areas and to make written recommendations. In particular, his expertise was sought in evaluating and making recommendations about the internal operations of the society because it was decided that no one on the board or staff had sufficient objectivity to conduct this assessment. Furthermore, a group of the staff was assigned some areas and it prepared position papers that were submitted to the planning committee for regular review and comment.

☐ *Oversight of the planning process.* It was clear that such a complex process, involving so many volunteers, would require a kind of project management group to be sure that deadlines were met and to reassign work that wasn't getting completed on schedule. The planning committee was responsible for this oversight function. In order to be sure that there was proper liaison between board and staff, the executive director served on the planning committee.

☐ *The role of the staff.* It was clear that staff members had to be involved in the planning process if the plan was to be effective and realistic. But the planning committee felt that it was equally important that the staff not dominate the process of planning. Staff members were therefore asked to serve as "resources" to the committees with at least one staff member assigned to each committee. Staff also tended to logistical details, making sure that meetings were scheduled and materials were prepared and sent out. Finally, staff reviewed and commented on all materials, and helped the consultant prepare documents for the final board meeting.

Integrated Planning

There are other approaches to planning that rely less on a predictable sequence of steps and emphasize instead an ongoing process, one that is integrated into the regular operation of the organization. Such integrated planning models do not have predictable beginning and end points nor do they assume that one step in the planning process determines subsequent steps. Rather, this approach utilizes the concept of strategic fit, suggesting that the various components of planning must fit together to make a coherent whole. To accomplish such a fit, every detail in the planning process must be capable of influencing every other. As a result, all components of planning—mission statements, goal formulation, the development of objectives and targets, action plans, implementation, and evaluation—must take place constantly so that as information is generated from one area it can influence decisions and choices made in another.

In linear planning, information flow tends to be in one direction. Thus information about mission determines goal formulation but not the other way around. Goals determine objectives, objectives determine strategies, and so on. In integrated planning, information flows in several directions because every planning component is interdependent and can affect and be affected by any other. An organization's mission is tied inextricably to its actions, to the evaluation of those actions, to available resources that often determine strategies, to the needs of the constituency as defined in many of the goals, and so on. As a result, integrated planning must be informed by various kinds of ongoing information gathering. It is not sufficient to collect information for a particular phase of planning only once. Information must be collected continually as other phases of the planning process redefine the original questions asked.

An integrated planning model is best represented visually by a circle that resembles a wheel with spokes (figure 9.2). The planning coordinator or

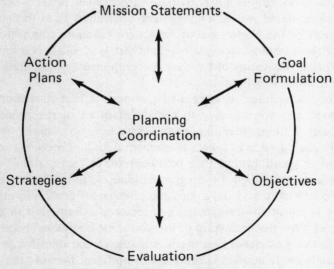

Figure 9.2. Integrated Planning

coordinating group sits at the center of the wheel collecting information from and communicating it to the wheel's perimeter via the spokes. At the perimeter, various people are working on specific tasks. These tasks are already familiar to us—one group may be evaluating current activities, another might be reviewing statements of purpose, a third might be survey-ing the organization's membership to formulate new goals for the future, a fourth might be talking to potential funders, a fifth might be working on budgets relating to specific action plans, and so forth. (In some cases, one group or even one individual might take on several of these tasks.) In order for the wheel to turn—representing the organization's forward progress in planning—the planning coordination process must take place at the center. This involves three types of activity: collecting information from the plan-ning groups at the wheel's perimeter, communicating relevant information back to these groups, and ultimately fitting all the pieces of information into a coherent plan.

Integrated planning is by its very nature an ongoing process. Like the wheel that serves as the visual metaphor for the process, it has no beginning point and no end point and is continually moving. For this reason, inte-grated planning tends to emphasize the *process* of planning. This is one of its advantages over linear planning. Unlike linear planning, an integrated process enables an organization to be immediately responsive to change, opportunity, and setbacks. It does not have to begin the process of planning all over again in order to respond to a sudden change in the funding environment, political reversals, or in staffing and governance that could lead to new opportunities and activities. Rather, when changes occur, goals can be reformulated and action plans can be drafted all at the same time. It is the role of the planning coordinator (or planning committee) to see that all of these tasks are completed, that there is adequate communication flow, and that the results of the various components of planning dovetail to make a coherent whole.

A second advantage of integrated planning is that it encourages the board, staff, and constituency to remain involved in the process in an ongoing way. In linear planning, people often have only one or two oppor-tunities in each decade to take a fundamental look at missions and goals. They tend to spend a lot of time being careful to "get it right" and then the discussion is dropped. In integrated planning, the process drives itself forward continually and the discussion of mission, goals, objectives, and strategies is repeatedly revisited. Furthermore, a discussion of strategies does not wait for the discussion of mission to be completed because there is no such thing as closure on that discussion. What does happen is that a continually evolving plan is drafted and updated. Because the plan can always be revised as the planning process moves forward and because the various planning components fit together, no air of finality hangs over the draft passed along. It is true that there is rarely a comprehensive planning document as in linear planning. However, there are working policies adopted by the board periodically, goal statements (reviewed at least annually), as well as objectives, strategies, and specific activity schedules to guide the actions of the staff.

A third advantage of integrated planning is that it tends to move more quickly toward action. Linear planning models, as we have seen, are slow because they assume that distillation is the essence of planning and that in any planning decision, every reasonable alternative should be considered. Although this does lead to informed choices in planning, those choices may be a long time in coming. Integrated planning cannot claim to be as comprehensive. What it gives up in comprehensiveness, it gains in time.

The very advantages of integrated planning suggest the disadvantages. Its lack of comprehensiveness can lead to uninformed decisions that result in rash actions, its flexibility can have a negative effect on people's confidence in the organization's long-term plans, and the emphasis on process usually means that a carefully organized, well-documented, written plan is a second priority, one that is often not addressed. What does an integrated planning process look like? The following example may be helpful.

THE COMMUNITY FOUNDATION

The Community Foundation, a broad-based, grant-giving nonprofit organization in a midwestern city, has used integrated planning for a number of years. The trustees decided on this approach for several reasons:

☐ Donors were establishing restricted funds at the foundation and additional monies were being added to the endowment at unpredictable times; thus it was extremely important to be able to review the foundation's philosophy, goals, and programs regularly in light of available resources.

☐ Community needs appeared to change rapidly; issues such as AIDS and drugs required quick and decisive responses and the board was not comfortable in reviewing its priorities every five years as would have been the case with linear planning.

☐ The board wished to discipline itself about looking toward the future; they found in the past that linear planning allowed them to relax in years when a structured planning process was not moving forward but they preferred to force themselves to debate future needs and activities every time the group came together.

To do effective integrated planning, the foundation established a planning committee composed of some trustees, staff members, and, occasionally by special invitation, resource people from outside the organization. The role of the planning committee was to collect and organize material that could be presented to the full board for discussion and action according to a predictable annual schedule. In addition, the planning committee developed built-in liaison with other committees so that it could coordinate the planning of each group and organize all of the specific plans into a coherent whole.

The foundation's planning committee decided that it was necessary always to be considering three time frames as it went about its work: the immediate future, the medium-range future, and the long-term future. At each meeting, different emphases were placed on each of these time frames depending on where the group found itself in the annual planning cycle. For example, at one meeting held in 1990, the planning committee spent almost the entire time talking about a single long-term planning issue—education after the year 2000—and did not discuss anything relative to the foundation's activity in the decade to come. At its next meeting, the discussion focused on a three-year strategy for dealing with the homeless. The determining factor for the agenda in each case was the needs of the full board. If it was necessary for the trustees to have specific action items relating to the immediate future, the planning committee had to have all the information ready with preliminary recommendations well in advance of that meeting. Thus the committee's work was completely coordinated with the decision cycle of the board itself.

Several features of the foundation's approach to planning should be highlighted:

☐ The foundation's planning committee was under constant pressure to produce material for the full board to discuss and act on. It could not sit back and have general philosophical discussions leading nowhere. Rather, it needed to come to closure and complete very specific assigned tasks. As a result, the meetings of this group were highly structured and very efficient. Every member of the committee was given an assignment and reports were prepared in advance of meetings for everyone to read and discuss.

☐ The foundation's planning committee relied on others to do much of its basic research and work. It called on special *ad hoc* committees of the foundation to bring recommendations on specific activity areas such as education, the homeless, cultural activity, AIDS, drugs, and so on. It also depended on information provided by the finance committee on short- and long-term budget trends. From time to time, consultants or staff members provided additional information at the request of the committee.

☐ In many organizations, the work, which in this case was done by the foundation's planning committee, is carried out by the executive committee. The foundation's board decided not to use the executive committee in this fashion inasmuch as nonexecutive committee members might have felt a sense of disenfranchisement from the important issues and decisions the organization faced. By setting up a separate planning committee, many more board members became involved in critical issues. Nevertheless, all of the planning committee's work was reviewed by the executive committee before being circulated to the full board. It was the executive committee that was responsible for placing this material in the context of the full agenda for board meetings.

WHICH MODEL TO CHOOSE?

The extensive discussions in the second half of this chapter about linear and integrated planning—and the two case studies of the Craft Society and the Community Foundation—have demonstrated that each approach offers advantages and disadvantages for particular kinds of organizations in particular situations. For this reason, *a single organization may end up utilizing both linear and integrated planning at different times in its development.*

Most organizations should attempt to complete a linear planning process at least once every decade (many of the best run organizations carry out such plans at five-year intervals). If an organization is moving in new directions or undertaking a controversial activity or an activity that will require broad-based support, the *comprehensiveness* of a linear approach is probably appropriate. If the emphasis of planning is the written product (to satisfy the board, the community, funders, or others), the linear approach will again make good sense.

On the other hand, an integrated approach to planning is certainly better for deliberations about the future that allow the board and staff to have an *ongoing* structured planning process as well as a continual focus on planning issues. Integrated planning is also useful for organizations that find that they must often respond quickly to change. This is one reason why a very new organization often does well with integrated planning. Until the organization stabilizes, it is essential that the board and staff monitor events, take advantage of opportunities, and respond to threats in a timely manner. For older organizations too, especially those experiencing crises and reversals, the responsive nature of the integrated approach is beneficial. Finally, integrated planning establishes a kind of discipline on the part of board and staff members, forcing them to look continually at the future and chart the course of the organization in a responsible manner.

In the end, every organization should decide on a planning approach that seems right for the time, the situation, the people involved (both within and outside the organization), and the organization itself.

MAKING DECISIONS

One of the greatest hurdles in a planning process is getting from the phase of generating ideas and recommendations to the stage of making choices and final decisions. Achieving closure on the process of planning and effecting the transition from planning to action requires discipline. But it also requires a system which encourages swift movement on items about which there is general agreement.

One of the best systems yet devised is the so-called *consent calendar*, which is extensively used in decision-making meetings of public bodies but can be easily adapted for private nonprofit organizations. The procedure associated with consent calendars involves several steps:

1. A planning report should be written and proposed actions should be condensed into a series of recommendations. Each recommendation should be followed by a brief justification and explanation. This work can be done by the planning committee, a consultant, a staff member working with the planning group, or anyone else designated by the board.

2. The planning report should be sent to members of the decision-making group (e.g., the board) with a response sheet. On the response sheet, each recommendation is written out in full and is followed by three words: *Agree, Disagree, Discuss.* Board members are asked to circle their choice for each of the recommendations and return the sheet by a certain date. If an individual is completely comfortable with a recommendation, he or she should circle "Agree." If clarification is needed, if a recommendation is confusing, or if someone feels that a recommendation is so important that it merits full discussion, then the word "Discuss" should be circled. If someone is in complete disagreement about an item, then the word "Disagree" should be circled.

3. By prior agreement, a predetermined percentage of "Agree" responses will be sufficient to put a particular question on the consent

calendar. Once a recommendation is on the consent calendar, it is removed from the agenda for discussion and all such recommendations are simply voted on as a block at the meeting in which the plan is to be approved. A 60 percent "agree" rate should be an absolute minimum for inclusion on the consent calendar though 75 percent is preferable. Some organizations might wish to see the figure as high as 90 percent.

4. At the meeting at which planning decisions are to be made, all other recommendations other than those on the consent calendar are placed on the agenda for discussion. They can either be taken in the order in which they appear in the report, or, if there is overwhelming consensus on recommendations that should *not* be approved, these can be taken first.

The consent calendar system has many advantages. It streamlines the decision-making process by eliminating discussion where there is no controversy. It points out those areas where there may be confusion or disagreement at a point in time when corrective measures may be possible. Because the response sheet requires people to make their opinions public before the meeting, there is usually sufficient time to discuss specific points with individuals whose opinions might be swayed or even changed. Finally, the consent calendar prevents one or two people from filibustering, prolonging discussion, and preventing approval of actions that the majority believe is appropriate.

For any organization setting up a planning process, the following comments may be especially useful to keep in mind:

☐ The simpler the planning process, the more likely it is to succeed.
☐ There is no one right way to plan; the best planning processes are those custom-designed to fit the needs of an organization and the working styles of board and staff.
☐ The primary benefit of planning is often the process itself; planning is a structured way of involving a number of people in thinking about the future, and this is often its chief value.
☐ Planning is not necessarily a synonym for growth; scaling down activities (or eliminating them) may often be an appropriate planning decision.
☐ Planning produces conflict and anxiety; no one can completely control the outcome of a planning process and this can cause tensions among board and staff (this feeling is often augmented by frustration over the amount of time required in planning).

☐ The desire for consensus almost always impedes the planning process; it is important to hear everyone's views but it is not advantageous to incorporate every minority opinion into a plan.

☐ To be successful, a planning process must have the strong support of top-level staff, key trustees, and others of influence in the organization.

☐ Planning should not be left completely to professional planning consultants; staff and board must be involved so that the decisions reached are their own.

☐ Perhaps most important, there must be a climate of enthusiasm within the organization toward planning; without it, a planning process has little chance of success.

CHECKLIST QUESTIONS FOR CHAPTER 9

1. Do planning activities in your organization include a review of the mission statement, the development of goals and objectives, the formulation of an action plan, the development of a timeline, and the preparation of appropriate budgets for purposes of analysis?
2. Is some kind of evaluation scheme built into the planning process so that the plan can be adjusted if things do not work out as predicted?
3. Are both board and staff involved in planning activities? Have appropriate ways been found to involve volunteers, constituents, funders, and other important community representatives?
4. Are consultants being used by your organization in planning? Are their responsibilities clearly defined?
5. Does your organization have a fully documented process for planning with clear deadlines? Is it well understood by all participants?
6. What is the strategy for garnering support for long-range planning in your organization? Is there an effort to develop a climate of enthusiasm around the process of planning?

10
Managing Information

In 1988, Fred Coolidge took over as the executive director of public radio station WYXZ. After less than a month, he concluded that his staff was behind on paperwork and could not keep up with the information needs of the organization. In 1988, WYXZ—an affiliate of National Public Radio located in a rural state—had roughly 7,000 members who contributed a minimum of $25 and provided about 70 percent of the organization's income. Keeping track of these members was a tremendous burden for the staff of six full-time and two part-time workers. But that was only the beginning. There were program and production schedules that had to be organized and distributed. There was the mass of correspondence that seemed to pile up. There were accounting records, financial reports, and budgets. There was program information that had to be organized for the monthly program guide. There were fund-raising proposals that had to be written for government agencies, foundations, and businesses and the final reports that these institutions required. The list went on and on. Hard-working staff members always seemed to be racing to catch up and always looked exhausted. Staying ahead of the paper flow—and managing the information it contained—seemed beyond their capacity.

Fred Coolidge's dilemma was not unique. Nor was his sense that the ability to manage information was going to be a critical factor in determining the success of his tenure. Indeed many experts consider the effective management of information as one of the hallmarks of sound organizational administration. In many nonprofit organizations, information management is so important that it is regarded as part of their distinctive service to the public—they collect information, analyze it, and disseminate it to members, public officials, or constituents. In others, information may not be central to their missions, yet their staffs end up spending a tremendous amount of time working on it in order to keep the institutions functioning smoothly.

In the last two decades, there has been a revolution within nonprofit organizations with respect to information management. The unprecedented development of office technology has changed the way even the smallest organizations do business. The reason the situation has changed so dramatically, particularly since 1980, has much to do with the advent of small, powerful (and increasingly less expensive) computers. Managing information electronically has become a possibility—in fact, a necessity—for virtually all organizations, regardless of size.

The purpose of this chapter is to offer some sense of how computers can be used most effectively in the nonprofit environment to improve administration. It will also detail how to choose a computer system that can meet a nonprofit organization's needs. While there will be some description of specific equipment that is available, it should be pointed out that many books and magazines regularly update information on computer hardware and software and these should be consulted for listings and evaluations of the most up-to-date products. In this chapter, the emphasis will be on the strategy of computer selection and usage. We will follow Fred Coolidge of radio station WYXZ as he addresses the information management needs of his organization and undertakes to implement a computer system.

Like many nonprofit administrators considering a decision about computer systems, Fred Coolidge did not feel competent. His one trip to a local computer store so intimidated him that all he did was buy a computer magazine. After reading this magazine and others, he talked to friends who used computers in their offices. Each was a self-proclaimed expert and each sang the praises of his or her system. Fortunately, one of the radio station's board members, Maria Calderon, worked in the data processing department of a bank and also sat on the board of the local historical museum, which had recently been involved in a successful computer installation. Over several months, Coolidge was able to work with Calderon to develop a clear picture of the needs of the station, the priorities for computerizing various tasks, as well as the method for selecting and purchasing computer equipment and bringing it into the organization with a minimum of disruption.

The first thing Coolidge learned was that there were three categories of items associated with computer systems that he should know something about:

- Computer *hardware* (the actual components of the computer itself including the monitor, keyboard, and microprocessor)
- *Peripherals* (such things as printers, modems, networks, and tape back-up drives)
- Computer *software* (the electronic programs that provide the instructions for the hardware to operate)

HARDWARE

The computer needs of most small- to medium-size nonprofit organizations can be easily met by today's microcomputers. But there are really three different types of computer, distinguished primarily by size, speed of operation, and the number of individuals who can use them simultaneously. The distinctions among these computers have become blurred in recent years. But because the terminology is still in use, it is wise to understand the general differences among the types.

Mainframe computers. In the early days of computers, only large machines, called mainframes, were available. They are still common in large institutions such as city governments, major universities, hospitals, and research institutions. They often support 200 or 300 terminals simultaneously, as well as many printers and other devices. Frequently, organizations with mainframe computers will rent out time, storage space for data files, and programs to other organizations. Called *time-sharing,* the practice is becoming obsolete with the introduction of continually less expensive, and more powerful, smaller computers.

Minicomputers. Minicomputers have less capacity and are considerably less costly than mainframes, but still provide a great deal of computing power. They have more than one microprocessor, are very fast, and regularly support up to 100 individual users. These computers are not uncommon in medium- and large-size nonprofit organizations with budgets in excess of $2.5 million. In general, minicomputers require full-time data processing staff and frequently require specially designed software, which will increase the cost of operation.

Microcomputers. The smallest of the three types of computer, microcomputers are usually stand-alone, single-user systems. In the past several years, the capabilities of microcomputers have grown so substantially that there is virtually no information task in an office environment that they cannot perform. It is not uncommon to find these computers serving many users by linking several of them in what is called a *network.* In general, the majority of nonprofit organizations use microcomputers, with the larger among this group employing networks.

Each computer is made up of several components: the *keyboard* (through which information is input, or put, into the system), the *central processing unit* (the part that performs the actual operations), the *monitor* (a device that provides the user with a way to view the computer's output), and the *mass storage devices* (the floppy and hard disk drives that provide permanent storage of the electronic data). In explaining the components to Coolidge, Calderon made several important observations:

☐ Computer *keyboards* vary from one brand to another both in the layout of the keys and the touch. If an organization is considering purchase of more than one type of computer, it is important that a standard keyboard, or at least a common keyboard layout, is selected. Staff members should get the feel of different keyboards before a selection is made.

☐ The *microprocessor* used in the central processing unit will determine the speed with which calculations are performed, and the more recent processors are considerably faster than older ones.

☐ *Monitors,* which look like television screens, display the data the computer user is working on. They come with a variety of options, including monochrome or color, low or high resolution, and regular- or large-size screens. Coolidge quickly learned that while computer prices in general have come down dramatically in the past decade, newer high-quality monitors can still cost a great deal. The range he discovered was astonishing—when he was looking, a simple black-and-white monitor cost under $100 and a large-screen, high-resolution color monitor cost over $2,000! Calderon raised some important concerns. "Make sure," she said, "that the monitor you buy has only the features you really need. Also make sure that the person or people who will be using the computer have some say in the monitor that is chosen—they'll be staring at it, and they should feel comfortable with it."

☐ *Storage devices* are the parts of the computer system on which the electronic data are kept when they are not being used by the computer itself. There are two kinds commonly used: portable diskettes or disks, which can be put in and taken out of the computer, and hard disks, which are built into the computer.

    ☐ *Portable diskettes or disks* store data on an electronically sensitive material. The older variety are called "floppy disks" and are 5¼ inches square with centers that are cut out like 45 rpm records. The newer versions are 3½ inches square, are solid, and are made of much harder material and hold much more data than the older types. The more durable, smaller disks, which hold the most information, are preferable.

    ☐ *Hard disks* are internally mounted in the computer and the disk material is never removed. While this might seem a limitation, it is minimized by the fact that hard disks can hold from 10 million to 120 million bytes (or *megabytes*) of information.[1] It is also a more secure method of storing data and allows the user to have ready access to computerized information without the inconvenience of finding the appropriate disks and putting them into the machine. Calderon's advice was to get a computer with a hard disk. An important question was how large the capacity of the hard disk should be. Unless there is a clear and obvious need—for example, a large database, a networked computer system, or software-intensive applications such as desktop publishing—a moderate-size hard disk is usually sufficient.

☐ It should be pointed out that *tape* is also used for data storage outside a computer. Because it holds a great deal of data, it is especially helpful for archiving or "backing up" data contained on a large-capacity hard disk. In a microcomputer system, tapes are not used to store data that require frequent access.

SOFTWARE

Having seen the basic components of computer hardware, Fred Coolidge and his guide Maria Calderon turned to computer software. Software is the electronically coded set of instructions that controls the computer, allowing it to perform the required tasks. Different kinds of software allow the same machine to do things that are as different as word processing, complicated mathematical calculations, and graphic design, among many others. The person who writes software is called a *programmer* and software is simply another name for a collection of computer *programs,* or machine instructions.

Calderon surprised Coolidge when she told him that software was the key part of his computer system. "Hardware is important, of course, but if there is not appropriate software to get the machine to perform the functions you need, the machine is useless. Most experts agree that it is best to choose the software that will fit a user's needs before making a decision on hardware."

Coolidge had read enough about software to be confused by phrases such as "easy-to-use," "easy-to-learn," and "user-friendly." There is an ongoing debate, he discovered, among software purchasers about whether to opt for programs that are:

☐ Easy-to-learn, which tend to provide a great amount of explanatory text on the screen and offer what are called *menu choices,* allowing the user to pick and choose his or her way through the program to the task to be performed; the problem with these programs is that once learned, the text and menus become tedious and slow down the experienced user.

☐ Easy-to-use, which tend to offer shortcuts to get quickly to the particular operation or functions to be performed; unfortunately, these shortcuts require memorization of certain key strokes and thus are more difficult for first-time users.

Calderon suggested a useful way for the radio station to resolve this debate. "Consider your staff and those who will use the computer in the future. If the office has a high turnover rate among those people who will use the software, it may be wise to use software that is easy-to-learn; if you think employees will stay a while, ultimately they will much happier with software that is easy-to-use once the learning process is complete."

As Coolidge discovered when he began looking at software carefully, the boundaries between software categories have blurred, with features associated with one type of software showing up in other types of application. For example, he saw some so-called data base software that not only allowed the user to organize and store information according to various categories (as is common in most software of this type) but also performed spreadsheet and graphing functions; he saw some word processing software that included typesetting capabilities. Should he gravitate toward these *integrated* software packages (perhaps just one or two) that could solve all the radio station's needs?

According to Calderon, the answer was probably no for several reasons:

☐ Integrated packages are more difficult to learn; these combined programs can become very complex and it is time-consuming to work around the additional features, particularly if many of them are not needed.

☐ Integrated packages can cost an organization more money in the long run because many features that are purchased may never be used.

☐ Integrated packages use more of the computer's memory and can slow down or overwhelm a smaller system. Because the special additional features of an integrated software package are usually tangential to the primary purpose of the software, they frequently are not complete enough for the serious user. ("I found this out when I bought a word processing program with desktop publishing," said Calderon. "Unfortunately the desktop publishing was not sophisticated enough to do my bank newsletter so I had to buy another specialized publishing program anyway.")

Software purchased from a dealer is usually ready to operate. However, Fred Coolidge knew that many of his associates at other nonprofits mentioned that they had found it a good investment to have some customizing done to the software. Customizing generally involves hiring a consultant or software vendor to write short programs to simplify some software functions. This can be as simple as formatting a word processing program to get it to print on business envelopes or as complex as setting up standard reports for an accounting program. According to Maria Calderon, "Customization can be a wise investment in many cases; however, it is important to check the credentials of anyone who offers these services. The more complex the customization, the more care that should be taken in locating someone who understands not only the software being employed, but the business in which the organization is engaged."

By this time, Coolidge was thoroughly overwhelmed. "I understand that software is important, so I should start there. But every time I go into a computer store, I see rows and rows of boxes with software—and each package has a price tag in the hundreds of dollars." Calderon suggested that she guide him through the basic types of software, pointing out features that she thought were important.

Types of Software

She started by distinguishing two general software categories, *system* and *application* software. System software,[2] sometimes referred to as the computer's operating system software, provides the computer with the instructions it needs to perform a wide range of internal housekeeping functions, including such things as keeping track of where data and program files are stored, making sure the proper characters appear on the computer's monitor, overseeing the transmission of data to the printer when required, and allowing the user to copy and delete files from the hard disk.

Application software is designed to perform a specific task or function for the user. There are many major areas of application software types such as word processing, data base, spreadsheet, accounting, graphics, and desktop publishing, as well as several less common areas, such as project management, communications, outlining, and others. In addition, there are *utility* programs that work to simplify some of the procedures performed by the operating system software. Each of these software categories has from several to hundreds of packages, many quite complex, to perform a wide range of functions within that category. Among the most important types of application software for nonprofit organizations are the following:

Word Processing. Word processing software is designed to manipulate text. "On the most basic level," said Calderon, "a computer with a word processing program can be used like a typewriter. However, unlike a typewriter, adding, changing, and deleting text can be accomplished without retyping the full text of a document. In addition, blocks of text can be moved around in the same document or moved to new documents." There is, of course, much more that a fully featured word processor can do. Some of the most important features are:

- Formating complex documents, using easily altered margins, columns, tab settings, as well as various styles and sizes of type
- Providing on-line checking of spelling, automatic outlining, footnotes, and thesaurus capabilities

- Creating a personalized form letter by merging specific information and blocks of text with a list of names and addresses
- Compiling tables of contents, indexes, and tables of reference automatically

Data Base (or List Management).[3] An important consideration for any nonprofit organization is the management of its lists—including lists of members, subscribers, donors, trustees, press contacts, and clients. Coolidge recognized the importance of being able to track these individuals more easily. "One of our most important nonfinancial assets is our lists. The people on them and the information about these people is our lifeblood, and it is important to be able to keep the lists up-to-date easily." Data base (or list management) software is designed to store discrete pieces of information such as names, addresses, organizational affiliations, and fund-raising information (including dates and amounts of pledges) in a way that allows for their ready retrieval. A data base program will let you select the specific kinds of information you want (for example, a list of all of an organization's members who contributed more than $100) and to sort the information in a variety of ways (for example, in zip-code order). This can be an invaluable aid, even more important than the ease of making address changes or generating mailing labels.

Calderon explained to Coolidge that there are two distinct kinds of data base programs, the simpler *list management* types, which allow for straightforward manipulations of data including simple selecting and sorting abilities, and the more complex *relational* data bases. "A relational data base program is one that will allow you to define connections between different data bases, so that updating information in one will update all instances of that information on another. For example, you might set up a data base for your complete mailing list and subsidiary data bases, one for members, and another for subscribers to your program guide. If you were using a relational data base, the subsidiary data bases could be 'related' to the mailing list data base. One person might appear in all three and if an address were updated in one place, the change would be reflected in all of them."

Spreadsheet. Considering how much time Coolidge spent working on the various program budgets at the station, Calderon was surprised that he wasn't familiar with spreadsheet software. She described it to him by suggesting that he visualize a giant accountant's columnar pad with numerous vertical and horizontal lines that create rectangular boxes, or *cells,* for data entry. "The computer allows you to look at sections of the 'spreadsheet' from the 'window' of the computer screen. Imagine a columnar pad as big as a wall with 500 columns across and several thousand rows down. These intersecting columns and rows define the cells, and because the rows are numbered and the columns are identified by letters, it is possible to describe the location of any cell on the entire sheet by a letter and number. You can enter data of various kinds—words, numbers, or formulas. Furthermore, you can specify that numbers in a column or row should be added, subtracted, multiplied, or divided."

Spreadsheet software is an excellent tool for developing budgets and other financial reports, because it is quite simple to change numbers as additional information becomes available. It can also be quite useful for making projections of income or expenses, for example, by using a formula that includes percentage increases from year to year. Two features that might prove useful in a spreadsheet program include the ability to:

- "Link" cells in one spreadsheet with cells in another to develop consolidated statements and to overcome memory limitations
- Sort data alphabetically or numerically

Calderon commented that it is quite common for spreadsheet software to incorporate rudimentary data base functions as well as the ability to generate graphs from its data. Such features, particularly the graphing, are useful, although, she pointed out, the serious user will probably want the full range of features available in stand-alone graphing and data base software packages.

Accounting. Having addressed the budgeting and financial projection capabilities of computers, Fred Coolidge was prepared to examine the advantages of computerized accounting. Accounting software allows the user to automate many of the aspects of a bookkeeper's job that involve entering and manipulating numbers. There are obvious advantages, primarily in the ease of entering data and of getting specific financial reports on a timely basis. The scale of the organization will determine in large part what software is most appropriate. For the smallest organizations, simple single-entry bookkeeping systems are available that duplicate the functions of a checkbook register and simple ledger. For larger organizations, a wide range of double-entry accounting systems are available. Most accounting software is sold in modules providing separate programs for particular accounting functions, such as general ledger, accounts receivable, accounts payable, payroll, and so on. For most organizations, it makes sense to start by automating the general ledger.

Desktop Publishing. Also called typesetting or page layout software, desktop publishing software refers to a range of packages that allows computers to be used to provide typeset-quality material from special high-quality printers, called laser printers (which are discussed later in this chapter). The ability to use a microcomputer with special typesetting software and a laser printer to create newsletters, reports, and other design-quality material that is camera-ready for printing is a major new benefit for small- to medium-size organizations.

Many people get very excited about the possibilities inherent in desktop publishing but Calderon told Coolidge that there are several caveats to keep in mind:

☐ *Specialized equipment.* Although some of the software can be run on simple computer configurations, it is likely that the serious user will decide on a program requiring a computer with a fast processor, a great deal of RAM (internal computer memory used temporarily to store programs that are in use), and a large-capacity hard disk. These features, which will allow the user to produce professional-level work much more quickly, can double or triple the cost of the computer. In addition, a large-screen, high-resolution monitor is almost mandatory, as is a laser printer and a mouse (a mobile tracking device connected to the computer and used to input information and work with software in conjunction with the keyboard). Finally, other special equipment, such as digital scanners (which allow the user to incorporate photographs and other visual images into documents) may be worth considering.

☐ *Software.* The range of software options is very broad, and prices range from the low-budget level (which might be sufficient to prepare a newsletter in a standard two-column format) all the way to fully featured programs costing several thousand dollars (which would provide sophisticated formatting options and document management techniques). Additional software might be required to handle such things as creating graphs, organization charts, tabular material, and other illustrations. Because all of these programs use the monitor's and the printer's capabilities quite extensively, they usually require careful programming to work properly with the hardware *and* with each other. Thus it is not uncommon for the user to hire someone (often the software vendor) to program the software to work with his or her specific computer/printer configuration.

☐ *Training.* Because this software—even the simpler programs—tends to be very complex, users will probably need assistance to master it, as well as the other graphic-oriented software that may be employed to create camera-ready text. In addition, there are many smaller, utility programs that may be necessary (for example to translate tabular material, graphs, and other illustrations into a format that can be used by the page layout software). Thus there are likely to be several software packages with which the user must become familiar. To ensure that the system works effectively and that the greatest benefit is gained, a comprehensive training program should be planned.

☐ *Design.* Generating typeset and camera-ready material will not benefit an organization if the graphic design of that material is confused, unappealing, or sloppy. Thus it is often a wise investment to get the assistance of a graphic designer to ensure that the output is consistent in visual quality with the organization's graphic image. The designer should create some common formats for different uses (for example, press releases, reports to trustees, program notes, fact sheets). If an organization is starting from scratch to develop consistent graphic layouts for all its presentation materials, this step may be costly and time-consuming.

Even with these concerns, the benefits of desktop publishing are considerable. Simple brochures and announcements can be turned around in days rather than weeks, and perhaps more important, they can be of uniformly high quality. In addition, because text can be moved directly from the word processing software to the publishing system, there is less likelihood of typographical errors, and proofreading is minimized.

Graphics. Graphics software is designed to assist the user in creating a wide range of visual presentations, ranging from simple graphs of financial data to organization charts, bulleted lists, or financial tables for complex slide presentations. Because there is a wide range of software available, it is crucial for an organization to define its needs carefully before choosing. "At the bank," said Calderon, "our financial department has found it very valuable to take data from our budgets and make graphs, so that we can easily explain where our money comes from and how we spend it for our annual report. Our real estate department staff has designed a slide presentation that shows architects' models of certain buildings. We used graphics software to create a visual representation of our new organization chart when we acquired another bank."

Other Software

There are many other types of software that are not as universally used but are important to know about. Calderon felt the radio station might be interested in some of the following.

Utility Software. This software simplifies user interaction with the computer and the housekeeping tasks associated with the computer's operating system. In certain cases, this can be invaluable. Some examples of utility software include:

- Software to streamline the process of backing up (making copies of) program and data files on the computer; this encourages more frequent back up, thus minimizing the risk of lost or missing files
- Software to assist the user in relocating, recovering, and restoring data files that have been inadvertently deleted; this can be a virtual lifesaver when a power failure or an accidental key stroke deletes a long manuscript or a complicated graphic from the computer
- Software to rearrange data on the computer's hard disk in order to increase the computer's speed
- Software that creates a more accessible interface between the user and the computer's operating system to make it easier and safer to perform basic computer functions, such as copying or deleting files, formatting disks, or organizing files on the hard disk

Communications Software. This software is used with a device called a modem and allows computers to transmit data over telephone wires. This is very useful when an organization has more than one location or when the staff wishes to work on a group project with computer users in other places.

Fund-Raising Software. This software is generally a customized version of data base software and allows an organization to keep donor and member records, track pledges, and organize a fund-raising or membership development schedule.

Project Management Software. This software allows the user to track projects or events and coordinate the tasks associated with them.

OTHER COMPONENTS OF COMPUTER SYSTEMS

Printers
Fred Coolidge realized that there was still one piece of the computer puzzle missing from his review. Maria Calderon hadn't said anything about *printers.* When he called her, she suggested that they meet at the local computer store and she would give him a quick tour. "The problem—if you want to call it that—is that the technology is changing so quickly it's hard to keep up," she said when they met. "Even a few years ago, the standard high-

quality printer for most users was a *daisy wheel,* or letter-quality, printer. It worked much like a typewriter, except it was considerably faster—up to about 50 characters per second. If you wanted to print faster or you wanted to print something other than letters and numbers, you could get a *dot-matrix* printer, which printed at up to 350 characters per second, but you had to sacrifice the quality of the visual material. The choice of which of these printer types to purchase was usually a decision based on the needs of the organization and the funds available, and it wasn't uncommon for computer installations to have both kinds of printers available. But all that has changed with the advent of *laser* printers."

Laser printers use a photocopierlike technology to produce near-type-set–quality material. A laser printer works much like a dot-matrix printer, but it has several dramatic advantages:

- It produces output at a higher resolution, typically 300 dots per inch, which looks almost as good as a commercial print job
- It can print approximately eight pages of double-spaced text per minute, considerably faster than a letter-quality printer
- It prints with virtually no noise
- It has a variety of typefaces built into it, so that it can print in standard serif and nonserif type styles; in addition, using special software, it can print an almost unlimited range of typefaces

By the mid-1980s, laser printers began to be mass marketed to microcomputer users and in the next several years the costs dropped by more than 50 percent. By the end of the decade, they had replaced daisy wheel printers in many computer installations. "If the radio station is serious about desktop publishing, a laser printer is mandatory. But even if that isn't a major concern, it might still make sense. Considering the small size of the offices at the radio station, and the likely demand on any printer, the fact that the printer is very fast and the fact that it is almost absolutely quiet are important features."

Networks
A *network* is a system of hardware and software that allows a group of personal computers to work as a single system. Different users can share data files and equipment, such as a laser printer, a tape backup drive, or a modem (a device that allows computers to send and receive data over telephone lines). Simply put, each computer user on the network is able to have access to the files of any other machine on the network and is able to print his or her documents on any network printer. Calderon explained why this could be useful at WYXZ. "Sharing files might be a significant

benefit, for example, if the station gets so many new names and pledge amounts to add to its lists during pledge period that you want two people to work on entering the information at the same time. They can both be working on the same list from two different computers. Or you and the development officer might want to trade edits on a draft of a grant application or a proposal. In addition, if you end up getting several microcomputers, as I think you will, all of you can access a single laser printer from your own computers."

But there are some reasons not to rush into the purchase of a network:

☐ Networks are expensive; a fully functional, midpriced network can add as much as 20 percent to the total cost of computer hardware, not including the cost of installation, and it is frequently necessary to buy special network versions of your software, which will add a significant sum as well.

☐ Network operating software in some cases will use a large portion of the computer's memory; this may slow down the computer system or it may make it impossible for some of the chosen software packages to run without additional memory being added to the system—another expense.

☐ Network software adds another layer of complexity to the computer system; the amount of time necessary to handle the usual housekeeping chores on the computer will increase, so training someone to take care of them will be increasingly important.

☐ There are some inexpensive ways to accomplish many of the same advantages of a network: A simple switch box can connect several computers to a single laser printer for very little money, an external, portable backup tape drive unit can be used for backing up all the computers, and, of course, it is possible to hand carry diskettes from one machine to another to share data files, a system humorously referred to as a "sneaker network."

☐ A network will generally require additional staff time to make it function smoothly, so it is important to analyze the office staff to determine if there is someone who has the interest, aptitude, and free time to become the "network administrator"—the person in charge of computer headaches.

IMPLEMENTING A COMPUTER SYSTEM

To Hire or Not to Hire a Computer Consultant

Having completed his review of computer hardware, software, and other related issues, Coolidge was eager to begin putting what he had learned to use to figure out the details of the computer system the radio station needed. Calderon suggested that it now might be time to call in a consultant to assist with the remaining steps in implementation. "Whether or not to call in a consultant and deciding when to do it is a judgment call," she explained. "It is important to keep in mind the various ways a good computer consultant can help you and the kinds of tasks you can expect him or her to do."

What kinds of work might a consultant undertake? Among the range of activities consultants are commonly called on to do are the following:

- *Needs assessment* to determine precisely what kind of hardware, software, and peripherals will meet an organization's needs
- Writing a "request for proposals," which documents in technical terms the complete computer systems (or specific additions, such as backup systems, networks, integrated fax/modems) that the organization wishes to acquire (the request for proposals is subsequently sent out to firms that might wish to sell the system to the organization)
- Assistance with *equipment purchase,* including the selection of hardware components, configuration of all equipment to the client's specifications, and installation (especially if no request for proposals has been prepared)
- *Software customization* for specific applications, such as accounting systems, data base and mailing list, fund raising, and prospect tracking
- *Documentation* writing for customized systems
- *Technical support* services, which might include maintaining particular hardware or software training sessions for staff

There are some questions that will help determine whether the services of a consultant are necessary. These include:

☐ How complex will the computer system need to be? If an organization is going to purchase a single computer and printer for word processing only, a consultant is not necessary. However, systems requiring more complex and integrated solutions may benefit substantially from a consultant's help.

☐ How much time is available, and how much interest is there within the organization to research the existing internal needs and potential computer alternatives? If someone on the staff is interested in computers, can provide the objective assessment of needs, *and* has the time, it may not be necessary to consider the services of a consultant.

☐ How much money is available in the budget for computerization? The specialized expertise of a consultant may be cost-effective, but if the budget is limited, it may be more sensible to purchase equipment and software rather than advice.

Calderon shared her concern about the skills of some individuals working as computer consultants. "Beware of consultants who are out to sell a specific product or who are new computer users with more enthusiasm than experience. There are good consultants out there. Locating a suitable computer consultant is much the same process as locating any other sort of consultant—ask colleagues for recommendations, check with other stations, write or call organizations that know about computer professionals. We need to find someone who has worked with an organization of roughly our size, preferably a nonprofit . . . although a background in radio is probably not critical. We need to make clear what we want done and by whom, and we want to be sure to specify a completion date. Data processing consultants—particularly programmers—are notorious for taking longer than promised to complete work. We should consider penalties for late delivery of work. Of course, all agreements should be put in writing."

Needs Assessment

After several phone calls and three interviews, the radio station hired Arthur Johnson, the consultant who had helped the historical society with its computerization project. Johnson's first task was to determine precisely and systematically what the radio station's information requirements consisted of. At the outset, he explained that he didn't want to assume that the solution to every information problem was a computer. "There are a lot of ways you get at information around here. I like to think in terms of *information systems*—the information itself and the procedures to utilize it effectively. There are certainly several information systems at WYXZ that should be left alone. Your rotary file is a good example. It functions fine and it would be silly to get rid of a convenient quick reference system that is meeting your needs. Another good information system is the notebook you use to keep copies of your correspondence in chronological order. My task is to help you identify all the information systems at the radio station and decide which will be made more effective by the use of a computer."

Johnson then explained what makes an information system effective. Whether a system is complex or simple, manual or computerized (or some combination of the two), to be effective it must be *accurate, reliable, efficient, secure,* and *cost-effective.* It should improve the quality of work that is accomplished and increase productivity by allowing more work to be completed in less time. In order to develop systems that are effective, a process called *systems analysis* is used to answer a basic question—How do things get done?

For the next several weeks, the staff of WYXZ conducted, with assistance from Johnson, an analysis of how their existing information systems worked. Each person at the radio station tracked the number of letters, forms, and grant applications mailed out, counted the number of names on mailing lists, determined the kinds of special printing formats presently in use, analyzed the way budgets were prepared, and compared financial report formats. They also made estimates of what the station's information requirements might look like in five years, because it was clear that a new computer system should accommodate growth.

The next step was to take the results of this analysis and determine precisely what kind of computer setup might best meet the radio station's requirements given a range of budget options. The questions to be resolved at this point included:

☐ What are the *priority applications* for the computer systems (e.g., mailing and membership lists, routine correspondence, and accounting)? What are secondary applications that would be desirable after the priority applications are implemented?

☐ What is the *volume* of the information to be handled? For example, it would be important to know whether the mailing list has 500 or 50,000 names on it.

☐ What is the *frequency of demand* for this information? For example, will the radio station want to get reports from its mailing list four times a month, four times a week, or four times a day?

☐ What is the *changeability* of the information? For example, will it be necessary to enter address corrections on a mailing list once a week or quarterly?

☐ What is the required *speed of access?* For example, is it acceptable to have the computer take an hour to sort a mailing list in order to generate labels or must that function be accomplished in a considerably shorter period of time?

Writing a Request for Proposals

Johnson's contract included the preparation of a request for proposals (RFP) for the purchase and installation of the computer system. This document was to be circulated to data processing equipment vendors who would in turn be invited to bid on the installation of the system. Johnson promised that his RFP would provide a description of the organization and its activities, as well as a statement of what the desired computer system, when fully implemented, was supposed to accomplish in broad terms. It was also to include a more specific outline of the radio station's information requirements (a summary of the research put together in the needs assessment phase). Additional information that is optional for smaller organizations with simpler computer system requirements was also to be provided with the radio station's RFP. This included:

- A detailed statement on the structure and content of the various subsystems (for example, accounting, development, and membership), including data specifications and report formats
- A parallel statement on equipment requirements, including general types of computers, network configurations, number of terminals, printers, modem, and so on
- A further description of other technical requirements, including computer storage, speed of processing, types of communication lines (if any) service requirements, and future upgrading possibilities

The decision to include the preparation of the RFP in Johnson's contract was made after Coolidge had spoken to someone at another radio station about her experience in implementing a computer system:

We had done all the research about our computer needs, but when we started looking, we found one dealer that handled two of the software packages we were looking for, but not the others. Furthermore, that dealer sold the computer we wanted, but not the printer. It took us quite a while to find a dealer that sold all the items we wanted to buy and the store was quite far from us. We ended up buying our software from a mail-order house, the printer from one dealer, and the computer from another.

Everything seemed to be working out fine at first, and we had saved a great deal of money. But problems started cropping up when we tried to get the printer to work with some of our software. We called the dealer who supplied the printer and were told the problem was with the software. We called the dealer from whom we bought the software who told us our computer dealer should have configured the system so that it recognized the software. I don't know how, but it was finally resolved. Then, the computer's monitor stopped working. We called the dealer, and it took three days and one threatened hysterical fit to get a replacement, even though we were well within the warranty period. I wasted several days on unnecessary computer problems, and that accounted for a considerable part of the money we thought we had saved.

In the end, WYXZ's request for proposals included the comprehensive list of systems to be computerized and the detailed specifications for the computer system. It included three computers networked together, with both a laser printer and a dot-matrix printer, as well as specific software for word processing, spreadsheet, data base, general ledger, and desktop publishing.

Reviewing Proposals

Once completed, the radio station's RFP was circulated to a list of companies and individuals recommended by the consultant, other nonprofit organizations, and computer companies. Fifteen individuals and firms were sent copies of the RFP, seven individuals called for more information, and three submitted bids. Johnson warned that the proposals, when they came in, should be read carefully. In reviewing the proposals, he felt that there were two areas that required particular attention:

Hidden costs. It is too easy to overlook costs that the vendor will not build into his bid unless it is specifically requested in the RFP. There are all kinds of basic supplies: some printers require special paper, others need special feeder trays; the initial purchase will also probably include an inventory of disks (or diskettes and tapes), printer cartridges, lamps, and even special furniture. Most organizations find it prudent to safeguard each computer by investing in power surge protectors and an uninterruptable power supply. If the computer system is to include a modem, special software will be required as well as access to telephone lines. Network software may require the purchase of additional memory capacity. Sometimes it will turn out that the physical facilities will have to be partially rewired to accommodate the additional power and grounding requirements. And, finally, there is the whole issue of service contracts, which might be purchased on many of the hardware components.

Compatibility. With the proliferation of computers and software, and with few universally accepted standards in the industry, the issue of compatibility is very important. Inexperienced computer system buyers often assume that any component can be plugged into any other and that all software will run on any machine. This is not the case even when machines are specifically sold as compatible with standard brands. It is essential that a dealer be required to specify in writing that the hardware will all be compatible and will be able to operate the software specified. Better still, the dealer should demonstrate how the system operates before the purchase is made.

Coolidge decided that it was too risky to make a decision without help, so the proposals were sent to Johnson for his advice. Johnson sent a letter giving his reasons for recommending one of the vendors over the others. He advised that the final contract with the vendor insist on deadlines for the completion of work and include penalties if the work was not completed on time.

At the end of the next month, a contract was signed for the purchase and installation of all hardware and software. Equipment was delivered three weeks later and the network and various software were installed by the vendor and tested. After all hardware was in working order and software had been demonstrated, the staff at WYXZ was ready to begin using the system.

Beginning to Use the Computer

A milestone had been reached. It had taken almost a year for Fred Coolidge to plan a successful computer installation. But Maria Calderon advised him that he still faced a long process of incorporating the computer system into the operations of the radio station. She warned him that it would not be a simple process and that some planning would make it less trying for the staff. She recommended the following steps:

☐ Choose one or two systems to computerize initially that will show an immediate productivity gain when they are implemented. The psychological boost from getting some instant benefit will be very helpful. The systems should be important to staff, but should also be ones that are relatively easy to implement. Word processing or simple list management is a good place to start.

☐ Where actual system design is necessary, do it carefully—computers will only increase efficiency if information systems are well designed. This means thinking through things as obvious as developing a system for naming documents in word processing. It means choosing appropriate "fields" in a data base system and, if necessary, assigning specific codes to summarize categories of information (e.g., in a fund-raising system, *y* might stand for yes; *n*, for no; *1*, for active current member; and so on). It means developing and providing numerical codes for the chart of accounts in an accounting system. Often the area of system design is another place where a consultant can come in for a few hours and be quite helpful.

☐ Begin entering data. Do it carefully and systematically, allowing plenty of time. After some data are entered, they should be edited and corrected. Procedures for updating information will have been established (in the previous step), and they must be implemented so that once the information is computerized it will be kept current.

☐ Operate both the old manual systems and the new computerized systems together until it is clear that the new ones work (this is called running parallel). While testing out the new system and looking for things that are not working properly *(bugs),* the staff must also manage their lists, mailings, bookkeeping, and correspondence in the way they did before there was a computer. An organization cannot afford to trust the computer until it has proven itself.

☐ Document the new systems completely. This means writing down everything someone needs to know about the new system: what data go into it, how the equipment works, how to generate reports, which staff member is responsible for what task, and so forth. The system should be so well documented that if everybody on the staff left, an entirely new group of people could come in and teach themselves how to operate it.

Training, Backup, Scheduling, and Maintenance

There are some additional areas that need to be thought about as soon as the computer system is in place.

Training. There is much new information to master when computers are brought into an organization and it is therefore necessary to plan a comprehensive training program. Such a program will have several components. The first, which might be called "computer basic training," should cover:

- An overview of the equipment, including the basic operation of the computers, printers and other peripherals, scheduling procedures, maintenance, and supplies
- The use of the computers' operating systems, including copying and deleting files, formatting disks, creating subdirectories, and backing up files
- An overview of the important features of the most commonly used software, including loading and saving data files, printing, and exiting

This training should *never* be overlooked. Many people who claim to be computer experts have never received this introductory information in a formal and inclusive session. It is wise to offer this training and to make it mandatory to prevent bruised egos.

The second part of the training program should be much more specific. It involves detailed explanations of how to use specific software packages that the organization has acquired—word processing, data base, spreadsheet, and so on. Staff members must learn the nuts and bolts of the software, but training must be geared to the users' level of skill, interest, and need.

There should be one staff person who takes responsibility for the computer systems and this individual, ideally, should also oversee (although not necessarily provide) the training. If a particular staff member is already thoroughly conversant with a certain software package and has the time, he or she can assist in training. In fact, for each major software package in use, it is ideal to have someone in the office who can answer tough questions and troubleshoot problems. Finally, outside training resources should be used if it seems appropriate. In addition to consultant and vendor assistance in this area, there are workshops, classes, and publications—many devoted exclusively to certain software packages.

Backup. Because data stored on hard or floppy disks are in electronic form, any disruption of the electronic field can potentially cause loss of data. In addition, it is quite possible to delete data accidentally. Thus backing up data—making duplicate copies of all data files—is just common sense. Backup can be done in a variety of ways. One way is simply to copy the contents of one disk onto another (often this is done using a simple software program that compresses and copies all the files to a floppy disk). Another way is to utilize a built-in tape drive unit that can copy the contents of hard disks to portable tape cassettes.

A good rule of thumb is to back up frequently enough that it would never be inordinately difficult or time-consuming to reconstruct the data that have been entered since the last backup was done. For example, if an organization added to and corrected its mailing list once a month, it would make sense to do backup after each batch of entries. If, however, it processed these additions and changes a few at a time, whenever they came in, it would make sense to do backup at a regular time each week, perhaps every Friday afternoon. While backup does take some time—the actual amount of time will depend on the number of computers and the number and size of files on their hard disks—it is absolutely essential.

An ideal procedure for backing up involves having two complete sets of back-up tapes or disks. One is stored off the premises, the other in the office. Each time backup is done, the off-premises copy is brought in and updated and becomes the new office copy while the old office copy is taken off premises after backup is completed. This way, the most recent backup is in the office when it is needed, but another set is safely off-site in case a real disaster such as a fire destroys the office copy.

Staffing. It is important to have adequate staffing to handle the various computer-related tasks such as backing up, training, scheduling the use of the computer, and taking care of routine maintenance. Depending on the scale of the computer installation, this responsibility may be part of a regular staff person's job, or it may involve hiring a full time director of information management. It is important that *one* person be designated as responsible for these areas to ensure that critical tasks such as backing up are not overlooked and to coordinate scheduling. In addition to training and backing up, which were already discussed, this person should be responsible for:

☐ *Scheduling.* When a new computer system is acquired, there is a tendency to assume that the equipment will be available for anyone who needs to use it at any time. Very quickly, it becomes clear that priorities and schedules for usage are required. There should be clear written policies regarding priorities for usage and procedures for scheduling of computer time. Weekly staff meetings are ideal times to discuss timing of major projects (sizable mailings, or writing of grant proposals) and negotiating computer availability. Because regular backup is a priority, it should *not* be skipped because someone wants to get on the computer. Everyone, even those with their own machines, must learn to schedule their computer time carefully.

☐ *Maintenance.* The person serving as information manager should be in charge of maintenance of all equipment and software. He or she should research and make recommendations on purchasing of service contracts on hardware. (Service contracts are most needed on hardware with many moving parts, such as printers.) The individual should also ensure that all software registration is completed in a timely manner and that any software updates are obtained and installed. This information manager is not necessarily the one to actually perform computer maintenance, but he or she should be familiar with whom to call for both hardware maintenance and software support.

Two years after joining WYXZ, Fred Coolidge could look back with pride on a successful computer installation, one achieved with a minimum of dislocation and inconvenience. The productivity level of the staff had increased dramatically and the organization was managing information quite efficiently. But Coolidge made an interesting discovery. As productivity levels increased, so did the demands on the computer system. The staff discovered a variety of new applications that they wished could be added to the system. Indeed, less than a year after paying the last bill to Arthur Johnson, the computer consultant, Coolidge invited him back to do another small-scale needs assessment for additions to the system. But far from being discouraged, he was elated. For Fred Coolidge had come to appreciate that the wise use of technology in managing information could greatly enhance the effectiveness of his organization.

CHECKLIST QUESTIONS FOR CHAPTER 10

1. Does your organization have access to people who are fully qualified to make judgments about computer hardware, software, and peripherals? Are these people sufficiently objective or will they simply recommend those products that they personally sell or use?

2. Has your organization done a complete computer needs assessment that defines what kinds of hardware, software, and peripherals are needed? Has this needs assessment been done within the last three years?

3. Have existing information systems been fully documented? Could new staff come in and operate these systems based on the documentation?

4. Is there adequate technical expertise available to support and service your organization's information systems and provide training when necessary?

5. Has your organization identified data processing professionals who can be hired as needed to assist with programming, developing requests for proposals, reviewing proposals, and advising on equipment purchases?

6. Has your organization developed proper systems for backup, scheduling, and maintenance of the computer systems? Are there adequate provisions for staff training as needed?

11
Making Things Better

Jack Fox and Martha Whitney left their respective nonprofit organizations on the same day. Jack had been a volunteer at his church for two years. Martha had been employed as executive director of a shelter for battered women for four years. Both had begun their work with a feeling of optimism and a sense of service. But as the months and years had passed, each was troubled by the fact that things were not always going smoothly in their respective organizations.

At the church, Jack couldn't quite put his finger on what was wrong. Certainly the shrinking membership base and the constant need for money were challenges, but he wasn't sure whether they were symptomatic of larger problems that no one in the church was willing to face. In Martha's case, she was able to diagnose what was wrong—there were not enough paid staff members, the building was inadequate, and the board was unwilling to raise funds—but she felt helpless to do anything about these problems.

Jack Fox and Martha Whitney are typical of many individuals in nonprofit organizations. They are good, committed people. They care deeply about the work their organizations are trying to do. But they feel stymied and frustrated, either because they cannot seem to use their talents effectively or because their organizations seem adrift and on the wrong track. Often the organizations are operating close to capacity with staff members overworked to the point of burnout and budgets strained to the breaking point. There never seem to be enough hours or sufficient money to identify and solve problems. People like Jack and Martha do not want to initiate personal conflicts, hurt people's feelings, or rock the organizational boat in any way. It is simply easier and less stressful to walk away from the organization and its problems.

The purpose of this chapter is to provide an alternative scenario for those who are committed to nonprofit organizations and want to make them better. These people should not be lost to the nonprofit world—they are too valuable. They should be encouraged to stay and contribute. This chapter will provide guidance on how to participate in a process of evaluation and assessment, which can lead to improvements in an organization's operations and programs over time.

THE EVALUATION PROCESS

No nonprofit organization is governed or managed perfectly and most have serious shortcomings in several areas. The ones that are most successful are able to get the board and staff to commit to a process for evaluating problems and developing a systematic way for making things better. This is done by taking a few important steps:

1. Accurately diagnosing the organization's current situation and identifying areas in which there are opportunities for positive change
2. Separating the problems into those that need immediate attention and those that might be dealt with later
3. Building board and staff consensus so that the identified problems can be dealt with honestly, forthrightly, and in a timely manner
4. Developing a realistic, affordable, multiyear schedule for implementing change
5. Continuing the diagnostic, evaluation, and self-improvement process year after year

Assessing Strengths, Weaknesses, Problems, and Opportunities

The diagnosis of an organization's current strengths, weaknesses, problems, and opportunities involves making assessments in several areas and evaluating the organization from several points of view. The process involves asking questions about how well the organization measures up to a predefined ideal. The following checklist provides an excellent starting point for a process of organizational assessment.

Mission, Image, and Case for Support

A. Mission. A strong organization is one whose purpose is relevant to current needs of the community it serves and to the requirements of a broad and well-defined constituency.

☐ Is the mission statement up-to-date or out-of-date (i.e., how closely does it actually conform to what the organization seems to be about)? How might the mission statement be reworded so that it is more reflective of the organizational purpose?

☐ Is the mission itself still relevant to the needs of those served (i.e., is there a compelling reason for the organization to exist)? Can this be demonstrated in a concrete way that would convince a skeptic? Should the mission be broadened or changed in some way to become more relevant to contemporary needs?

☐ Who is being served (i.e., who are the clients)? Is this constituency sufficiently diverse or is it too narrowly focused on a small group? If the constituency should be broadened, what concrete steps might be taken to accomplish this?

B. Image. The organization should be well known and well respected in its community and among its constituency.

☐ Does the organization's name mean anything to people in the community? How familiar are people with its activities? Are there people who should know about the organization but don't? How can the organization's profile be raised?

☐ What is the organization's reputation? Is it well respected? Is there any old history or controversy that plagues its image? How can this be taken care of?

C. Case for support. The organization should present a compelling case for support both to its clients and to its contributors.

☐ How convincing is the organization's pitch to its users and its funders? Are the services, activities, and programs of the organization described in a way that will entice full participation?

☐ How clearly and simply are the financial needs of the organization outlined?

☐ Are contributors given a varied enough menu of giving opportunities? Are donors offered a way to meet their own objectives for name recognition or other needs?

Manpower Issues (Board, Staff, and Volunteers)

A. Board. Board members should be active, assuming general oversight of the affairs of the organization, taking responsibility for fund raising, and allowing staff to carry out the day-to-day operational affairs of the organization.

☐ Do board members know what is expected of them (does the organization have a trustee job description or board manual)? Do board members attend meetings regularly? Do they give and solicit money? Do they assume proper oversight of the budget? Do they engage in program and organizational planning?

☐ Are the bylaws structured in such a way that inactive or ineffective board members can be rotated off the board quickly and painlessly? Are there specific board members who should be encouraged to resign to make room for others who are more active?

☐ Do the officers assume proper leadership roles? Is there an effective committee structure?

B. Staff. The organization should have a qualified and well-trained staff that is large enough to carry out the tasks allotted to it. The organization chart should maximize the potential of the work force and there should be clearly documented personnel policies that reflect a sense of fairness leading to good morale.

☐ What are the skills and qualifications of individual staff members? Does the organization have the best possible people for each job? If not, is the problem related to compensation, poor recruiting and hiring, or something else?

☐ Are there enough staff? Are their job descriptions complete and up-to-date? Is the organization chart appropriate?

☐ Are there personnel policies? Are they written down? Is there a regular procedure for staff evaluation? Does it work? What is the level of staff morale? How can it be improved?

C. Volunteers. In organizations that rely heavily on volunteers, these individuals should be committed, given clear tasks, and rewarded for the work they do.

☐ Are there enough volunteers? Are there skills that are not being met by the current volunteer pool? How can more volunteers be found in the right areas of need?

☐ Are volunteer tasks and activities well organized and properly assigned? Are tasks described in writing? Is there a system of review and follow-up to make sure tasks are completed properly?

☐ Are volunteers serious about their work? Are they committed? Have they been oriented and told about the importance of the work they do? Is there a system that rewards them?

Finances

A. Financial management. The organization's finances should show prudent management, appropriate oversight and controls, and proper systems for predicting and tracking revenue and expense.

☐ Are the financial records kept accurately and statements produced frequently and promptly? Do key members of the board provide proper oversight and review the reports? Are there controls in place that meet generally accepted accounting standards? Is there an outside review of the books?

☐ Do the balance sheet and the income statement show a history of prudent financial management? Is there an accumulated deficit and if so, what strategies are there for eliminating it? Is there a cash reserve? An endowment?

☐ Are budgets prepared well in advance of the fiscal year? Is budget reconciliation done frequently enough to anticipate problems? Are cash flow projections available? Can revenue and expense projections and reports be analyzed for each activity and program? Are multiyear budget projections available?

B. Income and expense. Except under unusual circumstances, the organization should earn and raise enough money each year to pay its operating expenses.

☐ Is there an appropriate balance between earned and contributed income? The ratio will vary depending on the kind of organization. Is there a sufficient source of unrestricted income? Is the organization too dependent on a single donor or a few large contributors?

☐ Are costs reasonable given the service or product provided? Are there systems for analyzing and controlling costs?

☐ Does the organization operate at a surplus or deficit after all income (contributed and earned) is considered? If there is a pattern of operating deficits, what can be done to change this pattern?

☐ Is the fund-raising program well organized? Do board members and other volunteers carry out their responsibilities? Is information about donors collected, updated, organized, and used strategically? Are donors appropriately courted and properly thanked?

Activities and Programs

A. Resource audit. The organization's programs should meet the needs of the constituency and the community. They should be well administered.

☐ Are the programs and activities of this organization really needed or wanted and if so by whom? How much would people suffer if the organization went out of business?

☐ Which programs, services, and activities does the organization do best? How well do they meet the needs of clients and community? How can they be improved?

☐ Which programs, services, and activities does the organization do less well? Should they be dropped? If not, how can they be made more successful?

B. Positioning. The organization should appear to offer unique advantages to those who utilize its programs and services. It should be well regarded with respect to its competition.

☐ With which entities and activities does the organization compete? How well are its programs regarded in relation to its competition?

☐ How can the organization broaden its appeal to a wider group of constituents and strengthen the loyalty of current users?

Planning and Evaluation

A. Planning. The board and staff of the organization should be involved in both short- and long-term planning at all times.

☐ How well defined are goals, objectives, and strategies for the next two years? The next five years? Is there a well-articulated plan that is providing a blueprint for action?

☐ How effective is the planning process? Who is involved and who is left out? How involved are the board, the staff, the constituency, and the community? Are new activities properly planned and piloted before moving into full implementation?

☐ Does the planning process take financial realities into account? Are conservative revenue and expense projections available? To what extent does planning involve multiyear budgeting?

B. Evaluation. Evaluation systems should measure performance against preestablished targets and standards. From time to time, evaluation should utilize the objectivity and expertise of outside professionals.

☐ How are the organization, in general, and its specific activities, in particular, evaluated? Are evaluations based on preestablished quantitative targets?

☐ How often are evaluations carried out and by whom? Are outside experts used in this process? To what extent is their advice heeded?

☐ Are planning and evaluation linked? How are the results of ongoing evaluation utilized in long-range planning?

SELF-ASSESSMENT VERSUS OUTSIDE EVALUATION

The diagnostic process just described can be done as a self-assessment, which relies on the talents and abilities of an organization's board and staff; alternatively, it can be done with the assistance of outside evaluators, utilizing the talents and knowledge of one or more professional who are not associated with the organization in any way.

Self-assessment has many advantages. Those involved generally know the organization well. It doesn't take them a long time to get up to speed about the organization's history, community, constituency, and internal politics. It is inexpensive, because it does not require that large fees are paid to an outside consultant. It also can serve as a consensus builder inasmuch as those involved in the assessment process are the same individuals who will be responsible for making the necessary changes.

Yet some of these very advantages of self-assessment can work against the organization in the long run. Because those who are involved are close to the organization, they may suffer from institutional myopia. Because they have seen things operate in certain ways for so long, they may not be able to understand that there are novel alternatives that would actually lead to improvements. Additionally, they may, either consciously or unconsciously, be attached to certain individuals, procedures, programs, and activities that are not, in the long run, in the best interests of the organization.

For example, one would not expect a trustee who had underwritten a series of school-based public affairs programs for ten years to conclude that these programs were not as effective as similar ones offered by other organizations. An executive director who had spent several years training her assistant, with whom she feels a close personal relationship, might not feel inclined to look at an alternative staffing structure that excluded this individual.

Another danger with self-assessment is that there may be strong factions on the board or among senior staff, each with strongly held and differing opinions about particular issues. The factions will probably choose to disagree both about problems and solutions, and they may become quite personal in ascribing blame to individuals in the other camp. This is destructive and divisive and it usually means that someone from the outside, with a fresh, objective vision should be called in to perform an organizational assessment or evaluation.

Sometimes organizations resist calling in an outsider because board members or staff think they cannot afford the services of a consultant. However, it is important to keep in mind that there is a growing trend among institutional funders, such as foundations and public agencies, to pick up all or part of the cost of outside evaluation and assessment services. From the funders' point of view, money given for such projects—which in the end may lead to improved management, governance, programming, or planning—can be an exceptionally sound investment.

Regardless of whether or not an outside paid professional is used, it is always helpful to bring in an individual who is neither a board member nor a staff person to help out during the assessment period. Such a community member can aid in bringing objectivity to the evaluation process, spot areas of internal conflict, and lend a calming voice to the process of problem identification.

Building Consensus for Future Action
The process of building consensus among board and senior staff is critical as the organization moves toward a solution to its problems or decides to take advantage of new opportunities. The results of an organizational assessment can make people very nervous, particularly if it reveals problems. Unfortunately, some may regard these problems as a sign of personal failure even though, in many cases, the problems stem from very different sources—external changes in the community, new sources of competition, shifts in the priority of funders and underwriters, rapid organizational growth, staff turnover, or the failure of some new administrative procedure or system. In any case, an effort should be made to make everyone feel comfortable with the diagnosis of the problems. There must be broad consensus on what is wrong before the group can take effective action to do something about it.

One of the most effective ways to build this consensus is through a group meeting, such as a retreat, involving board and senior staff. Typically, a retreat is led by a facilitator who has special training in group process and is fully familiar with the organization's problems and the options that are under consideration for the future. The best of these meetings are those in which the participants are not simply there to receive information but are being asked to help formulate policy and direction. However, it is important if decisions are to be made at the meeting the issues be clearly articulated, the options well structured, and the decisions formulated within predefined limits.

This chapter has offered some strategies for bringing about change and making improvements in a nonprofit organization. It has suggested that there are ways a nonprofit organization can set about diagnosing problems and making things better. As we have seen, several areas need to be analyzed in the process of evaluation and change. The evaluation process itself can reveal organizational strengths and weaknesses and can provide the basis for developing goals and objectives for the future. Different names are sometimes attached to the evaluation process to indicate differing kinds of emphases (e.g., management review, program evaluation, marketing audit, and financial assessment), but the overall intent is the same—to establish a baseline of consensus around organizational problems and to identify areas in which there are opportunities for positive change.

Evaluation, either through self-assessment or outside evaluation, is generally a positive experience, but there are certain inherent dangers. One is the tendency for board and staff to become discouraged because they have been overly self-critical. They forget that they are measuring themselves or being measured against an ideal that no organization ever achieves. As the assessment process unfolds and they compile long lists of organizational deficiencies, they begin to question their own competence and the judgments of others. This can be dangerous and destructive. The purpose of the assessment is not to be negative. It is to develop an agenda for change.

It is also extremely important to realize that organizations cannot be changed overnight and the process of problem solving and change is generally best managed on a gradual and ongoing basis. Certainly every nonprofit organization can do what it does more effectively. Put another way, every nonprofit organization has room to make improvements. The challenge for trustees and staff is to manage the changes in such a way that the effects are positive and long lasting.

Notes

CHAPTER 1

[1]Two excellent reference books on the nature of nonprofit organizations are Burton A. Weisbrod's *The Nonprofit Economy,* (Cambridge, MA: Harvard University Press, 1988) and Walter W. Powell, ed., *The Nonprofit Sector* (New Haven, CT: Yale University Press, 1987). Many of the statistics in this chapter are drawn from these books.

[2]This figure represents the total number of nonprofit organizations including those (such as trade associations and country clubs) that are not eligible to receive tax-deductible gifts. The universe of so-called charitable nonprofits is about a third as large (there were approximately 366,000 in 1985).

CHAPTER 2

[1]The word *trustee* is used here to describe a person serving on the board of trustees. Sometimes this group is referred to as the board of directors, in which case those who serve are called directors. However, the directors who serve on the board are not to be confused with a staff person with the same title such as an executive director, a program director, or an artistic director. In general, directors who are board members do not serve on the staff and are not paid.

[2]According to the American Association of Fund-Raising Counsel, individuals gave $66 billion to nonprofit organizations in 1985. If we assume that deductibility of the average dollar contributed was at the 20 percent level (tax bracket), then over $13 billion was lost to the treasury in foregone taxes.

[3]While statutes governing nonprofit or charitable corporations do not specify that trustees may not be compensated, it is generally expected that the majority of trustees will not be. In some cases, the IRS, in reviewing applications for tax-exempt status from certain types of organizations, will require that a provision be included in the corporate charter specifying that trustees may not be compensated. In some nonprofit organizations, the chief executive officer and the artistic director (both of whom collect a salary) do sit on the board *ex officio,* often without a vote. In almost all nonprofit organizations, however, the vast majority of board members are not compensated so the spirit of independence from financial self-interest on the part of the board is maintained.

[4]In many cases, creditors threaten to sue individual trustees if their claims on the organization are not met. However, given the laws in most states, they have no legal standing in this regard even if they can prove gross negligence.

[5]For those interested in a fuller treatment of this subject, there is the excellent book by Daniel L. Kurtz, *Board Liability* (Mt. Kisco, NY: Moyer Bell Ltd., 1988). It is strongly recommended for anyone interested in the subject of boards of trustees in nonprofit organizations.

CHAPTER 3

[1]Generally, the board of trustees hires the executive director. The executive director hires other staff. In large organizations where staffs are sizable, division heads often hire the people that work under them. In the most decentralized organizations, where each

employee is hired by his or her immediate supervisor, it is advisable to involve staff colleagues working in the same department in the recruitment and interviewing process. No matter what hiring procedure is used, it is always advantageous to have more than one person forming an impression of prospective employees even if one person ultimately will make the final selection.

CHAPTER 4

[1]The term *benefits* as used here may include, but is not limited to, vacations, sick days, personal days, maternity and paternity leaves, other leaves of absence, medical insurance, private retirement plans, life insurance, disability insurance, and other forms of nonsalaried compensation. Social security, workmen's compensation, and unemployment insurance may also be considered benefits to the employee, although they are not discretionary—that is they are the employee's right by law.

[2]Employees of nonprofit organizations are covered by unemployment insurance by virtue of their employment. The organization itself, however, must be careful to understand its options and liabilities. At the federal level, the organization is exempt from paying unemployment taxes (FUTA). At the state level, laws vary and it is important for a nonprofit organization to check the procedures. In many states, the organization has an option to participate in the unemployment insurance program. If state unemployment insurance (usually assessed as a percentage of total employees' salaries) is paid regularly, and an employee is subsequently laid off, the state pays the unemployment compensation and the organization pays nothing. If the organization does not pay into the state unemployment insurance fund (and nonprofit organizations usually have the option of not participating in the system) and the employee is laid off or fired, the state pays the unemployment benefit and then charges the organization the full cost of the claim. Nonprofit organizations that are certain they will have no employees collecting unemployment may decide not to pay into the system. Others may wish to do so. Still others may wish to establish their own self-insurance fund, putting aside a certain portion of the employees' salaries into a separate bank account for a time until they feel confident that they are protected against unemployment liability. (Note: Unemployment benefits cover only salaried employees, not independent contractors.)

[3]When an employee works according to a *flextime* schedule, he or she substitutes one set of working hours for another but works the same number of total hours. If the employee works *overtime,* he or she works additional hours beyond the number originally required.

[4]The individual's title may be executive director, administrative director, artistic director, general director, or something else, but he or she is at the top of the organizational chart.

CHAPTER 6

[1]Technically, it is not permissible to use restricted funds for purposes other than those specified by the individual or organization imposing the restriction. However, organizations occasionally are tempted to borrow from their restricted funds to cover short-term cash needs. The rationale is generally given that the organization will pay back the restricted funds prior to needing them and in the meanwhile such a temporary transfer of funds helps the organization avoid more expensive borrowing. This practice is common among nonprofit organizations, but is it legal? According to one accountant

consulted on this matter, the practice is legal so long as the organization has secured a letter of credit from a lending institution (or individual) that commits sufficient funds to replace the restricted funds should the organization be unable to repay the restricted obligation.

CHAPTER 7

[1]Usually the fund balance or equity figure portion is adjusted only at year end; it does not change during the year and the changes in the total fund balance are reflective of the net income (or loss) from the income statement. Again, for a profit-making corporation, this equity could be the owners' original investment, which is augmented or reduced by any profit or loss that the corporation makes.

[2]The balance sheet allows someone to calculate the equity of property owned by the organization. The value of the property is shown under Assets and the outstanding debt on the property is shown under Liabilities. The amount of equity in the property is the difference between these two figures. Thus in figure 7.3, the equity is calculated as $50,000 minus $25,221, or $24,779. Interest payments do not appear on the balance sheet but are shown on the income statement.

[3]This income statement is typical of one that would be included in a year-end audited statement. Accordingly, it is an income statement showing changes to the fund balance as well as income and expenses. On a regular monthly financial statement for Morse School, changes to the fund balance would not be included, but a line for net income (or loss) would be. A regular monthly statement also would not show changes in market value of investments. However, it often does include a comparison of year-to-date figures with the annual budget.

CHAPTER 8

[1]In this section, the term *corporations* refers to large business concerns that have organized giving programs. While smaller local businesses, described earlier in this chapter, are also corporations, the nature of their philanthropy is quite different from what is described here. It is on a much smaller scale, is primarily restricted to the local giving area, and is generally not as carefully organized as the giving programs of larger corporations.

CHAPTER 10

[1]One byte is the equivalent of one character—a single letter, number, or space. A megabyte is a million bytes and is the unit that is used to describe the capacity of hard disks (e.g., a ten-megabyte hard disk).

[2]Operating system software is usually proprietary to the computer manufacturer, although the generic version of IBM's PC-DOS operating software, known as MS-DOS, has become one of several de facto standards on microcomputers. Other operating systems have achieved some degree of acceptance as standards—Pro-Dos for the Apple 2 series of computers; the Macintosh operating system, which functions on all Apple Macintosh computers; and the UNIX operating system, which was initially developed on AT&T computers, but which is being considered by an increasingly wide range of manufacturers. One other operating system, OS-2, was introduced by IBM in the mid-1980s in conjunction with IBM's new line of personal computers.

[3]In a computerized data base system, a *field* refers to a single item of information, such as someone's name. A collection of related fields that are logically treated as a unit (for example, in a mailing list, the fields referring to one person's name, address, city, and state) is called a *record*. A *data base* is a collection of related records, such as the complete mailing list, that is organized in some meaningful way.

Index

303